SIX SIGMA
EXECUTION

SIX SIGMA EXECUTION

How the World's Greatest Companies Live and Breathe Six Sigma

GEORGE ECKES

McGraw-Hill

New York   Chicago   San Francisco   Lisbon   London
Madrid   Mexico City   Milan   New Delhi
San Juan   Seoul   Singapore
Sydney   Toronto

Copyright © 2005 by George Eckes. All rights reserved. Printed in the United States of America.
Except as permitted under the United States Copyright Act of 1976, no part of this publication
may be reproduced or distributed in any form or by any means, or stored in a database or
retrieval system, without the prior written permission of the publisher.

1 2 3 4 5 6 7 8 9 0   DOC/DOC   0 9 8 7 6 5

ISBN 0-07-145364-4

McGraw-Hill books are available at special quantity discounts to use as premiums and sales
promotions, of for use in corporate training programs. For more information, please write to the
Director of Special Sales, Professional Publishing, McGraw-Hill, 2 Penn Plaza, New York, NY
10121-2298. Or contact your local bookstore.

This publication is designed to provide accurate and authoritative information in regard to the
subject matter covered. It is sold with the understanding that neither the author nor the publisher
is engaged in rendering legal, accounting, or other professional service. If legal advice or other expert assistance is required, the services of a competent professional person should be sought.
—*From a Declaration of Principles jointly adopted by a Committee of the American Bar Association and a
Committee of Publishers.*

This book is printed on recycled, acid-free paper containing
a minimum of 50% recycled, de-inked fiber.

To Susan Ayarbe and Andrea Price.
You make me think.
You make me laugh.
You make me feel.
I love you both.

Contents

Acknowledgments

This book would not have been possible without the contributions of many people. First, to the McGraw-Hill team for their contributions on editing and publishing this work, particularly Jeanne Glasser and Sally Glover.

To Jennifer McClellan, my office manager, who inspires me each and every day. Your work ethic, attitude, and enthusiasm in the face of so many challenges makes me want to be a better person.

To Andrea Price, my senior vice president and friend. I don't know what happens first each day we are together—a laugh moment or one of your great ideas that makes me or my company better. Having you in my life again has been my greatest blessing. To Susan Ayarbe. You will always be the greatest human being I have ever known. It's one thing to say to a friend, call me anytime, even at 2:00 in the morning. With you I know the offer was true, and after last year you do too.

To my father, for your support in recent years. I will always crave your approval. To Gayle Thompsen for her never-ending encouragement during trying times. You will always be a friend. To Ross Leher for his undying support, encouragement, and ability to make me think. To David Felton for his epicurean genius. To Joseph Della Malva. I dote on your every phrase. To Dave Schulenberg, my Captain, whose friendship and support is valued beyond words. Working with you never seems like work. I won't tell the client if you don't.

To the "Pumper." Thank you for showing me your definition of love, commitment, honesty, respect, affection, hard work, and trust. I will take those lessons you taught me to the grave. May you receive all you deserve.

To Joe and Temo. In the last 20 years I have done two things right. When you look in the mirror, you will see one of them. Finally, to Debra Lee... 143.

Six Sigma Execution

Execution is a systematic process of rigorously discussing
hows and whats, questioning, tenaciously following through,
and ensuring accountability.

—Lawrence Bossidy, *Execution*

Introduction

IN HIS BOOK, *Execution*, Lawrence Bossidy characterizes the best
leaders as not necessarily being the most charismatic but those managers who spend the most time executing the strategy, operations, and,
most importantly, the people processes of an organization. He makes
an important point not to see this effort as simply tactical, advancing
the argument that true leadership is devoted to execution. I completely
agree with this premise, and this leads me to the assertion that the
execution of Six Sigma is identical. What prompts me to make this
statement is what I have observed in my 20 years of consulting with
business leaders both in the United States and across the globe. I have
been fortunate to be positioned to see firsthand both the results of execution as well as a lack of leadership.

In recent years, I have grown increasingly optimistic about the
presence of business leadership in our industry's largest corporations.
In the early 1990s, my optimism was brief but well-founded, as I saw
business leaders like Bob Galvin at Motorola and Lawrence Bossidy at
AlliedSignal endorse Six Sigma as not just a cost-cutting measure, but
as a true management philosophy. My optimism reached its zenith in
1995 when Jack Welch adopted Six Sigma as his management philosophy. As a Six Sigma professional and author on the topic, I have observed the tremendous growth in popularity of the approach. Those,

like Bossidy and Welch, who adopt Six Sigma as a management philosophy should be applauded. But my optimism wanes when I witness executives using Six Sigma as a silver bullet, and when the quick fix doesn't take, just as quickly abandon the method.

This book is intended to create Six Sigma leaders at every level who will use the approach to guide the strategies, operations, and culture of their organizations. My method throughout the book is to simulate the training sessions offered by myself and my colleagues at Eckes and Associates. In this chapter and those that follow, I will take you through the discussions, explanations, and exercises that we at Eckes and Associates have used with our own clients. The goal is to provide you with the dialogue, tools, tactics, and cautionary advice that you can then use to deploy a Six Sigma effort of any size. And perhaps the sessions that I duplicate in these pages will assist you in creating and training your own Six Sigma teams and departments.

Step One: The Quiz

My sessions with executive clients typically begin with a simple quiz that is designed to determine the current levels of effectiveness and efficiency of their organizations. The quiz has five questions.

Question 1: "How much time do you spend in an average day reworking something someone else has started?" This usually averages about 20 percent of a person's day.

Question 2: "How much of your day is spent doing something someone else has to redo?" Ironically, in 10 years of asking this question, I don't think I have ever had someone say his or her number is higher than the response to question one. The answer to 2 usually averages about 10 percent. While I might joke about this in my seminars, I am always perplexed at how this subtle question, even among executives, leads to the conclusion that it's someone other than the executives themselves that contributes to the overall inefficiency of the organization.

Question 3 asks for the definition of value-added activity. To be a value-added activity, three criteria must be met. First, the customer of the activity must consider it important. Second, there must be some physical change to the product or service being worked on. Third, it must be done right the first time.

Asking the audience member to exclude the portion of his day that he included for questions one and two, I then ask him to review the portion of his day and rate the percentage of his day that is non value added. This usually is rated around 20 to 30 percent. I then ask him to add up the answers to questions one, two, and three. In the last several years, that sum has averaged around 50 percent.

In Question 4, I ask each executive to think of *his or her* personal most important customer. For most executives that would mean other employees in the organization but rarely does a person think that way. Instead she thinks of her biggest account, the external customer who pays an invoice.

In the final question, I ask her to project how that customer would rate her performance in meeting the needs and requirements of the products and/or services provided to him. For the last 10 years the average result of question number 4 have averaged 7 out of 10, or 70 percent. When my youngest son, Temo first saw this, he responded pointedly, "Dad, 70 percent... that's a C in my school." Using their own assessment, they have just confessed to wasting half their days and being evaluated as being " 'C' students."

I created this quiz to show my clients that they had to change the way they managed. How could they expect to continue wasting half their days and receiving poor evaluations from their customers? If their organizations were profitable, they were profitable in spite of themselves, rather than because of something they were intentionally doing. But pointing this out to my clients proved problematic.

Resistance

While I was quick to point out to quiz participants that they personally were not ineffective and inefficient, it often did not matter. In most seminars, the quiz was attacked. Executives of all kinds questioned its integrity and subjectivity; this despite the subjectivity of their own perceptions and answers. Some focus on the fact they thought they were too hard in grading themselves. Still others begin to talk about the hard economic times and how that explains their poor scores. Yet how can a poor economy explain why an organization isn't as effective and efficient as it should be? Turbulent economic times only exacerbate the preexisting flaws of a company.

Regardless of excuses, I had just shown them that their organizations were broken. I used this quiz to highlight the concept of process, a series of steps and activities that take inputs, add value (we hope), and produce outputs for customers that meet—and preferably exceed—requirements.

I reminded my audience of the *I Love Lucy* episode where Lucy and Ethel decide to impress their husbands by showing them they could be gainfully employed outside of the house. They take jobs at a candy manufacturer where they are to package candy. Of course, for those who remember this episode, the manufacturing line is broken, somehow stuck on warp speed. They work furiously to package candy, only to stuff candy into their clothing, try to stop the line, and even begin eating the candy themselves.

Not once, but twice a supervisor comes in to scold the girls. They commit to trying harder, but the same thing happens each time the supervisor leaves. Pure and simple, this is a broken process.

I use this example to highlight that a 50-percent inefficiency and 70-percent effectiveness rating indicates that there are broken processes afoot that must be improved. Of course, I use the *I Love Lucy* example to emphasize that it wasn't the worker's fault that performance was so bad. Management is responsible for the broken manufacturing process, and it is management's responsibility to see that it's fixed. So logic follows that the quiz participants with poor effectiveness and efficiency ratings have the responsibility to get their numbers more in line with a high-performance organization. According to most experts, a high-performing or functioning organization usually has less than 10 percent inefficiency and a rating of 9 percent or higher for effectiveness (an "A" using my son's grading scale).

What amazes me is the resistance against setting these lofty but doable goals. Clients call these targets unrealistic and say no organization can be classed in these categories, despite the GEs, Southwest Airlines, and Federal Expresses of the world.

No Silver Bullet

Several years ago I received a call from a CEO of a major Midwestern fast food chain. He had recently read my first book, *The Six Sigma Revolution: How GE and Others Turned Process into Profits* and said that he would fly anywhere I was to have dinner and talk about how Six Sigma could transform his organization. First, I was impressed with his passion and dedication to coming to see me as quickly as possible. While I tried to remove my ego from the proceedings, I probably failed. To have a CEO want to travel to see you can be a heady experience. I now see it as an act of desperation, not commitment.

This particular dinner went very well and I was highly impressed with this CEO. He was a former high-level GE business leader who had left GE just before GE's commitment to Six Sigma in 1995. He had become the CEO of a Midwest-based fast food chain with locations all over the United States, from Ohio to California. At the dinner it became apparent he had not only read my first book but had highlighted portions of his obviously dog-eared copy. During our first meeting he had talked about the organization's need for more effectiveness and efficiency, particularly in his industry where profit margin was paper thin. He talked with passion about how Six Sigma could be the vehicle for his company's market supremacy. His comments truly inspired me; I was always on the lookout for committed, involved management that didn't want a quick fix or use Six Sigma as a simple cost-savings initiative, of which I was seeing more and more.

At the end of our meal, the CEO candidly referenced his main problem. He used the sports metaphor of "poor bench strength." I had heard this before from other newly anointed CEOs to describe organizations with less-than-sterling direct reports. Pleased with this CEO's commitment to utilizing Six Sigma, I agreed to his next request. He wanted to arrange a dinner with all his direct reports in six weeks. This informal meeting was a part of their next off-site management retreat. It would take place in Denver where I lived.

The events that transpired during the direct reports dinner have repeated themselves time and again and are the context behind one of the concepts stressed throughout the book. Leaders often attempt to reach a consensus before making a commitment. In times of trial, true leaders must place a stake in the sand, commit to a management approach, and lead, rather than attempt diplomacy.

The dinner began with introductions and a few standard questions designed to test the consultant. What was unusual about this dinner was how quickly the CEO attempted to hold a meeting. He wanted me to immediately begin teaching the mechanics of Six Sigma over drinks and appetizers. I knew this was a mistake and instead began asking the vice presidents about their headaches and struggles in making this organization function in spite of a wafer-thin profit margin. As with the five-question exercise, I was trying to compel this group of executives to look at their business in a different way.

It soon became apparent that seven executives out of the nine were dead set against even acknowledging any organizational problems. As I attempted to help this group see that they were neither as effective nor efficient as they could be, I started to encounter the type of resistant questions I have heard for years, which helped me to determine the extent of their resistance.

"What about Motorola? I have heard they started Six Sigma, but look at how poor their business is today."

Anyone who asks this question in recent years has no real interest in my answer. They are against Six Sigma, and Motorola's situation is simply a way for them to justify their opposition. In direct response to these negative perceptions, I point to the fact that General Electric and AlliedSignal have generated billions in cost savings by using Six Sigma. Instead of asking how a proven methodology can be applied to a fast food chain across multiple states, they immediately ask a question to validate their fear and resistance.

Aware that my answer is irrelevant, I still counter with a summary of the technology issues at Motorola, the fact that many Motorola executives indicate there might not be a Motorola today without the implementation of Six Sigma in the 1980s, and most importantly I provide a pragmatic analogy about results. I maintain that implementing Six Sigma does not guarantee success, just as leading a healthy lifestyle is not a guarantee of longevity. Finally, I argue that while Motorola was the first organization to use Six Sigma, the pioneer in an industry rarely perfects it.

The second theme of questions focuses on my fast food experience. Other than a brief stint in high school flipping burgers, I tell them I haven't had experience implementing Six Sigma in a fast food chain. These types of questions spotlight the "we are different" school of resistance. This means that executives believe that they have the toughest job imaginable, and that an outsider could never have encountered the problems of these poor managers. What I have learned working in varied environments implementing Six Sigma is that processes are processes; there are unique obstacles and opportunities in every business.

Other first-hour questions focused on motivating hourly workers and franchisers who fail at operational management and often work long hours for paltry pay. I did see this as a unique situation but stressed that an ineffective and inefficient set of processes only increases the frustration of poor pay and long hours. Somehow, this reasoned approach was falling on deaf ears.

When engaged in a dinner conversation with multiple resistors, you're constantly on the defensive. By hour two of this dinner I had moved into identifying possible opportunities where Six Sigma could benefit these managers. Also, I conveyed how impressed I had been with the CEO when we had dined alone about his commitment to the method and was trying my best to make the case for realizing his vision. I dutifully laid out the proper way to implement Six Sigma. I described the strategic element of Six Sigma, wherein key executives link key processes to strategic business objectives and then select high-impact, low-performing processes to improve through the tactics of Six Sigma. I went on to stress that uniformity of process performance across so many of their locations would increase repeat business, stressing the recent problems of McDonald's, where variation across locations had negatively impacted their repeat business and hurt their business model of uniformity of customer expectations. A philosophy of Six Sigma is removal and/or reduction of variation in all a business does. Zero variation is paramount in the fast food industry, where often wait time is of more value to the customer than the food itself. If I wait 2 minutes in the drive thru on Monday, 20 minutes on Tuesday, 8 minutes on Wednesday, and 14 minutes on Friday, it matters little that the average wait time is 11 minutes. I feel the variation in the process.

By the end of the second hour I had become noticeably aware of the CEO's silence through much of the conversation. After two hours of what I felt was an arduous dinner I called on him for his perspective, asking what his thoughts were on the discussion thus far. He replied that the discussion was very interesting, but he wanted me to tell the group more about how Six Sigma can help us.

One Six Sigma tool is called the boomerang and happens when a question is thrown back to the inquirer. In this case the boomerang was thrown back to the consultant. Clearly, I was expected to do more selling of Six Sigma. Another tool in the Six Sigma toolbox is the moment of truth, that period of time between supplier and customer where either a positive or negative experience occurs. For me, this was the beginning of my negative reaction to this CEO. A passionate, dedicated leader had somehow transformed into a weak, facilitating consensus builder.

I feebly attempted to comply with his wishes. We spent the next 20 minutes immersed in details as minute as how Six Sigma could help keep meals warm, and how line workers could perform better maintenance. Finally, the CEO intervened as coffee and dessert was served.

"All right, we have heard from George about what Six Sigma can do for us. What I would like now is each of your reactions, whether or not you think we should do this."

My amazement was only surpassed by the feeling that I was on trial, and within earshot of the jury deliberations. For the next 45 minutes each of the nine vice presidents said that Six Sigma was too bureaucratic, would take too long, wasn't applicable to their type of business, or simply that they were doing fine without it.

After this litany of complaints was aired in detail, the CEO looked at me and asked if I wanted to respond to their comments.

The moment of truth had come for me. I wanted to respond not to their assessments, but to the CEO's style of management. "Actually Frank, I want to tell you something. In 1995, I doubt seriously if Jack Welch gathered his direct reports from the various business units and had them listen to a consultant pontificate on Six Sigma and then asked their opinion. Once Jack had gathered enough information on his own, he told each and every person who reported to him that GE was committing to a Six Sigma strategy and that he was making Six Sigma one of only three strategic initiatives in his 20 years at GE. I can assure you that if he had polled his direct reports about whether GE should commit to a Six Sigma strategy, the answer would have been no."

While Frank's face began to show shock and dismay, far more apparent was the laughter from the nine vice presidents. His financial officer commented, "Frank, I think he just challenged your manhood."

"No, I didn't challenge his manhood. I just challenged his leadership."

After paying the bill, Frank and I walked out of the restaurant. We exchanged pleasantries. He seemed apologetic about his lack of leadership, explaining that his management style was based on consensus building. I briefly explained that consensus building with a "weak bench," as he described his management team, was a flawed decision. I reluctantly informed him that a team would never rally around Six Sigma without a strong commitment from the CEO.

Needless to say, this organization neither worked with me nor built a reputation for customer service.

Summary

The theme of consensus building does have its place in leadership, but not when embracing something as dramatic as Six Sigma. This is the purview of the leader and his or her vision for the organization. In later chapters we will address how consensus can be a part of great leadership, but the point of this sad story is leaders must lead and take their organization forward, even when other executives have doubts.

Key Learnings

- Six Sigma when done correctly is a management philosophy aimed at improving the effectiveness and efficiency of an organization.
- Most Six Sigma initiatives fail due to the lack of vibrant management commitment and involvement.
- The commitment to a Six Sigma deployment cannot be achieved by attempting to develop a consensus decision among key business leaders.

The History of Six Sigma: How Motorola, Allied Signal, and General Electric Each Contributed to Making Six Sigma a Management Philosophy

> Victory has a thousand fathers, but defeat is an orphan.
> —John F. Kennedy

Introduction

JOHN F. KENNEDY'S words at a press conference after the failed Bay of Pigs invasion reminds me of the history of Six Sigma. It reminds me, of course, in the opposite way that prompted JFK's now famous quote, uttered in 1961 after he blindly trusted the CIA and Defense department experts claiming that a group of Cuban insurgents could overthrow the Communist regime of Fidel Castro without U.S. military involvement. Of course it wasn't that simple. JFK balked at providing the military assistance of the United States, which ultimately led to the Cuban invasion and a huge political and military failure.

Instead, Six Sigma is like the first part of JFK's quote. A study of Six

Sigma's 1980's beginning shows many people taking credit for its inception. Originally a set of disciplined quality tools to reduce defect rates at Motorola, Six Sigma evolved both within Motorola and later at AlliedSignal and General Electric. This chapter will show that this evolution has resulted in Six Sigma becoming more than a quality toolbox, instead becoming a management philosophy and a cultural phenomenon when properly implemented.

There is the parable of the three blind men and the elephant. Each is asked to identify what they are touching. The first touches the tusk of the elephant and identifies he is touching a spear. The second touches the torso and claims what he is touching is a wall. The third touches the tail and thinks it's a snake.

This parable parallels Six Sigma. As its popularity has grown, different "experts" have marketed Six Sigma to fit their needs, not necessarily that of their customers. Of course, Six Sigma includes significant amounts of statistical tools. But many see Six Sigma as only statistics. They are wrong. Touch part of the work that constitutes Six Sigma and it will look eerily similar to other quality approaches. Touch another part of Six Sigma and it only vaguely resembles a quality approach at all. This chapter is aimed at enlightening the reader to seeing that as Six Sigma has evolved during the last 20 years, it has been modified, adapted, and augmented into more than a quality toolbox. Our goal with this chapter is to see how three different organizations helped to create and change Six Sigma so that your implementation efforts don't repeat the mistakes of others.

The Origin of Six Sigma—The Motorola Story

In the mid 1980s Motorola quality was considered poor by any measure. A meeting was held among the top executives with Bob Galvin, their CEO at the helm, discussing a company in chaos. Reject rates among customers were high and internal defect rates were bleeding the electronics company of badly needed profits.

Galvin had responded well to an internal memo written by Bill Smith, an engineer at Motorola. Bob Galvin was a visionary leader who believed strongly in the concept of customer satisfaction and never-ending improvement. Smith's memo, written in 1985, statistically proved the relationship between product field life and how much rework occurred in the manufacturing process.

Ted Zucconi worked at Motorola in the 1990s as a business leader in their computer group, as technical director. He went on to Motorola University before retiring in 2002. In a July 2004 interview with Andrea Price and me he recalls that critical meeting among management.[1]

"I don't know if you heard the famous story about the vote we had at that senior meeting. Everybody was giving their reports and saying how well everything was going and someone stood up and said, *'No, you are all wrong, our quality sucks.'"* [2] Zucconi continues by saying a spirited discussion followed with Galvin finally asking for a vote among the 12 senior managers present. The vote centered on whether they were going to start a formal quality initiative. The vote was 11-1 against with the one positive vote generated by the only one that counted, Galvin himself. Six Sigma as a formal initiative was ready to be conceived.

The initial formula used by Motorola was MAIC, which stood for measure, analyze, improve, and control. An underlying assumption was that a project was already well defined and chartered, the right people had been assigned, and that proper sponsorship was in place to ensure success of the project. Sadly, that was not always the case.

Nonetheless, Motorola reduced manufacturing costs from the inception of Six Sigma in 1987 through 1994 by 1.5 billion dollars. Through the summer of 2004, Motorola claimed cost savings of 15 billion dollars. This is in keeping with experts who claim that an organization can save anywhere from 1.2 percent to 4.5 percent of the organization's revenue.

Much discussion has centered on the true originator of Six Sigma. Mikel Harry must be given major credit for packaging and commercializing Six Sigma as a vibrant quality-improvement methodology. To Harry's credit, he claims it is Bill Smith who should be given the moniker of Six Sigma founder. But it was Harry who formulated much of the details of Six Sigma methodology. Harry first published *The Nature of Six Sigma* in 1986. It was also Harry that went on to publish *The Strategic Vision for Accelerating Six Sigma* within Motorola and was later appointed the first head of the Motorola Six Sigma Research Institute.

While much discussion centers around who created Six Sigma, little has been said about the deployment of Six Sigma, first within Motorola, and then later at AlliedSignal, and then General Electric.

Much credit should be given to Motorola for their efforts in pioneering Six Sigma. However, the approach Motorola took toward implementing Six Sigma was virtually all at the tactical level. This means that Six Sigma was primarily used as a defect reduction tool, not the ultimate management philosophy championed by AlliedSignal and GE. Further, because defect reduction was the goal of Six Sigma at Motorola, the focus was on the manufacturing floor. Virtually ignored was the waste and inefficiency generated by other areas of the business, from backroom operations like accounting to more prominent areas such as sales and marketing. This "find and fix it" approach to Six Sigma utilization totally ignored the design areas of Motorola. This failure to address both the backroom operations and design elements of Six Sigma tactical application ultimately resulted in the complaints about Motorola and Six Sigma in the late 1990s and early twenty-first century. It wasn't that Motorola had abandoned Six Sigma as some had suggested. Instead, it simply never reached certain areas of Motorola that would have made the company the true hallmark of Six Sigma deployment.

Further, Motorola did not use Six Sigma strategically. As we shall see shortly, organizations like AlliedSignal and General Electric eventually saw the power of utilizing Six Sigma strategically. This included but was not limited to using Six Sigma as an enabler to enhancing revenue, growth goals, and ultimately customer satisfaction.

When I questioned Ted Zucconi about how much Six Sigma pervaded the culture of Motorola, his answer highlighted the above.

> **It became part of the culture, but more at a tactical level. The focus was so much on growth, numbers, and manufacturing. Six Sigma never directly dealt with customers or how we designed things even though designers were educated. Even though people sent reports up to corporate, it doesn't mean that they truly embraced it as a part of doing business.**
>
> **Sometimes certain business units did absolutely the minimum. There wasn't a uniform set of expectations and if you were meeting your numbers the corporate expectations seemed voluntary.[3]**

One aspect of Six Sigma that General Electric brought to the table was the emphasis of it being an expectation of every business unit. I asked Ted Zucconi to what extent that was the case at Motorola.

> **There was a corporate edict that you had to do Six Sigma but
> you had the option of doing it your way. For example, our semi-
> conductor business was caught up in the boom-or-bust business
> cycle. In the boom they were busy increasing capacity and figur-
> ing out allocations. During the period of excess capacity, they
> worried about cost reductions, some of which were quality im-
> provements. Having worked for more than one semiconductor
> company I observed that apparently sometimes it is difficult for
> managers to see the connection between quality, yield, and ca-
> pacity. I know Intel does, but most don't.[4]**

I inquired into what comprised the corporate edict.

> **The corporate edict was centered on education and reporting of
> defect levels. I never saw an edict around expectations of number
> of projects or so many master black belts or black belts.[5]**

Another Motorola business leader, Arnold Klugman, agrees.[6] The
Chief Manufacturing Officer for the Motorola Computer group in
Tempe, Arizona, Klugman notes that Six Sigma's focus on manufacturing could be explained by its being an engineering company. "Since it
was an engineering driven corporation the tag line was, 'We don't want
to minimize creativity.' Thus the focus was driving out defects, not
building quality in at the design stage."[7]

As it relates to corporate edicts, Klugman also agrees with Zucconi.
"At GE with Jack Welch it was truly top-down driven. There was no
optionality. At Motorola there was massive optionality."

Klugman then goes on to talk of this optionality. "There was no
doubt that Bob Galvin was a believer and pushed it. But if a business
unit was very successful and returning the revenue plan and achieving
their numbers and growing market share the business leader has no difficulty saying leave me alone and I will do Six Sigma the way I choose.
The optionality was pervasive."[8]

AlliedSignal

The concept of the originator not ultimately being associated with its
perfection is not unusual in business. The food processor was invented

in France, but not by the organization that perfected its application, Cuisinart. Raytheon created the microwave in 1949, but I don't see a Raytheon microwave in many of the kitchens I visit.

Thus it was two other companies that transformed Six Sigma into what it is known today. Ironically, without the success of another quality initiative at Motorola, it is possible that Six Sigma would have remained a Motorola-exclusive phenomenon.

In 1988 Motorola was the first organization to win the coveted Malcolm Baldrige Quality Award. Created in that same year and named for the former Commerce Secretary, the Malcolm Baldrige award was presented by the President of the United States to a small group of organizations that meet certain quality criteria. Those organizations interested in obtaining the award file a comprehensive application and, if a finalist, are visited by Baldrige examiners who review the application and its documentation. In November 1988 Motorola was awarded the first Malcolm Baldrige award. A criteria of winning the award was that each recipient had to agree to share information about their quality activities with interested parties. Thus, it was winning the Malcolm Baldrige award that propelled Six Sigma beyond the Motorola borders.

One of the first organizations to inquire about Six Sigma from Motorola was Unisys. Cliff Ames, a Unisys plant manager, was one of the first individuals to attempt to leverage those individuals with Six Sigma knowledge into greater positions in the organization. Prior to Unisys, those with Six Sigma knowledge were not necessarily designated as experts in their field. It was at Unisys (in conjunction with Mikel Harry at Motorola) that the term Black Belt was coined. Both Ames and Harry were martial arts enthusiasts, and they thought it made sense to designate a martial arts moniker for team leaders who had acquired the statistical skills necessary to guide a project team toward completion of the Six Sigma methodology. Thus in the late 1980s Six Sigma as a career path began to take on more prestige and attracted high-potential individuals to its implementation. This subtle but critical change in the perception of a quality career track is yet another difference between Six Sigma and other quality initiatives.

Previous to Six Sigma, the quality arena was often a dumping ground for poor performers. There was clearly no glamour associated with a quality career prior to the 1980s. Often seen as a necessary evil, quality prior to Six Sigma was focused on inspection efforts where quality control was seen as a cost to an organization, not a potential for profit enhancement.

Six Sigma changed that. While we have chronicled the limitations of Motorola's effort, nonetheless working on defect reduction resulted in cost savings that contributed to the bottom line. Thus, working on MAIC projects brought some level of stature to those who participated. That typically was not the case with more traditional quality activities.

In addition to Unisys examining Six Sigma as a quality initiative, Texas Instruments began implementation efforts. Both Unisys and TI had marginal success, but in 1993 two additional companies began Six Sigma activities, Asia Brown Boveri (ABB) and more importantly, AlliedSignal.

The work at ABB was important because Mikel Harry and his colleague Richard Schroeder were now reaching the right audience to make Six Sigma more than a defect reduction effort. Whatever the origins of Six Sigma, credit must be given to both Harry and Schroeder for attracting the attention of executive management. It was Kjell Magnuson, an ABB business unit president who first began to see how Six Sigma could be used as a strategic tool. Instead of just a defect reduction program, Six Sigma began to be seen as an enabler to assist a business leader achieve his or her business objectives.

It was at this time that Harry and Schroeder formed the Six Sigma Academy, their full-time consulting organization. One key element of their program was to begin to sell Six Sigma not as a quality program but as business enabler. Ever the salesmen, their approach was focused on the business leader, not the quality leader. This is yet another differentiator between Six Sigma and other quality initiatives. Prior to Six Sigma the message about quality improvement was aimed at and implemented by the quality professional. With Six Sigma the business leader was usually the prime target for its implementation. In 1993 their message was heard by the person who was eventually going to become its greatest disciple to date, Lawrence Bossidy.

Lawrence Bossidy had come to AlliedSignal in 1991, having years of experience at General Electric. A close friend of Jack Welch, he had been smart enough to know that Welch was not leaving GE anytime soon and his chance at being a CEO rested elsewhere. His chance came in 1991 when the troubled conglomerate AlliedSignal tapped him to be their next CEO.

Anyone who has spent time with Bossidy knows him as a nononsense, bottom-line type of leader. A person who had a reputation that impugned quality programs for the their lack of contribution to the bottom line, it was surprising to some when Bossidy formally committed to implementing Six Sigma in 1993.

AlliedSignal's success with Six Sigma came relatively quickly. Instead of just measuring defect reduction rates, Bossidy attempted successfully to tie Six Sigma activity to business metrics. One key metric was operating margin. In single digits when Bossidy arrived, Six Sigma helped AlliedSignal to achieve a record operating margin of 14.1 by the middle 1990s.

This subtle but powerful addition to the approach to Six Sigma highlights Daniel Laux's comments in an iSixSigma discussion forum. Laux, the president of the Six Sigma Academy, was responding to the host of those who criticized or were taking credit for the origins of Six Sigma.[9]

> . . . I believe every Six Sigma practitioner, consulting firm, and black belt has contributed to the evolution of Six Sigma. We should therefore focus our time and resources, not on diatribe and who should get credit for Six Sigma but rather on continuously improving upon the strategies and tactics that result in business excellence.[10]

It was Bossidy and AlliedSignal that helped evolve Six Sigma in three other important ways. One was how projects were selected. The second was the focus on process. The third was to establish a link between Six Sigma and the customer.

At Motorola, projects tended to be selected informally, often chosen based on problems that surfaced and Six Sigma tactics were applied. At AlliedSignal, Bossidy got high-level executives involved. His first step was in training the high-level executives. Once they were trained, these executives played a pivotal role in project selection. At the urging of Bossidy, executives were told to choose projects that affected their financial objectives. Thus, Six Sigma took on a strategic element, becoming part of the business model rather than the initial "find it and fix it" approach made successful at Motorola.

Dr. Mina Gabriel, Director of Six Sigma Plus for Design and Growth

Processes at Honeywell (the merged name of AlliedSignal and Honeywell today) agrees.[11]

We had done particularly well squeezing lots of dollars in first projects, first in the manufacturing areas and then in our transactional applications. But we quickly realized that we had to move to the front end of the business and find projects that would impact our strategic business objectives. We wanted to transcend Six Sigma into areas that impacted innovation and apply a similar robust approach to technology, and impact such processes as marketing and business development as well as engineering.[12]

Project selection, as mentioned earlier, became very strategic whether at the engineering level or into the more nontraditional areas that Gabriel referenced. Some of the reason behind that was the greater expectation of Six Sigma of business leaders at AlliedSignal under Bossidy. Gabriel notes the directness of Bossidy's expectations:

Bossidy believed in Six Sigma and went out and demanded it. It was not an option. AlliedSignal was in a precarious position. We were not making our numbers in the early '90's and we were acting as a host of different companies. Bossidy basically used Six Sigma to create a culture that unified the company.[13]

Thus, AlliedSignal began to transform Six Sigma into an enbabler toward achievement of business objectives.

The second key element popularized by Bossidy was getting the organization to see the business through a series of processes rather than through traditional functions or departments. While not relinquishing the concept of the organizational chart, it was at AlliedSignal that business process management became successful.

A cursory reading of Bossidy's book *Execution* shows the focus he has on process.[14] A process is a series of steps and activities that take inputs, add value, and produce outputs for a customer, whether that customer is internal to the organization or the ultimate external customer. Processes by their definition cut across functions and departments. Thus, those that see an organization through the process lens are viewing their organization horizontally rather than through the vertical organization chart.

In my experience, I have found that business executives either immediately capture the concept of process thinking or they never do. When they do, they transform the organization, particularly if they marry process thinking with managing those processes with Six Sigma measures.

Bossidy embraced the concept of process. In *Execution* he discusses that in any organization there are three core processes: the people process, the strategy process, and the operations process. A core process is defined as the highest level of steps or activities that directly impact the organization. Thus, those three core processes were directly related to not only how business objectives were met, but how an executive manages a business.[15] Therefore, what Bossidy brought to Six Sigma was more process thinking, management, and what we will describe in Chapter 3, the strategy of Six Sigma.

The third and final element of how AlliedSignal modified the rollout of Six Sigma was around becoming more customer focused with their Six Sigma activities. Again, Dr. Gabriel nicely frames the evolution of Six Sigma at AlliedSignal as it affected the customer:

> **We realized very quickly that we could do all the efficiency based projects in the world and squeeze costs but we aren't going to grow . . . we wanted to touch the customer interface and touch it in a way that we had credibility with a truly robust structured approach but nonetheless allowed for flexibility and innovation. We found very quickly that there is no conflict between using the Six Sigma structured approach to help us identify some major customer issues and at the same time continue to drive process efficiency and allow for innovation.[16]**

1995—The General Electric Six Sigma Revolution

I began consulting with General Electric in 1991, thanks to being invited to work with the Destra Consulting firm. Pam Dennis, their founder and retired CEO, had asked me to work with them on a project at GE Plastics. GE Plastics was engaged in a series of process improvement efforts and was looking for a more quantitative approach to their work.

One of the things I learned early on working with GE was their highly competitive, results-driven culture. If work didn't contribute to the bottom line, then it was considered a waste of time. A true meritocracy (usually an oxymoron for a large company), the company abhorred bureaucracy. In the initial months of my work with GE, time and again I heard the refrain that whatever we were doing in small pockets of GE Plastics would never be taken to a corporate level because Jack Welch associated quality activities with bureaucracy, something verboten in GE circles.

However, one characteristic of General Electric in the 1990s was the concept of benchmarking. Benchmarking, or "Best Practices" as it is called at GE, is the set of activities associated with learning from other organizations. For example, if an organization wanted to learn about improving inventory turns, regardless of whether they were in retail sales or not, they might visit Wal-Mart based on their remarkable reputation for inventory management. If you wanted to learn about turnaround time, you might interview NASCAR pit crews, even though your business would never visit a racetrack.

Jack Welch was a big proponent of "Best Practices" and personally involved himself in that concept. Of particular pride to Welch were the executives who (secure in the knowledge that Welch was going to stay at GE into the twenty-first century) went out on their own to be CEOs of other companies. One obvious person he kept close contact with was Lawrence Bossidy, the former leader of GE Plastics who not only was one of his best direct reports, but a personal friend as well.

Therefore, it was not unusual for Welch and Bossidy to begin a dialogue in the mid 1990s regarding Six Sigma as AlliedSignal began to show significant results from their implementation efforts. Rumor has it that the discussions began in earnest over a game of Ping Pong they were notorious for playing. On a bet, Bossidy was going to be required to visit GE and talk about Six Sigma if he lost the game, which he apparently did since a meeting for corporate executives was planned for the summer of 1995 at the famous "Pit" at GE's corporate education center in Crotonville, New York.

The "Pit" is a sunken auditorium that is scheduled for very important meetings. Therefore when Bossidy returned for his 1995 meeting in the "Pit," the GE executives knew attendance was important.

Under promise of anonymity, I spoke with a GE executive who

attended this meeting. His views might have represented the thinking of most in attendance. "I was personally skeptical. While I deeply respected Jack, I also knew he was a man of many ideas, many of which didn't make sense for our organization. I didn't know Lawrence Bossidy but was aware of his reputation. I can't say I went with an open mind but was impressed with what Bossidy had to say."

Missing from that summer 1995 meeting was Jack Welch. As chronicled in his autobiography, *Straight from the Gut*, increasing fatigue and chest pains resulted in the treatment for a heart ailment.[17] Bossidy, to his credit, had offered to postpone the event because he didn't want the impression formed that he was returning to GE with some magic potion when Jack was ill, essentially undercutting him. Welch demurred and the summer session went off without a hitch.

By the early fall of 1995, interest in Six Sigma had begun in earnest. The GE culture was one of "getting things done yesterday." When Jack Welch had decided to implement Six Sigma, he contacted the Six Sigma Academy and hired Mikel Harry and Richard Schroeder to begin the first rounds of training of corporate overviews.

By late 1995, Nigel Andrews, a man I knew from my work with GE Plastics, was now running a significant part of GE Capital, the financial services arm of the worldwide conglomerate. I gave an overview of Six Sigma, discussing some of my work with Motorola suppliers in the 1980s. I gave what I thought was a thorough yet entertaining overview of Six Sigma, making sure to include the strategic element that AlliedSignal had contributed to the evolution of Six Sigma. It was my impression that the session went well. I even received several comments about my portion of the one-day overview to key GE Capital professionals. I left that day to visit a non-GE client in a neighboring state.

The next evening I returned to my hotel room and found a message from Nigel Andrews' assistant. It indicated that Nigel wanted to talk to me as soon as possible. I checked my watch as it approached 6 p.m. Knowing that a GE executive who leaves by 6 p.m. is considered to have worked only half a day, I started to call Nigel's number. As the phone rang, I arrogantly thought perhaps Nigel wanted to commend my performance the previous day. Nothing could have been further from the truth.

"I wanted to give you feedback on your speech yesterday." Nigel said with an air of somberness. "I thought it too glib, too much time spent on jokes, and not enough meat. I trust in the future you will do a better job."

Mumbling an apology, the brief phone conversation ended with my assuming that my Six Sigma consulting time with GE was very short lived.

I learned several painful lessons about the GE culture as a result of that phone conversation. First, I learned about the no-nonsense, results-driven culture of GE. I had experienced that to some degree working with GE Plastics on and off from 1991. But nothing had prepared me for the professional tongue lashing Nigel gave me that early fall day in 1995.

In my seminars I have what is described as a set of "Eckes-isms," parables that try in a sentence or two to impart some key learning. Eckes-ism #1 taken from my team dynamics course is "Feedback is a gift; some gifts can be returned." That night over another room service meal I honestly reviewed my performance and decided to open Nigel's gift. He was right. My speech could have been lighter on entertainment and heavier on content.

Third and most importantly, I knew from the seriousness of Nigel's message that GE was going to be serious about implementing Six Sigma. Selfishly I worried I wouldn't be a part of that implementation.

What I didn't know at the time of Nigel's call was the fact that Jack Welch had taken an inventory of reactions from those attending the Bossidy session in the Pit. The response was enthusiastic and Welch had made a commitment to implement Six Sigma. Ever the competitor, he asked Bob Galvin how long it had taken Motorola to make Six Sigma a part of the Motorola culture. Mind you, Motorola still saw Six Sigma as a tactical tool aimed at taking out defects. Welch, with his unique leadership style, wanted to make Six Sigma even more pervasive. He wanted to roll it out as a full cultural phenomenon at G.E. As he stated in *Straight from the Gut*, Six Sigma would end up one of the three most important initiatives during his helm at GE. When Galvin informed Welch that it took 10 years for Six Sigma to fully integrate at Motorola, he committed to its full realization at GE within 5 years.

Fortunately for me, not all of the attendees at the GE Capital overview had the same impressions as Nigel Andrews. By December of that year I had participated in a small Billing and Collections pilot for the Accounts Receivable department. During that pilot, Mike Markovits, the head of the division later known as the Center for Learning and Organizational Excellence (CLOE), audited the Billing and Collections training. Markovits personified the GE culture. In my years of consulting I never encountered a more dedicated worker. During the next several years working with Mike, I don't think I ever saw him put in less than a 15-hour day. A man of significant curiosity and dry humor, Mike was eventually tasked with the assignment of creating and delivering the first series of training and implementation courses on Six Sigma to GE Capital.

By late 1995 and early 1996, CLOE had developed a core group of consulting firms that would be responsible for creating the first course materials and delivery systems for DMAIC. Among the consulting firms represented in those first development sessions were Interaction Associates (to provide the materials and delivery of the facilitative skills portion of the pilot), Joiner Associates, and Oriel Consulting. And then somehow there was me.

This core consulting group was given the task of course material creation in anticipation of a large-scale pilot that would be taught to more than 100 GE Capital participants.

It quickly became evident that there were too many chefs for this soup. I felt for Markovits and others representing GE as they listened to a litany of consultants pontificate on their specialized approaches to Six Sigma. Now, I enjoy a good intellectual scrap, but there were major-league arguments over the approach GE Capital should take. This issue was more problematic at GE Capital than any other division of GE. Within Plastics or Appliances, the transition to Six Sigma was smoother because of their experience with total quality management, statistical process control, and re-engineering. At these divisions the concept of process thinking and improvement were not foreign. At GE Capital there was an old adage that if GE Capital had competition they didn't fight them; they bought them. Mergers and acquisitions were the order of the day, and while processes at GE Capital were abundant, they just didn't think in terms of process improvement.

In the more than 90 days before the March pilot, I recall losing far more battles than I won. I valiantly attempted to include the strategic element of Six Sigma but lost badly when it was decided that we had to jump quickly into projects. We needed fast results to justify GE's initial consulting investment (hey, good Six Sigma consultants don't come cheap).

To the group's credit, we included team dynamics elements and extra materials on the Define step of DMAIC that had been missing in Motorola's initial materials. In each element of DMAIC there are a series of levels or "tollgates" that teams must pass to improve effectiveness and efficiency. The course development team made the first tollgate top heavy with emphasis on the team charter, including such elements as design and management of project scope, creation and communication of the business case, and management of milestones.

These were mentally exhausting days. While we were doing good work, the pieces didn't flow in a coherent manner. By this time I had sensed my input wasn't as valued as the rest of the teams. Mike Markovits thought my course materials weren't as extensive as some of the others. Philosophically I felt that course materials should be an adjunct to good Six Sigma training, but as time progressed I felt we were creating a manual that included the kitchen sink. I recalled Ronald Reagan's joke about the optimistic boy plowing through a pile of manure under the Christmas tree because he knows there must be a pony in there somewhere.

Finally, in late March of 1996, we were given our teaching assignments. It was much like scene in *The Godfather Part 2;* the cake was being sliced, metaphorically giving pieces of the business to the other godfathers. I looked at dismay at my plate. I wasn't given a large role in the pilot. At the time I had mixed feelings. I wanted to do more but I also knew that this pilot was a disaster waiting to happen.

I was right. The feedback from the participants, a cross-section of the more than 20 business units that comprised GE Capital, made Nigel Andrews' comments seem tame. Fortunately for me, many of my predictions about the pilot were prescient enough that it gained me increased respect from Mike Markovits and the rest of the CLOE team.

We began modifications in earnest the next week and by midsummer the newly crafted GE Capital DMAIC course was a hit. Among modifications was the inclusion of the change management materials that GE Capital's in-house expert Beth Galucci nicely modified to fit with Six Sigma tools and techniques.

By 1997 CLOE had added the talents of Bill Lindenfelder and Dave Schulenberg, who added their breadth of experience to the tactical success of the DMAIC training by including a more formal set of training elements on the strategic elements of Six Sigma, business process management. This was formalized under the tutoring of Mo Cayer, who developed and delivered a business process management seminar that garnered great reviews and, more importantly, the active involvement of GE Capital business leaders.

1997 and 1998 also brought more mandates directly from Jack Welch that helped distinguish and add luster to Six Sigma, conveying it far from its roots as Motorola's set of defect reduction activities. These major changes are listed below.

The Focus on the Customer

One of the many arguments I fought and lost during the initial course design work was to deemphasize the focus on cost savings. I felt that cost saving was an important by-product of project success; however, I did not want it to be confused with the main goal of improving effectiveness. At its core Six Sigma is attempting to improve both effectiveness and efficiency.

There are costs associated with obtaining both effectiveness and efficiency. But obviously there are far greater costs in being ineffective or inefficient.

Costs associated with inefficiency are far easier to quantify. Inefficiency costs like rework, labor, downtime, and others are far easier to calculate than the cost of a lost customer. Therefore, when management wants to see a quick return on investment (ROI), there is a bias in terms of picking projects that impact efficiency. Unfortunately, when an organization makes a public commitment to Six Sigma (like GE did), customers are going to want to see how Six Sigma affects the products and/or services they purchase from the Six Sigma company.

My feelings were influenced by my brief contacts with W. Edwards Deming in the early 1980s. Deming, who influenced management worldwide during his days as the premier quality consultant to countries and companies alike, had told me once over breakfast that many cost savings that occur through process improvement are harder to quantify than others. He rhetorically asked me how an organization could calculate the cost of a lost client or that client informing others not to buy your products or services.

Therefore I took some solace in 1998 while attending the all-managers meeting in Puerto Rico when an edict from Jack Welch himself stated that all DMAIC projects going forth would have to have an external customer touch point. He had indicated that in recent months prior to the Puerto Rico meeting he had received repeated calls from major customers saying they weren't seeing Six Sigma's effects in their dealings with GE.

And why not? Of course the focus on hard cost savings resulted from projects. It is possible to calculate effectiveness costs, but often those take longer or can only indirectly be attributed to Six Sigma activity.

For example, it is possible that the strategic business objective of revenue or growth can be affected by Six Sigma projects but there will be other factors in a business affecting these measures. Sometimes businesses have to take as an article of faith that improving effectiveness will positively impact these measures even though there will be a lag time in terms of seeing improved revenue or growth measures. Because of this tendency I inform my clients to have a bias for efficiency-based projects in year one of their launch only to have a bias for effectiveness-based projects after they have seen the benefit of first-year efficiency-based projects adding to the bottom line.

To GE's credit, the 1998 edict from Jack Welch helped to push the customer front and center in terms of what Six Sigma added to an organization's reputation.

Formalization of the Strategy of Six Sigma

The strategic component of Six Sigma first became apparent when Bossidy was becoming more process focused in his management. At AlliedSignal, project selection was becoming more formalized through the application of the Strategy of Six Sigma. The Strategy of Six Sigma is called Business Process Management (BPM). BPM is a set of carefully calculated steps that identify and link key processes to business objectives. Then key measures of effectiveness and efficiency are measured for those processes. Finally, projects with the worst performance and highest impact to the business are selected for the tactics of Six Sigma, DMAIC (this book addresses the creation of the business process management system in Chapter 3).

To their credit, AlliedSignal began utilization of business process management activities, but it was GE Capital that began to be the prevalent organization to practice BPM, the key strategic element of Six Sigma.

In 1997 Bill Lindenfelder, Beth Galucci, and I formatted the Green Belt for Champions course materials that included the BPM elements. The course went on to be the most popular at GE Capital because management was able to see a pragmatic vehicle toward achievement of not only good project selection, but also their involvement in sponsoring those projects.

Formalization of Using Six Sigma as a Business Enabler

While it was AlliedSignal that first began to use Six Sigma as a business enabler, it was GE that formalized using Six Sigma as more than just a cost-savings initiative.

In 1997 GE formalized their Six Sigma for Sales program. Sales and marketing groups were expected to use Six Sigma to obtain more business for GE and achieve growth goals. They also began to see Six Sigma as a solutions tool for customers.

Modification of Systems and Structures

Perhaps the largest contribution of GE to making Six Sigma a cultural phenomenon was how they modified the systems and structures within GE that forced the organization to see Six Sigma as more than a set of quality tools.

Systems and structures typically are focused around six major working areas that define the culture of the organization. Table 2.1 shows the six items. We will briefly describe with examples each of these six elements.

The first element of changing systems and structures centers around hiring. As it relates to Six Sigma, this includes what initially is perceived as added bureaucracy but in reality is the infrastructure for successful implementation.

First, GE hired an army of consultants. At one point there were 62 different consulting organizations working within GE Capital alone. The first order of business was creating the course curriculum, but most organizations need outside help with the first course delivery, and GE was no different.

Table 2.1   Systems and Structures Six Major Working Areas

Working Areas
Hiring
Development
Rewards/Recognition
Performance Management
Communication
Job Description

The actual infrastructure of Six Sigma includes hiring Six Sigma quality leaders, then master black belts (i.e., the internal consultants) and making the decision either to hire black belts or decide on green belts.

GE took the black belt approach. Full-time Six Sigma project leaders were trained and led three or four DMAIC projects per year.

The second element of changing systems and structures is development. What GE did better than any other organization that had committed to Six Sigma was indoctrinate everyone into the concepts of Six Sigma. Different courses were developed for each type of employee where the curriculum was tailored for their anticipated participation. For example, if a midlevel manager was expected to be a project champion, they would receive different training than a black belt. A four-week course was developed and delivered for master black belts who eventually took over the training first done by consultants.

The third and most tangible system and structure that GE imprinted on Six Sigma was changing their reward and recognition program to embrace Six Sigma. In 1996 Jack Welch dictated that 40 percent of a manager's bonus was dependent on participation in Six Sigma.

The fourth component of system and structure modification was performance management. Here GE excelled when Jack Welch committed to a promotion policy where only those with Six Sigma experience were candidates for better jobs in the organization. Successful black belts learned about a business leading three or four projects per year. Typically, a black belt career path lasted two to three years. They were then promoted into high-profile business positions. Not only did these black belts know the business, knowing participation in Six Sigma resulted in better career opportunities, they created a culture of greater buy-in to Six Sigma, and interest in being a black belt.

Perhaps the boldest move Jack Welch made was in his communication about Six Sigma. Not only did he make a public commitment to Six Sigma for GE, Welch announced it to the financial community. A surge in stock price quickly followed his brash announcement. Once Six Sigma results began to materialize, the stock price rose even more. Finally, Six Sigma became part of some employees' actual job descriptions.

One reason for resistance to Six Sigma is the amount of time it takes to improve a process. This rationale disregards the fact that some employees cling to processes that are ineffective and inefficient. One GE solution to this issue was to add Six Sigma team participation to job descriptions, thereby making process improvement part of an employee's job, not "something else to do in addition to the job." In essence, Six Sigma became a mandatory component of all GE positions.

Summary

In 2000 I wrote the book, *The Six Sigma Revolution: How GE and others Turned Process into Profits*. In hindsight, Six Sigma has experienced an evolution since its inception at Motorola in the 1980s.

First used by Motorola as a tactical defect reduction quality tool kit, Six Sigma has evolved through its application by other organizations. It was AlliedSignal that first began to use Six Sigma as a strategic enabler to achieving business objectives and also initiated the use of managing by process.

Finally it was GE that not only added the strategic element of Six Sigma but also made it a cultural phenomenon.

Today, organizations need to apply Six Sigma in all three areas: strategic, tactical, and cultural. In our next chapter we tackle the first of these elements, the strategy, and provide you with how to execute the Six Sigma strategy.

Key Learnings

- Motorola is credited with being the originator of Six Sigma.
- Engineer Bill Smith was one of the first to propose Six Sigma, yet

it was Mikel Harry that generated widespread enthusiasm toward the concept and its application.

- Motorola used Six Sigma tactically as a quality improvement tool.
- Motorola's efforts were aimed almost exclusively on the manufacturing floor to reduce defects in products.
- Winning the Malcolm Baldrige Award required them to share their quality approach. This resulted in a host of other organizations like Texas Instruments and ABB learning about Six Sigma.
- AlliedSignal transcended the traditional approach to Six Sigma and began to utilize it as a means to accomplishing strategic business objectives.
- At Motorola, Six Sigma participation was expected of each business unit, but there was some "optionality" depending on an employee's current business performance.
- At AlliedSignal Six Sigma was not optional, and business leaders and managers played pivotal roles in selecting strategically important projects, focusing on more than what was broken on the shop floor.
- General Electric further defined Six Sigma as a true management philosophy by adding the final dimension: the cultural dimension.
- Among the elements that made GE so successful in implementing Six Sigma was their increasing focus on customers in selecting projects, expanding the strategic element of Six Sigma, and modifying systems and structures.
- Two major systems and structures that helped embed Six Sigma culturally at GE was making Six Sigma a part of the bonus program and making involvement in Six Sigma a condition of promotion.

Executing Your Six Sigma Strategy

The time to repair the roof is when the sun is shining.
—John F. Kennedy

Introduction

IN CHAPTER 2, we learned that Six Sigma was first launched as a set of quality tools at Motorola designed to reduce defects. As Motorola's success gained the attention of other organizations, Six Sigma began to evolve. In the early 1990s AlliedSignal contributed a strategic element, selecting projects that impacted business objectives. Thus Six Sigma migrated from Motorola's manufacturing floor to Allied-Signal's sales, marketing, and design departments. By the time General Electric launched their initiative, Six Sigma was a true management philosophy comprised of three key elements (strategy, tactics, and culture).

But improvement tactics are just one of the three elements. In later chapters we address the execution of those tactics as well as Six Sigma's cultural element, made popular by General Electric. In this chapter we teach the reader how to execute the first and most important element of Six Sigma, the Strategy of Six Sigma.

Background

I was born in Jersey City, New Jersey. Even as a boy I was struck by the majesty of the New York City skyline and with the World Trade Center Towers.

When 9/11 occurred I experienced the same emotions as any other American. This prompted my interest and involvement with congress to promote process management and Six Sigma in our fight against terrorism. I am now convinced that Six Sigma can be an aid to prevent terrorism.

In a *USA Today* article published on October 30, 2002,[1] Del Jones writes that the application of the data analysis elements of Six Sigma could have been used to sort through the mountains of intelligence data that the FBI and CIA face each day.

Jones's article stresses that review of data to determine what intelligence is valid and what intelligence data is not could use Six Sigma techniques. Later in this article Jones writes that government organizations could apply Six Sigma projects to drive significant cost savings in government that could be then be used to invest in more manpower or technical improvements to gather intelligence data.

I propose that while these two points are valid, the most important way Six Sigma can help in the fight on terrorism is through the application of the strategy of Six Sigma, a concept called Business Process Management.

Business Process Management and 9/11

The Strategy of Six Sigma is called Business Process Management, a series of activities taken by management to align their business by processes that impact strategic business objectives.

In today's business world, organizations are structured by functions. A business leader has a series of direct reports, typically vice presidents who in turn have directors and middle managers under them, visually displayed through an organizational chart. This organizational chart is represented in vertical fashion as seen in Figure 3.1.

Being structured by function has many advantages. It streamlines communication (within that function) and helps an organization manage budget adherence. Unfortunately, it hampers the organization with regard to its most important goal, being a customer-focused company.

To succeed, any organization must have customers or clients. These customers or clients buy a product or service from the organization. Customers are the lifeblood of any organization if that business is to be successful. Yet the problem not recognized by business leaders is their

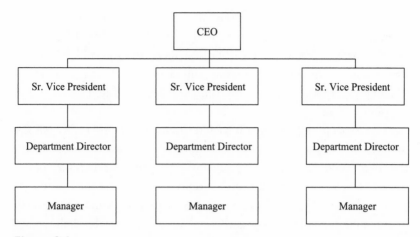

Figure 3.1

organizational models based on function get in the way of being customer focused.

At its core, Six Sigma attempts to make an organization both effective and efficient. Effectiveness is the degree to which an organization is meeting and preferably exceeding customer needs and requirements. Efficiency refers to the resources consumed in the attempt to become effective.

As we chronicled in Chapter 2, Motorola's first efforts were more efficiency-based projects, driving out non-value-added activities primarily on the shop floor. As Six Sigma evolved, the importance of the customer became paramount. As we indicated with the 1998 Jack Welch Puerto Rico meeting, projects had to have a customer touch point. Thus, the focus in the late 1990s was to have a bias for effectiveness-based Six Sigma work.

Those companies who attempted to focus on the customer soon learned that the traditional organizational structure hampered efforts to be customer focused. Why? A simple example will illustrate how the vertical nature of organizational structure gets in the way of being customer focused.

I recently experienced automobile problems with a leased vehicle. It was not the first time that I had experienced this problem, and I was frustrated by the constant need to take the vehicle in, arrange for a friend to pick me up, return, and fill out the unnecessary paperwork.

The good news is that the problem was finally fixed and the car was operational. The bad news is that along with this problem I had a host of other problems and was clearly dissatisfied with the vehicle. Therefore when a customer representative called and asked to take 5 minutes to complete a survey on how my vehicle was operating, I was only too happy to oblige.

The focus of the survey was to determine how happy I was with the maintenance of the vehicle. When I informed him I was dissatisfied with the vehicle and wanted to know my options about an early return of the leased vehicle, the customer service representative said that was out of his jurisdiction. He wasn't a customer service representative. Instead, he was a maintenance survey gatherer. This company, who shall remain anonymous but whose initials are BMW, was not interested in serving me, the customer. They only wanted to register good marks on how their maintenance was performed.

When I inquired as to whom I needed to talk to about an early lease return, I had to speak to three different people in three different cities before being told I was out of luck. I was stuck with this car.

The problem this represents is that the BMW organizational structure was vertically aligned. Yet, I as a customer wanted to proceed through the customer complaint process. A process is a series of steps and activities that take inputs (in this case my complaint), adds value, and produces an output (in this case a customer whose complaint was satisfactorily solved).

Thus, the vertical nature of functions or departments is at loggerheads with the concept of customer satisfaction. We are not advocating a dismissal of the organizational structure. As we have previously mentioned, it is imperative for function, communication, and budget adherence. However, without identifying, measuring, and improving processes that customers go through in your organization, you will ultimately suffer lost profits as customers look to alternatives, just as I now own a Mercedes instead of another BMW.

Fortunately, more organizations are starting to recognize the importance of process identification and management. The Westin hotels concept of "service express" is an example of process management (proudly, one of the locations where service express was piloted, the Westin Tabor Center is an Eckes and Associates Inc. client). Here the customer with a need, whether it is room service or a bulb replacement, calls one number (the service express button on her room phone) and the customer's need is met.

What is the implication of process management regarding terrorist attacks and 9/11? My analysis shows two areas where process management could have been of assistance. First, regarding the FAA's alignment of airline tracking and second, and more importantly, the management of information within and between information-gathering bodies like the FBI and CIA.

The U.S. airline industry is governed by the Federal Aviation Agency (FAA). The FAA has a series of Control Centers that are organized by region. Operational decisions about flights in the air are handled by these regional Control Centers and as a plane passes through one region into the next, there is a "handoff" of information relative to an individual flight. For problems in flight, air traffic controllers notify supervisors, who in turn inform their upper levels of management all the way to FAA headquarters in Herndon, Virginia, if necessary.

On September 11, 2001 the four hijacked planes were under the jurisdiction of four different regions at the time of the cockpit intrusions (Boston, New York, Cleveland, and Indianapolis).[2]

As the 9/11 Commission Report goes on to say on page 17.

FAA guidance to controllers on hijack procedures assumed that the aircraft pilot would notify the controller via radio or by 'squawking' a transponder code of '7500'—the universal code for a hijack in progress. Controllers would notify their supervisors, who in turn would inform management all the way up to FAA headquarters.[3]

The Commission report continues on what the chain of command was then expected to do once a hijacking was confirmed.

If the hijack was confirmed, procedures called for the hijack coordinator (who was the director of the FAA office of Civil Aviation Security or his or her designate) on duty to contact the Pentagon's National Military Command Center (NMCC) and to ask for a military escort aircraft to follow the flight, report anything unusual and aid search and rescue in the event of an emergency. The NMCC would then seek approval from the Office of the

**Secretary of Defense to provide military assistance. If approval
was given, the orders would be transmitted down NORAD's chain
of command.**[4]

The aforementioned protocols that call for inter and intradepartmental communication resulted in misinformation and considerable
loss of valuable time. For example, at one point the Boston region had
erroneously identified that Delta flight 1989 from Boston to Las Vegas
had been hijacked. At 9:41 a.m. the Boston Center called the Northeast
Air Defense Sector (NEADS) with a report that a Delta flight had been
hijacked. NEADS, taking that information provided by the Boston region, scrambled interceptors that eventually left Ohio for Michigan to
intercept the Delta flight.[5]

Ironically the time and confusion that followed regional air traffic
controllers, providing information to multiple resources and ultimately
going up and down the chains of command of various agencies, resulted in such misinformation and lost time that military response time
was virtually nonexistent. On page 31 of the 9/11 Commission report is
the following damaging data:

**As it turned out the NEADS air defenders had nine minutes' no-
tice on the first hijacked plane, no advance notice on the second,
no advance notice on the third, and no advanced notice on the
fourth.**[6]

Once the hijacking of four planes to be used as weapons of mass destruction took place that late summer day in 2001, a military response
was in order. But the vertical nature of command and communication
did not allow a quick response. A second plane hijacked in Boston, off
course and allowed to plow into the South Tower of the World Trade
Center, would not have occurred if a horizontal communication path
had been in place. While having Flight 175 intercepted by F-15s and
shot down would have been an untold tragedy, it would have prevented
the thousands of deaths of those working hard that Tuesday morning in
the South Tower of the World Trade Center.

Examine below the time line of events from the first hijacking of
Flight 11 that ultimately crashed into the North Tower to the demise
of Flight 93 that crashed into the ground in Shanksville, Pennsylvania.

7:59	American Airlines Flight 11 takes off.
8:14	Hijackers begin their assault on the cockpit of Flight 11.
8:14	Flight 175 takes off.
8:19	A call from an off-duty flight attendant informs American Airlines that a hijacking is in progress.
8:20	Flight 77 leaves Dulles Airport in Virginia.
8:23	American Airlines dispatcher attempts to reach Flight 11 unsuccessfully.
8:24	Boston Air Traffic Control becomes aware of hijacking based on hearing Mohamed Atta's instruction to passengers to remain quiet.
8:24–8:32	Boston Air Traffic Control begins to notify their chain of command about the hijacking.
8:32	The Air Traffic Control Command Center notifies the Operations Center at FAA headquarters in Herndon, VA. They do not contact NMCC to request a fighter escort per protocol.
8:34	Boston contacts the FAA office in Cape Cod.
8:37	Boston informs the military (NEADS) of a hijacking and the need to scramble F-16s for escort. Command Colonel Robert Marr phones Major General Larry Arnold seeking authorization to scramble F-15s.
8:39	Dispatcher contacts Boston Air Traffic Control, who indicates they already know of the hijacking of Flight 11.
8:42	Flight 93 takes off from Newark Airport.
8:46	Flight 11 crashes into the North Tower of the World Trade Center.
8:46	Hijackers begin their assault on the cockpit of Flight 175.
8:47	Air traffic controllers know something is abnormal as Flight 175 changes beacon codes twice.
8:51	Flight 175 deviates from flight plan.
8:52	Air traffic controllers unsuccessfully attempt to contact Flight 175.
8:52	Flight attendant calls United to inform flight has been hijacked.
8:52	Hijackers begin their assault on the cockpit of Flight 77.
8:53	F-15s in the air to track Flight 11. Not knowing specific vectors (for a flight that has now crashed into the World Trade Center) the F-15s are directed to circle off Long Island.

8:54	Flight 77 deviates from flight plan.
8:55	New York air traffic controller notifies his manager of a hijack of Flight 175.
8:56	Flight 77 disappears from Indianapolis radar.
9:00	Indianapolis Air Traffic Control attempts to contact Flight 77 by radio and then attempts to contact Flight 77 directly.
9:02	New York Air Traffic Control management notifies FAA headquarters in Herndon, VA.
9:03	Flight 175 crashes into the South Tower of the World Trade Center.
9:03	New York Air Traffic control notifies the military (NEADS) of a hijacking of Flight 175.
9:08	Indianapolis contacts Langley Air Force base about a missing plane assumed to have crashed; they are unaware of the two planes that crashed into the World Trade Center.
9:09	Indianapolis Air Traffic Control notifies a FAA regional center about Flight 77.
9:09–9:13	F-15s remain in a holding pattern off Long Island.
9:13	F-15 vectored to Manhattan after being notified of Flight 175 hitting the South Tower.
9:24	FAA regional center notifies FAA headquarters in Herndon, VA about the disappearance of Flight 77.
9:28	Hijackers begin their assault on the cockpit of Flight 93.
9:32	Dulles Terminal Control facility observes a "primary radar target tracking eastbound at a high rate of speed."
9:34	FAA headquarters notifies the military (NEADS) that Flight 77 is missing.
9:37	Flight 77 crashes into the Pentagon.
9:41	Cleveland Air Traffic Control loses transponder signal from Flight 93.
9:46	FAA headquarters in Herndon notified that Flight 93 is 29 minutes from DC.
9:49	FAA headquarters suggests that someone should decide about contacting NEADS.

FAA Headquarters: They're pulling Jeff away to go talk about United 93.

Command Center: Uh, do we want to think, uh, about scrambling aircraft?

FAA Headquarters: Oh, God, I don't know.

Command Center: Uh, that's a decision somebody's gonna have to make probably in the next ten minutes.

FAA Headquarters: Uh, ya know everybody just left the room.[7]

9:53   FAA communicates to NEADS about scrambling aircraft.

10:03   Flight 93 crashes into the ground in Shanksville, Pennsylvania.

While it cannot be said with certainty that Flight 175 and Flight 77 could have been intercepted by F-15s, it is fair to say that the amount of time for the three Air Traffic Control centers to run communication up their individual chains of command, then to transfer information to the FAA, who in turn had to pass information to the military (NEADS) appears to be the personification of the inefficiencies found in functional management. A more formalized horizontal process of direct communication with the military would certainly have increased the possibility of quicker military intervention and the subsequent increase in lives saved on September 11th.

The 9/11 Commission report also comments on how the same concept of command and control operated at the White House in the hours when the hijacking took place.

And none of the information conveyed in the White House video teleconference, at least in the first hour, was being passed to the NMCC (National Military Command Center). As one witness recalled, '(It) was almost like there were parallel decision-making processes going on: one was a voice conference orchestrated by the NMCC . . . and there was the (White House video teleconference) . . . In my mind they were competing venues for command and control and decisionmaking.'[8]

Figure 3.2 shows the geometrical path of going up and down the chain of commands at the various agencies that involve the hijacking of commercial aircraft at the time of 9/11. This vertical path of communication

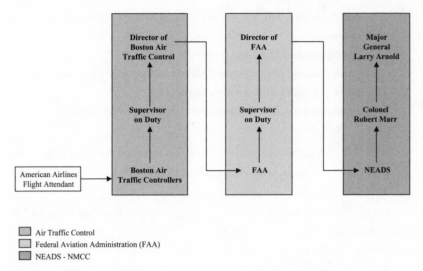

Figure 3.2

takes excessive time, and in the case of 9/11, it cost time that resulted in unnecessary loss of life. The concept of business process management (i.e., the strategy of Six Sigma) believes in a horizontal approach to communication. This horizontal approach takes considerably less time to complete. Figure 3.3 shows how that communication could have been accomplished in the case of 9/11.

Of far more impact is the cost to this nation of the functional structure that existed between the FBI, CIA, and other national agencies responsible for information gathering and dissemination that I claim could have prevented any plane on 9/11 leaving the ground with terrorists onboard.

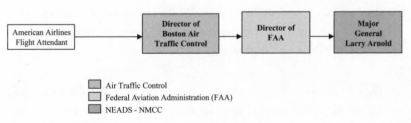

Figure 3.3 Hijacking awareness process

In the United States there are two major organizations responsible for counterterrorism, the FBI and the CIA. In an ideal world these two organizations would collaborate, share information, and be cohesive relative to counterterrorism. In reality they exhibited the same sense of silo management and fiefdoms that highlight many manufacturing and service organizations in the United States.

As stated in the 9/11 report, the FBI is a highly decentralized organization with most work done in a series of field offices (a total of 56 in all), each covering a specific geographical area of the United States. Prior to 9/11 each field office had a special agent in charge that reported to the Director of the FBI but was free to set her specific agendas and priorities as she saw fit for her field office.

Each field office was measured against such statistics as arrests, indictments, prosecutions, and convictions. Thus, if a field office director wanted career enhancement he focused on activities that would result in higher numbers being recorded in the aforementioned areas. Counterterrorism and Counterintelligence work often resulted in lengthy and tedious activities that do not result in arrests. Therefore, the FBI field offices focused on traditional work that pertained to drugs, white collar crime, and gangs. As the 9/11 Commission states eloquently, *"individual field offices made choices to serve local priorities, not national priorities."*[9]

As we shall see later in this chapter, the first element in creating the Six Sigma strategy is clear delineation of the strategic business objectives of the organization. The business objectives of an organization set the tone and guide the behavior of those in that organization. Thus, the focus on easily counted measures like arrests and convictions precluded the FBI from its most important job, protecting U.S. citizens from foreign invasion.

Making matters worse was that the FBI operated under what is termed an "office of origin" system. What this means is that one field office was always designated as the single point of contact for an entire investigation. The impact of the office of origin system was that other field offices that came across information other than the office of origin became reluctant to spend time on something because they had no control of the investigation and likely would not receive credit if an arrest or conviction transpired.

The 9/11 Commission Report also chronicles other inadequacies with the FBI and its priorities.

> In 2000 there were still twice as many agents devoted to drug enforcement as counterterrorism.[10]
>
> With a few notable exceptions the field offices did not apply significant resources to terrorism and often reprogrammed funds for other priorities.[11]
>
> ... the FBI did not have an effective intelligence collection effort. Collection of intelligence from human sources was limited, and agents were inadequately trained. Only three days of a 16 week agent's course was devoted to counterintelligence and counterterrorism and most subsequent training was received on the job.[12]

In July, 1995, Attorney General Janet Reno issued formal procedures dealing with FBI information gathering regarding counterintelligence and how that information should be communicated and managed by the Justice Department prosecutors. Like the Air Traffic Controllers, the FAA, and the U.S. military, each of these two divisions of government had a chain of command to follow. As such, procedures were often miscommunicated and took time, resulting in that information becoming outdated.

Again, because of the competitive nature of competing organizations, information sharing and coordination was faulty. In fact the 9/11 Commission Report states the procedures for sharing information between departments became known as the "Wall."[13]

This is significant because in the business world the concept of functional management and its resulting lack of cohesion between departments and functions has resulted in people quoting "throwing something over the wall."

A sad example of this "Wall" mentality was that one field office of the FBI (Phoenix) had information about Middle Easterners attending flight schools which was not passed on to either the Justice Department or the FAA. Further, in a *Christian Science Monitor* report (May 17, 2002), The White House now acknowledges that the CIA had informed President Bush in August 2001 of Al Qaeda's interest in hijacking planes. During this same time frame the aforementioned data on Middle Easterners attending flight school had surfaced. *The Christian Science Monitor* goes on to say that the Phoenix FBI office had warned in blunt language in an internal memo that Osama bin Laden and his Al Qaeda operatives had links between Middle Eastern men and their attendance at multiple U.S. flight schools.[14]

Further causing frustration was that in August 2001, two of the hijackers of Flight 77 (Khalid al-Midhar and Nawaq Alhazmi) had been placed on a CIA "watchlist," but the CIA did not share this information with the FBI.[15]

What is particularly painful is that in another FBI field office (Minneapolis), a French nationalist, Zacarias Moussaoui, had been arrested in August 2001. It was Moussaoui who had taken flight lessons in Oklahoma only to terminate his training in May 2001. He paid a Pan Am flight training school in Minnesota over $8000 to learn how to fly large aircraft. However, his interest in flying large aircraft without interest in obtaining a pilot's license drew the attention of the Minnesota flight school. The Immigration and Naturalization Service was notified and subsequently arrested Moussaoui on immigration charges because his visa had expired.[16]

If this arrest and its communication had been shared with information gathered by the Phoenix FBI office, a higher level of interest and research of other Middle Easterners taking flight lessons with no interest in obtaining a pilot's license might have occurred.

I contend that the misplaced priorities on the wrong strategic objectives and the way the FBI and CIA were organized prevented information from being shared. A hallmark of the strategy of Six Sigma (Business Process Management) attempts to link the key processes of an organization with the key business objectives. If the FBI and CIA had been practicing the concepts of Business Process Management, they would have identified among their key processes something akin to a "Terrorist Prevention Awareness" process. Processes by their very definition cut across functions and departments. They are horizontal, not vertical like an organizational chart. In the case of the hijackers, shared information would likely have averted 9/11.

A quote from the former CIA director, Stansfield Turner, seems to share my thinking. "There was an error here, in that the Phoenix and Minnesota indicators and analyses never got brought together. If they had, it's more likely that...an alarm bell would have risen high enough in decibels to attract somebody's attention."[17]

Charles Pena, a senior defense analyst at the Cato Institute agrees. "...there is a very large bureaucracy that is very compartmentalized... People literally don't talk to each other."[18]

Sadly, the simple steps to create the strategy for Six Sigma (Business Process Management) did not occur within our government. With it, I contend that September 11th would be considered just another day on the calendar rather than holding the sad remembrance of our nation's greatest tragedy that occurred on our soil.

We now address how to create those simple steps for your organization.

Executing the Strategy of Six Sigma

There are eight steps to creating your Six Sigma strategy and selecting high-impact, low-performing processes for projects. In the following pages we dissect those eight steps and teach you how to create your Six Sigma strategy.

The eight steps of creating your Six Sigma strategy are:

1. Creation and agreement of Strategic Business Objectives
2. Creation of Core and Key Subprocesses
3. Identification of Process Owners
4. Creation and Validation of Measurement Dashboards
5. Data Collection on Agreed Dashboards
6. Creation of Project Selection Criteria
7. Choosing First Projects
8. Maintaining and Managing the Business Process Management System

We tackle the first seven of these in this chapter and return to number eight in a later chapter on culture.

To execute the strategy of Six Sigma properly, there is a set of activities to conduct prior to the first two days the participants work together, a set of activities that can be accomplished in two days of executives working together, intersession work, and then a second two-day session to finish the first seven steps.

Work Prior to Your First Working Session with Executives

To simply show up one day and begin to create the strategy of Six Sigma would result in total disaster. One thing I have learned having done these sessions repeatedly is that the actual sessions reflect the culture of the organization. As such, these sessions can (and should) be different each time they are done. To reduce the variation in performance, it is crucial to have good preparation. Follow these simple but important steps to ensure that your session is a success.

Get the Right People in the Room

One of the keys to the success of Six Sigma is the active involvement of management. In previous quality efforts, the most that management did was give a kickoff speech and turn things over to the consultant. This was particularly the case with Total Quality Management (TQM), which had a lot of "T" and a lot of "Q" but not much "M." One of the advantages of Six Sigma strategy is that management not only creates the strategy, but it becomes the vehicle for their ongoing involvement.

Thus it is imperative that the strategy session coordinator must ensure the participation of the right people. Who should participate? In the first two scheduled days at a minimum the business leader and his or her direct reports should be present. The second two formal days should include the business leader and direct reports and other process owners (see process owner identification later in this chapter).

Getting the business leader and her direct reports in the same room for two full days can be a challenge. It is suggested that articles or books on the strategic element of Six Sigma first be shared with these individuals to create enthusiasm and need for their participation. We have found that the focus should be on the business leader first and foremost. Once they are on board, mandatory direct report attendance is almost assured. Appendix A has a generic letter from a business leader to direct reports requesting their attendance.

In addition to the main participants, it is also recommended that the Six Sigma infrastructure (one or two master black belts and the quality leader) be in attendance.

Choosing the Room and Working Materials

One often overlooked aspect of preparation is selection of the working area for the actual sessions. As you will soon see, these are highly interactive sessions where there is a need for participant mobility. Thus the first order of business is to have a room set up with tables that allow for access to a large wall space where the participants will work.

Why the need for a large wall space? Hard-charging executives can easily waste two valuable days talking issues as important as strategic business objectives and processes to death without gaining agreement. The purpose of the working sessions is to gain agreement on key issues facing the organization. Therefore, a tool I strongly suggest be the vehicle for the working session is the affinity diagram. The affinity diagram is a quality tool that allows for participation by all, allows limited discussion, and leads to gaining agreement on the elements of the Six Sigma strategy. Later in this chapter we will see a working example of the use of the affinity diagram as it is applied to the work of the business leaders. Suffice it to say, a large wall is necessary for the affinity diagram to be used effectively. Finally, check to see that Post-It notes will stick to the wall. If not, prepare the room by taping flip chart paper on the wall space so that Post-It notes will stick to the surface. Nothing is more frustrating than seeing a business executive's great idea hitting the floor when a Post-It note doesn't stick to the wall, only to be followed by other falling Post-It notes.

Additionally, the coordinator for this event must ensure that a proper and ample set of supplies are on hand. Appendix A lists the supplies that should be available in the working area.

Finally, the coordinator should arrange for three to five smaller rooms for the second day of work since the large group will be working in subgroups on Day 2.

The Premeeting with the Business Leader

A brief meeting should be scheduled with the business leader prior to the first working session. This session is imperative because certain agreements must be reached between the coordinator and the business leader. Among them are:

- The preferred method of decision making during the working sessions
- The amount, timing, and type of involvement on the part of the business leader

As previously mentioned, meetings among business executives can be laborious, rancorous, and unproductive. One reason for the unproductive managerial meeting is the tendency of executives to want to talk something to death rather than reach agreement. The psychology of most business leaders is that of a hard-charging, opinionated person who feels strongly about his position running a business. Therefore, without an agreed-to formal method to reach agreement, many a formal meeting ends in disagreement, only for decisions to be made in private in smaller groups.

Thus, prior to the working session the coordinator should meet with the business leader to gain agreement on the decision-making method to be used. Because the purpose of creating the Six Sigma strategy is to achieve agreement among the business leaders of the organization, we strongly suggest that the primary decision-making method be consensus. Consensus is misunderstood by many people who perceive it as 100 percent agreement. It is not. Consensus has two crucial criteria. First, all in attendance must participate. Second, all in attendance must agree when a compromise is proposed. The compromised agreement in all likelihood might not be the preferred decision by some, but they must agree to abide by the decision and not sabotage the decision at a later time. The advantage of consensus decision making is the buy-in that is created among those participating. There are two major disadvantages to consensus decision making. The first disadvantage is the time it takes to reach consensus. Second, and more importantly, sometimes consensus cannot be reached. When I conduct a Six Sigma strategy session I allow for liberal discussion on a topic and then ask the group whether anyone cannot agree to the proposed compromise. If someone says they cannot in good conscience support a compromise, then consensus cannot be reached and I then go the secondary decision-making method. The recommended secondary decision-making method is consultative decision making wherein the business leader makes the call on a decision.

Consultative decision making is defined as one person (the business leader) who makes the decision after taking input from others. The reason a premeeting is held with the business leader is to coach him or her not to proceed to this decision-making method prematurely. The coordinator should contract with the business leader that he or she should participate, but in the early stages of discussion play more of a passive role, allowing his or her staff to take the lead in discussions. This contracting is crucial on two fronts. First, many a Six Sigma strategy meeting can be derailed if it simply becomes a forum for the business leader's views. Second, the contracting is important to work out signals between the coordinator and business leader when they do need to intercede and make an executive decision when consensus cannot be reached.

Finally, in this premeeting, review the business leader's opening remarks for the kickoff of session one. Many times the coordinator will be asked to generate the speech given by the business leader. When I am asked for input I stress that the business leader should explain why the organization is pursuing a Six Sigma strategy, what's in it for the organization, and what is expected of her direct reports. Again the invitation letter found in Appendix A is a good starting point for this speech.

The Friendly Reminder

It is wise for the coordinator to remember that the absence of any key business executives can result in failure to execute the Six Sigma strategy. I have always found it helpful to meet briefly with each business executive invited to remind him of the meeting a week or so before the first working session and to review the agenda and desired outcomes for the two-day session. As the proverb goes, "a stitch in time saves nine."

The First Two-Day Working Session to Create the Six Sigma Strategy

Appendix A shows the specific and formal agenda for the first two days. Generally, the first two days are spent trying to complete the following items:

- Creation and Agreement of the Strategic Business Objectives
- Creation of Core and Key Subprocesses

- Identification of Process Owners
- Creation of Measurement Dashboards

On day one of the first session the coordinator should arrive at least one hour ahead of the start time. I recommend the start time be 8:30 a.m. so that the business executives can get in some regular work before starting the session, lessening their guilt about the time spent in the Six Sigma strategy session.

In that hour of preparation the coordinator should make sure that each table is set up with flip chart pens, Post-It notes, and writing tablets for each participant. The coordinator should further write out the agenda on a flip chart and prepare a set of recommended ground rules for the participants. While these ground rules must be agreed to by the participants, I have found the following ground rules, if agreed to, help the session go much smoother.

First, lay down a ground rule that everyone must stay in the room for the duration of the session. Typically when reviewing the agenda I build in breaks every 90 minutes for 20-minutes duration so that not only biological needs are met but the participants have a chance to check email or voice mail. However, it is imperative that each participant makes the commitment to stay for each of the 90-minute sessions and commit to prompt return from breaks and lunch. Insist that no cell phones or pagers remain on.

Another ground rule that should be suggested is "No stripes in the room." This indicates everyone is an equal (except if the business leader is called to make a decision when consensus cannot be reached) and that each individual's ideas should be considered on par with everyone else's.

There are three other ground rules worth mentioning. First, sensitive information might be revealed, so confidentiality as a ground rule is worth consideration. The finished product of strategic business objectives, process identification, and measurement will be circulated to the organization as a whole, but getting there might result in discussions of a sensitive nature. Therefore suggest this to your key executives. Second, it has been my experience that some discussions in the creation of the Six Sigma strategy can become heated and even personal. Therefore, it's suggested that you set a ground rule that only one person may talk at a time. Further, hard-charging executives typically like to finish each other's sentences. Ensure that the group agrees to "look for each other's punctuation mark." Finally, sidebar conversations can be distracting to all involved, so suggest "Limit Sidebars" as a ground rule. Remember, ask for the input of the group for other ground rules and be sure the executive agrees with those you have suggested.

Review the agenda, noting to all participants that times are approximate. History has taught me that in some cases some elements of the agenda go quickly while other points take more time. Stressing this flexibility to the audience will save anxiety later and avoid a premature end to important discussions later on.

Once the agenda and ground rules have been addressed and the business leader has made some brief opening remarks, it's time for the session to become highly interactive. Address the first desired outcome of the day: reaching an agreement on the strategic business objectives.

Agreeing on the Strategic Business Objectives

The coordinator should be forewarned that it is likely there will be resistance to the first item on the agenda. Most business teams believe they have already identified their strategic business objectives. On more than one occasion I have been told that this agenda item is a waste of time. I strongly caution against skipping this agenda item. Many times I've discovered—painfully—that what is perceived as a strategic business objective really hasn't been understood by the management team or, worse yet, has been forgotten by the management team.

The coordinator should also be aware that when this happens, the business leader is apt to be more than a little upset. The leader wants to ensure that time spent in strategic planning has already been registered and absorbed by her direct reports. One failure of creating the strategy for Six Sigma can occur when the business leader's frustration with her direct reports curtails later involvement. Therefore, it sometimes is a good idea to prepare the business leader in advance for this possibility. One way I prep the business leader is to indicate that the times for addressing the strategic business objectives are approximate, and if there is clear sailing on this item we will proceed quickly to process identification. Of course, that kind of speed occurs only in a few cases.

The First Two Days—A Case Study

Author's note: Having completed many a Six Sigma strategy session, I have decided to share a case study. Because of the proprietary nature of this type of work, I have created a hybrid of several different companies. All of the examples used actually occurred across several companies, not just one. I have also created fictional names for the company I have identified for the case study. Everything I am about to share actually transpired in various Six Sigma strategy sessions.

The company in question is an international financial services organization. The company was more resistant to Six Sigma than most I had seen. The organization had several other initiatives going on, and most thought Six Sigma was just one more "thing to do." To his credit, the business leader did an outstanding job in his opening remarks to his direct reports indicating there was never a good time to implement Six Sigma, as well as referencing the fact that their work in implementing Six Sigma could assist with their other initiatives.

Knowing my time was seen as a nuisance, I attempted to convey an air of competence in my introductory statements about what Six Sigma could do for their organization. Quickly I taught them the basic concepts of the affinity diagram using a simple example taken from real life.

Learning the Affinity Diagram

"The affinity diagram is a structured yet informal tool that allows for all of you to participate in creating your ideas, sharing them with each other, and allows for discussion, but ultimately allows us to reach agreement. It's so simple I use this tool when my sons and I want to reach an agreement on where we should go on a summer vacation."

I then proceeded to tell them briefly about my two boys, Joe and Temo. I gave them information on their ages and interests and then told them at their working tables to take out a flip chart pen and Post-It notes and to write down some vacation spots that we might like to go on a summer vacation. Next, I instructed them to come to the large wall and place their Post-It note ideas on the wall in no particular order or fashion.

Within 3 minutes a host of ideas had been placed on the wall. Figure 3.4 shows what the wall looked like.

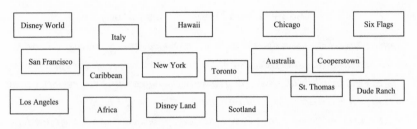

Figure 3.4

I then proceeded to read off each idea with the following understanding: if any of the participants disagreed with an idea, we didn't need to hear anything from them; if there was any confusion about the potential vacation spot, then participants could seek clarification.

As I read off each Post-It I started to assemble them in an organized fashion. Disney World and Disney Land were placed under each other. If I found a duplicate, I stuck them together. Within minutes most of the Post-Its were in four different categories (yet to be named) until we had gotten to the Cooperstown Post-It. Someone had inquired what makes this a vacation spot. Each time this happened I reverted back to the author, who gave an explanation. The author went on to say that given my initial information about my boys and I loving baseball, Cooperstown is the site of the Hall of Fame. No discussion ensued relative to whether it was a good idea or not, simply a discussion occurred to determine understanding.

Finally, I asked for a suggestion for a category name for each of the columns of ideas. Above Disney Land, Disney World, and Six Flags we placed the card "Amusement parks" (called a header card). Above New York, Chicago, L.A., and San Francisco we placed the card "U.S. destinations," and so forth.

Next we handed out sticky dots and told each table they had five dots (i.e., votes) as to which were the more likely places we should consider for vacation. After the multivoting exercise we were left with four "finalist" locations for consideration for the Eckes' family vacation. Those locations were Disney World, Cooperstown, the Caribbean, and a Dude Ranch.

To come up with one destination we then applied a set of criteria (in this case the father's) to decide on the final destination. In other cases, such as determining the strategic business objectives or key processes of an organization, multivoting might suffice.

Creation and Agreement on the Strategic Business Objectives

It was then time to use the affinity diagram on real work. I proceeded to instruct each participant to write silently as many ideas as they had about the strategic business objectives of this financial services organization. I attempted to practice prevention by also giving the two instructions. First, I asked them to think in terms of noun and verb/adjective. Second, I asked them to think in terms of the "what" of the business. In the case of the latter I often see some participants think ahead and state a process (the how) when at this point in the process they should think simply of the whats of the business.

At first, resistance was evident as the Chief Strategic Planner indicated loudly that this activity had been accomplished at their January off-site 10 months prior. I politely but firmly responded that we were not duplicating the January meeting and that if everyone had a common understanding of the strategic business objectives, this part of the day would go quickly. Reluctantly, the Chief Strategic Planner began writing the strategic business objectives that only he knew too well.

Within five minutes the executive team had begun approaching the working wall and placed their Post-Its with strategic business objectives. Just as we had with the vacation example, I began to read off each Post-It for clarification purposes while grouping duplicate ideas. During the clarification time, a rich discussion ensued over one card entitled "Profitable Assets." One person believed it meant Return on Assets while another believed it referred to Sustained Growth. I interceded with the ground rule that during the idea clarification period, we simply wanted to understand the author's reasoning so we could categorize the header card and resume discussion. I did shoot a knowing glance toward the Chief Strategic Planner who appeared to be frustrated that members of the staff didn't know what the real strategic business objectives were.

After clarifying and duplicating all Post-It notes, we were ready for the difficult assignment of naming the category header cards. Those engaged in this activity should be aware that healthy dialogue is expected and that the facilitator should err on the side of allowing a rich discussion before reaching a premature agreement.

During the naming of the header cards, various disagreements ensued. After a lengthy debate, Net Operating Margin was reached as the consensus decision for the financial related Post-Its. The Chief Financial Officer was pleased with that result and pointed out that it was slightly different than what had been determined at January's strategic planning meeting. The VP of Manufacturing pointed out that the use of the affinity diagram and the ensuing discussion had been missing from January's meeting. Instead a discussion by some of the participants in January's meeting had taken place. The affinity diagram was a vehicle to get everyone's participation as was the following discussion that I allowed to go on for some time. However, by utilizing the affinity diagram and then having this dialogue we not only reached agreement but the participants had gained greater buy-in to the use of Net Operating Margin as the financial strategic business objective of this organization.

It is common that the discussion around the financial strategic business objective is the lengthiest. In short order the group agreed to these header cards: Net Operating Margin, Customer/Client Satisfaction, Profitable Growth, and Portfolio Balance. There was some discussion about including one more header card focusing on employees. In the initial years of doing Six Sigma strategy work, I was astounded that many times I had to prompt the addition of some type of employee-related strategic business objective. Today the controversy centers more on what to call the employee objective. After our first break this team debated whether to call the header card Employee Satisfaction, Employee Development, or Employee Retention.

I have learned the hard way its better for an executive team to have buy-in to something they must later modify. However, the second of these labels (Employee Development) was a red flag that required an intervention from me. I was careful to point out that the executive team should not get ahead of themselves and reminded the group that we should focus on the "whats" not the "hows." I pointed out that Employee Development could later be a core process supporting either Employee Satisfaction or Employee Retention. The group listened respectfully and demurred to my input. At the same time I pointed out that if they had agreed to Customer/Client Satisfaction being a strategic business objective, why should employees be treated any differently? A healthy discussion followed, and I had an ally in the VP of

Human Resources. Finally, as we approached the lunch hour the group agreed on its final strategic business objective, Employee Satisfaction.

The following list shows the agreed to strategic business objectives for this financial services organization:

- Net Operating Margin
- Customer/Client Satisfaction
- Portfolio Balance
- Profitable Growth
- Employee Satisfaction

I have found that agreement to 5–7 strategic business objectives is best. Similar to the concept that phone numbers are best remembered because anything higher than 7 is difficult to remember; this client's list of 5 is quite manageable. In rare cases I have seen strategic business objectives extend to as high as 11. However, in most situations these businesses modify the list downward once it becomes clear that some of the objectives are really subobjectives, enabling the accomplishment of higher-level objectives.

Over lunch the group has become upbeat. They thank me for budgeting enough time for what they perceived as a valuable morning of reaching agreement on their objectives and indicate approval of the affinity diagram.

Creation of Core and Key Subprocesses

It was then my responsibility to get this group of executives to begin examining their business horizontally. Invariably this is a challenge for each group I work with for the following important reason. The former psychologist in me knows that all of the people in that room had risen to their high executive rank because they had mastered the concept of vertical management and the concept of command and control. Psychologically, we become used to doing what works. For the people in that room, functional management was a success, at least for them. What the afternoon promised was the need for them to create a paradigm shift in the organization. Every time I conduct the process management session, the move toward process identification is painful.

In the early afternoon I assigned the group several tasks to make the transition from vertical to horizontal management. They were as follows:

- Think and record a noun and some action word. For example Order Acquisition is indicating something that has to be processed (an order) and what happens to the order (it is acquired).
- Avoid the use of the word "and." Using the word "and" usually reflects combining two functions or departments.
- A process should at a minimum cut across two functions or departments. Once you feel you have identified a process, do a check to identify at least two functions or departments.
- Think high level. Our desired outcome of the afternoon session was to identify the five to seven "core" processes that had a direct impact on the strategic objectives from the morning session.

This group was more horizontally challenged than most. Despite my best intentions, the group used the affinity diagram basically to redefine the organizational chart. It is at this point someone like me switches roles, and instead of a facilitator plays the part of best practice sharer. I attempt to jump-start the concept of process thinking by sharing some examples from other financial service organizations that have already created their process management structure.

This can be highly dangerous. Just like the parent who might jump-start their offspring's homework by doing the first math problem or two, the organization can be lulled into having the consultant do all their work for them. The facilitator/consultant must also avoid the tendency to do the work of the group to avoid the frustration of getting the group to experience the paradigm shift that is crucial to later Six Sigma work. As my good friend and colleague Susan Ayarbe says, "Struggle is good." While painful to watch (and experience if you are the facilitator/consultant), struggle is important for group buy-in and to get everyone to start thinking critically and ultimately manage process.

Additionally, be aware that this exercise is rarely linear. I will sometimes tell the group to take an additional break in the hopes that clearing their minds can lead to a breakthrough moment upon their return. As a compromise, I often tell clients that if they can identify the noun, a fallback position is to use "management" as the temporary verb/process identifier. This was the case in this situation, and by 3 p.m. the group had identified and agreed to the following core processes:

- New Product Development
- Customer Acquisition
- Customer Relationship Management
- Employee Development
- Portfolio Management
- Compliance Assurance

There is one more important activity I strive to complete on Day 1. The last activity is to complete the alignment check to ensure that the right processes have been identified to support the right strategic objective.

The exercise is set up by having the facilitator/consultant list the strategic business objectives at the top right of the working wall. Next, the core processes should be listed down the left-hand column as Table 3.1 illustrates.

I break the executives into three to five groups of three to five each and ask them to rate the impact of the core processes against each strategic business objective on a scale of one to five, with one meaning there is little or no impact and five having major impact. For example, each table team would first rate how New Product Development impacts Net Operating Margin. I give significant leeway for each team in how to come up with their number. Some teams sense the day is nearly over and go around their table and simply produce an average, which they then put on a Post-It note and place in the appropriate area on the working wall. Other teams have a discussion and come up with a compromise number for the impact of that core process on the strategic business objective.

After all groups have given their numbers, I instruct each team to discuss what went well during the first day (called pluses) and what could have been done differently (called deltas). Once they have completed both tasks, they are free to go.

One reason I like finishing Day 1 with this assignment is it allows me to calculate the overall averages from each subgroup at my leisure in the evening rather than wasting the valuable time of the executives during the actual session. The averages are then posted and ready for the first discussion on Day 2. My remaining homework is to compile and prioritize the pluses/deltas for the day, which also will be part of the kickoff of Day 2.

Table 3.2 shows what the working wall looks like as we begin Day 2.

Table 3.1

	Net Operating Margin	Customer/Client Satisfaction	Portfolio Balance	Profitable Growth	Employee Satisfaction
New Product Development					
Customer Acquisition					
Customer Relationship Management					
Employee Development					
Portfolio Management					
Compliance Assurance					

Table 3.2

	Net Operating Margin	Customer/Client Satisfaction	Portfolio Balance	Profitable Growth	Employee Satisfaction
New Product Development	4.8	3.8	3.8	5.0	1.8
Customer Acquisition	5.0	2.5	3.0	4.7*	3.5
Customer Relationship Management	4.9	5.0	2.8*	4.0	3.5
Employee Development	3.2	4.0	2.2	4.0	5.0
Portfolio Management	4.5	3.0	5.0	4.2	3.2
Compliance Assurance	4.0	3.6	4.2	4.3	2.2

The second day begins like the first with a review of the agenda for Day 2 and reminding the participants of the ground rules from Day 1. The desired outcomes for Day 2 include aligning the core processes with the strategic business objectives, drilling down into subprocesses, and beginning the dialogue to define what the key measures of effectiveness and efficiency are for those processes.

Day 2 begins with a review of the pluses and deltas from the Day 1 participant assessments. The good news is that the vast majority of feedback was positive with participants feeling productive in regards to gaining a greater appreciation of the strategic business objectives and beginning to identify the core processes of the business. The only appreciative delta was a request of me to intercede quicker when there appears to be a logjam in terms of gaining consensus. This delta is always anticipated because I purposely err on the side of waiting to interject on Day 1 allowing more rather than less debate. However, this delta was duly noted and I commited to playing a more active role when I observe a failure of consensus.

Once we begin to tackle the real content of Day 2, I ask participants to observe the data collected at the end of Day 1 relative to the alignment of the core processes with the strategic business objectives. I ask them to analyze the data from three perspectives. First, does every strategic business objective have a "5" rating, which would indicate there is at least one core process that supports that strategic business objective? A check of Table 3.2 shows that indeed every strategic business objective has at least one "5." Next, I ask the team to analyze across each row to determine whether the right core processes exist. A failure to see a "5" across a given row would call into question whether that core process was necessary. That was the case with compliance assurance, which later was dropped as a core process. Finally, I point out averages with an asterisk. In my calculations done the previous night, any range of more than three (selected by me arbitrarily) is worthy of brief discussion about the table team subgroups who gave a rating at the extremes (one team high and the other team low). This financial services group had a brief discussion on Customer Acquisition's impact on Profitable Growth and Customer Relationship Management's impact on Portfolio Balance. In both cases one subgroup team had rated it low because currently the performance is poor. This is the most common root cause behind variations in ratings. I remind the team that current performance is irrelevant. The purpose of the alignment check is simply to ensure the establishment of proper relationships between processes and strategic business objectives.

Having successfully completed the alignment check, I moved to a flip chart with Day 1's list of each core process. I left some space below each process, allowing for three to five names to be written. I inform the participants that Day 2 will be slightly different than Day 1, as work will be done in subgroups. The first subgroup assignment is to create the detailed subprocesses that constitute each core process. This will be accomplished by taking each core process and identifying the subject matter experts associated with that process. We accomplished this task in short order, and I proceeded with a quick tutorial on process mapping.

Process mapping will be covered in more detail in a later chapter as it is applied to actual project teams. However, during the Six Sigma strategy meeting, I briefly conduct a tutorial using the mnemonic device known as SIPOC to help the executives find the right subprocesses for each core process.

SIPOC stands for supplier inputs, process output, and customer. There is a sequence to apply SIPOC to ultimately obtain the five to seven subprocesses that constitute each core process. Step 1 is to name the core process, which has already been done. Second, the subgroup attempts to indicate the start and stop points for the core process. In a more detailed application of SIPOC (see Chapter 5), the teams will identify outputs, customer, suppliers, and inputs. However, at this level of application of SIPOC I next instruct the subgroup teams to think of the primary customer that goes through the core process. I task them to think of the first subprocess they encounter, the second, and so on until they reach the stop point of the core process. Their desired outcome is to return to the main room in two hours with five to seven subprocesses that constitute their assigned core process.

During this breakout I visit each subgroup team to provide input when necessary. After the first round there is usually one team that I spend a disproportionate amount of time with because they might be struggling more than the other teams. In the case of this financial services organization, the team that was struggling the most was the Employee Development subgroup. I quickly review SIPOC and indicate the "P" of their SIPOC was the Employee Development Core Process. Their struggle seemed to be in indicating the start/stop points of the

Employee Development. After brief discussion they agreed on the identification of a hiring need, and after a lengthier discussion agreed that the employee's termination or death was the end point. This discussion was rich and the death argument came about when one person said that managing the employee's 401k after leaving the company labels death as the end point. While obviously this was an extreme end point, I saw that the employee development subgroup team had reached consensus and moved on.

With an understanding of start and stop points for the core process, I then asked each subgroup team member to start thinking in terms of activities that occur to or with employees. Words such as training, hiring, communicating, rewarding, recognizing, and firing came about. I then instructed them to see if several of these ideas could be combined into processes by putting the word employee in front of the action word. With minutes to spare before the large group report out, the Employee Development team had agreed to the following key subprocesses for Employee Development:

- Employee Acquisition
- Employee Training
- Performance Management
- Employee Recognition
- Succession Planning
- Leadership Development
- Employee Communication
- Employee Compensation

During the late morning large group report-out, each subgroup team reported its perceived subprocesses. Feedback was given by the large group and in several instances modifications were done, though I was quick to point out we were looking for gaps and overlaps in key subprocesses rather than wordsmithing. As often happens, a gap is identified where one function represented thinks another function is doing the work that potentially affects a strategic business objective. This occurred during the late morning when neither the Customer Acquisition nor the Customer Relationship Management report indicated anything about a supplier management subprocess. As was reported by the VP of Manufacturing, supplier management was a weak spot in this organization and he felt turning it into a key subprocess to manage and improve would make good sense.

The executive teams began to show greater enthusiasm for the tasks at hand and enjoy their second-day lunch before returning for the afternoon session where the first order of postlunch activity is determination of process owners.

Identification of Process Owners and Creating the Process Dashboard

I introduced the concept of process ownership during a brief tutorial to begin the afternoon session. I stressed that creating processes at either the core or key subprocess level means nothing if management doesn't go on to measure and improve those processes. I also told the participants that this doesn't happen through magic or delegation. Finally, I stress that a key distinction between Six Sigma and other quality initiatives is the amount and degree of management involvement and that being a process owner is physical evidence of that involvement.

It is anticipated that everyone present will be a process owner at some level either at the core or key subprocess level. Even with an average of two processes owned by each individual, people not present in the room will be designated as process owners. The main responsibility of a process owner is to ensure that the process' measures of effectiveness and efficiency are done completely and that the process is improved if chosen for a project.

There are several characteristics of a good process owner. First and foremost the process owner must be a subject matter expert. Second, they must be the person who experiences the most gain or pain if the process is working well or not. Third, the process owner does not involve a new set of offices or another organizational chart. He must persuade through the power of data and his own personality. Thus, a third characteristic is stature and respect within the organization. Finally, a good process owner should have at least some aptitude and attitude for process thinking and improvement. A resistant process owner accomplishes little in the position. I would rather see an enthusiastic process owner with few other characteristics than the other way around.

During our afternoon breakout I ask each team to return in two hours with two major deliverables. First, each subgroup team should return with its nominations for process ownership. Second, it should discuss and recommend one to three measures of effectiveness and efficiency for each subprocess.

I shared some effectiveness and efficiency measures with the participants. Effectiveness measures refer to those elements that measure how well the subprocess meets and preferably exceeds the customer's needs and requirements. Efficiency measures refer to those measures that tap into the resources consumed in achieving their goals.

I used the Employee Development subgroup team as a model, asking them to choose one of their subprocesses. They chose the Employee Hiring subprocess. The first question: who is the customer in the hiring process? This question might seem simple but soon proves to be a challenge. One participant suggests it's the hiring manager. Another participant suggests it's the potential employee. Both are right. Yet one should be the primary (or more important) customer. The other needs to be seen as the secondary customer. In short order it is decided the hiring manager is the primary customer and I instruct the teams to deal only with what they perceive as the primary customer for purposes of this next exercise.

With the knowledge that hiring managers were in the room, we asked them their needs and requirements. Needs and requirements are not the same thing. A need is the output of a process. The output of a process should be stated in terms of a noun. The output of the Employee Hiring process is an employee. There are characteristics (called requirements) of this employee that are important to the customer (the hiring manager).

A brief brainstorming session about those requirements reveals the following as important:

- A qualified candidate
- A candidate hired quickly
- A candidate who is not too expensive

If these are later validated by the customer, then these would become the vital few customer requirements that data should be collected on. The advantage, if the second requirement (a candidate hired quickly) is validated, is that it will qualify as both an effectiveness measure and an efficiency measure.

Efficiency measures are those that measure the resources consumed in attempting to be effective. There are typically four measures of efficiency. They are cost, labor, value, and time. Therefore, a candidate hired quickly would be considered a "two for one" measure. If validated by the customer as an important requirement, it qualifies as an effectiveness measure. At the same time it is a measure of efficiency. Teams are encouraged to look out for those types of measures because they are economically beneficial to the process owner.

Similar to the morning breakout routine, I visit each breakout room to ensure the teams are on track with the assignment. I inform the teams that a brainstormed list of requirements is all that is needed for the late afternoon report. I tell them not to agonize over this list because the next several weeks' work will determine whether they are right or not. It would be a waste of time to debate the items on this list because the ultimate decision will be through the "voice of the customer."

With 90 minutes left in our first two formal days to create the strategy of Six Sigma, we began sharing the report outs from the teams. I stressed that most discussion should center around giving feedback relative to the process owner nominations. They clearly should meet the aforementioned criteria and be considered among this organization's best and brightest. The discussions went well as I preempted the conversation by reminding them of our ground rule of confidentiality. I have found that if there isn't healthy disagreement around some of the nominees, then the group is probably going through the motions on this all important element of creating the Six Sigma strategy. There should be some healthy debate around the nominations, with my interjections centering around whether the nominees possess the right qualifications and if they are the "best and the brightest."

Intersession Deliverables

With half an hour left in our second day, I moved to a prepared flip chart that listed the intersession deliverables of the team between the close of the second day and when we return as a larger group in four to six weeks. (See Figure 3.5.)

The first deliverable focused on each core process owner (all of whom were present for the first two days of our work) to notify all subprocess owners of their responsibilities. Because these subprocess owners had not spent time with us in the first two days, it was also the responsibility of the core process owner to explain the concepts of Six Sigma and the strategic work that had commenced. I offered my

- Inform and Educate All Subprocess Owners Not in Attendance for Day 1 and 2 of Their New Responsibilities
- Validate that the Subprocess is Properly Named
- Validate the Process Dashboard
- Subjectively Evaluate Performance of Each Validated Dashboard Measure on a High-Medium-Low Scale
- Create a 10-Minute PowerPoint Presentation Regarding the Above for the Morning Session of Day 3

Figure 3.5 Intersession deliverables

assistance to work with these subprocess owners during the four-to-six-week intersession time to offer an outsider's perspective on what Six Sigma is, the strategic element of our work, and what is expected of the subprocess owner. It is common for me to contact several subprocess owners to help them understand that being a subprocess owner is a newly created, albeit noncompensated, role that is a great enhancement to their career aspirations.

The next item of business for each subprocess owner is to validate that the subprocess is properly named and to validate the process dashboards. This particular group did a good job of subprocess labeling, so all I anticipated was some minor wordsmith changes. The bulk of their work would be going through the validation of process dashboards. Invariably, what the executives think is that the customer requirements don't always correspond with the customers' actual requirements.

In the last half-hour I briefly instructed the audience on typical validating techniques such as one-on-one interviews, focus groups, and surveys (all covered in greater detail in later chapters). Because each technique has advantages and disadvantages, I encouraged them to use at least two methods to validate the process dashboard of effectiveness and efficiency.

Finally, I informed those present that each subprocess owner should plan to return in four to six weeks with a subjective evaluation of current performance against the process dashboard measures. I tell them to rank each measure of effectiveness and efficiency on a High-Medium-Low rating. This is a far cry from years ago when I would do a Six Sigma strategy session teaching cursory knowledge of Six Sigma and telling them to return in four to six weeks with baseline Six Sigma performance. Between the short time line and a low threshold to learn the intricacies of sigma calculations, I found too much resistance. At some point each subprocess should have actual data collected on performance, but in the short term it is satisfactory for just the subjective evaluations to be made for our work four to six weeks from now.

The roll up of the intersession deliverables include:

- Inform and Educate All Subprocess Owners Not in Attendance for Day 1 and 2 of Their New Responsibilities
- Validate that the Subprocess is Properly Named
- Validate the Process Dashboard
- Subjectively Evaluate Performance of Each Validated Dashboard Measure on a High-Medium-Low Scale
- Create a 10-Minute PowerPoint Presentation Regarding the Above for the Morning Session of Day 3

Report Outs on Intersession Work

At the West Point U.S. Military Academy, each class's cadets are expected to give presentations of homework. The theory is that the preparation for a presentation will make the cadet work harder and learn more. This is the same theory behind the morning session of the third day of creating the Six Sigma strategy.

Each subprocess owner is expected to give a concise but informative 10-minute presentation about validating process dashboards and give her subjective evaluation of current performance. Knowing you must give a presentation with the business leader in attendance tends to create a sense of urgency to look good to not only that leader but your peers as well.

Mark Twain had an adage that applies to these third-day report outs. He was once quoted as saying, "This letter I am sending you would have been shorter if I had had more time to write it." What I have found is that the best subprocess report outs are well within a 10-minute time limit, assigned 4–6 weeks prior to the presentation day. Those individuals who procrastinate in their preparations tend to go over the 10-minute limit. While I would never cut off a subprocess owner's presentation, I stress a new ground rule that only clarifying questions should be asked of the presenter during their presentation time. After he is done, feedback is given with the emphasis on what he has done well (pluses) before making suggestions for improvement (deltas).

There are usually between 25–40 subprocesses. Therefore the conclusion of the presentations will usually occur early in the afternoon. Experience has taught me that this is an eye-opening day based on the fact of process dashboard performance. In organization after organization, more than 80 percent of process dashboards are rated at a "Low" level. I always take several glances at the business leader during these report outs, and their discomfort during the day is palpable. Of particular importance is to draw the conclusion that it is impossible to achieve strategic business objectives if process performance is as bad as reported. At the same time I am quick to point out that such low performance makes our goals very clear. It is almost an assurance that process improvement and significant cost savings await this organization once we begin the tactics of Six Sigma. I sometimes use the analogy of low hanging fruit or even worse, saying there is fruit rotting on the ground ready to be simply scooped up.

Creation of Project Selection Criteria

We return to the use of the affinity diagram with the next item on our agenda, creation of project selection criteria. At first glance, virtually every process could be targeted for improvement through the tactics of Six Sigma. However, for a variety of reasons we want to pick 7–10 subprocesses for the first wave of Six Sigma tactics.

First, resources in any organization are limited. Between hiring an external consultant, taking project team members away from their "day jobs," and the amount of time needed for training and implementation, a limited number of projects should be targeted.

Second, your first projects must produce results. Skepticism is still to be expected during the first year of implementation. One of the goals of these first projects is to obtain such dramatic results that Six Sigma is embraced stronger than ever by the end of the first year. Thus, I like an organization to "cherry pick" the worst-performing processes that have the highest impact on the strategic business objective. Limiting the number of projects to 7–10 helps reach this goal.

Third, in the early stages of implementation, it is unlikely that a proper infrastructure has been built to support the amount of training necessary to make the tools and techniques second nature to the organization. There will be significant dependence on the external consultant not only for training purposes but assisting the project teams as well. Thus, instead of just training the team leader (called a black belt) and expecting her to learn, implement, and train the rest of the team, we recommend that the entire team take the tactical training. This is yet another reason behind limiting the number of first projects. When you think of each of the 7–10 teams having 6–8 members receiving training, we are looking at upwards of 80 people in the same room receiving tactical Six Sigma training.

Therefore, we need some mechanism to whittle 25–40 subprocesses down to 7–10. This mechanism is to apply the subprocesses to some project selection criteria to cull the list down to a manageable number.

Typically, there should be 3–5 project selection criteria. While I am flexible with many criteria that executive teams generate, I strongly urge the selection team to start with two that I recommend. The first is current performance. As previously stated, these first projects must generate success and save the organization money so that they become vehicles for future buy-in to Six Sigma within the organization. The more broken the process, the easier it is to improve it. The second project selection criterion should be impact on strategic business objectives.

Our discussion of how Six Sigma has evolved from a defect reduction program at Motorola to the management philosophy it became at AlliedSignal and GE explains why I always recommend the second project selection criterion. I know that in order for the organization to be transformed through Six Sigma, management has to be actively involved at all levels of the organization. Choosing projects that have poor performance and high impact to the business objectives that management is evaluated upon is a major motivator to gain not just their interest but their involvement as well. In Chapter 4 we see many of these process owners become project sponsors (called Champions in Six Sigma parlance). Thus, prior to using the affinity diagram to gain agreement on the project selection criteria, I offer these two suggestions for project selection and ask if anyone objects if we start with them. It is rare when an executive team disagrees.

At this point I task the team to brainstorm additional project selection criteria and write one project selection criterion idea per Post-It. With the inclusion of subprocess owners there might be between 20–30. Therefore, to make this a manageable exercise, I group the process owners into arbitrary teams of 3–5 and ask them to brainstorm a list of agreed-upon project selection criteria. I hasten to add that if someone feels strongly about an idea that the others dislike, list it nonetheless.

Ten minutes later we have a list of about 30–40 Post-It notes. We again practice the concepts of clarification and duplication. The good news is that when it comes to project selection criteria, there will be multiple duplicates. Once we had completed the affinity diagram there were three additional project criteria for this financial services organization:

- Impact on Resources
- Potential Cost Savings
- Chance for Success

Recognize that Potential Cost savings is similar in nature to one of the strategic business objectives of net operating profit. I don't discourage these additional project selection criteria. In fact, I encourage it. By its inclusion we have "weighted" impact on strategic business objectives. That only implies greater management involvement.

Choosing First Projects

At this point I had prearranged a separate Post-It note with each subprocess and listed them as they appear in Table 3.3. I then took the five total project selection criteria and placed them across the top of the working wall as you also will note is captured in Table 3.3.

With the large working group split into arbitrary subteams, I then asked them to discuss how each subprocess would be rated against the project selection criteria on a 1 (low) to 5 (high) scale. I noted that a poor performing process should be rated higher so that higher-rated numbers result in a higher probability for that process having been selected for a project.

I try to provide enough time for this activity so that the morning session ends with all subteams completing their ratings. In this manner I can spend my lunch doing the calculations and adding across each row to get a summation for how each subprocess is affected by the project selection criteria. Table 3.4 shows a partial list of the rated processes when judged against the project selection criteria.

Upon the team's return from lunch, our last afternoon session was ready to begin. I had completed the summations and asked the large

Table 3.3

	Impact on Strategic Business Objectives	Current Performance 5 = Poor 1 = Excellent	Impact on Resources	Potential Cost Savings	Chance for Success
Idea Creation					
Product Design					
Supplier Management					
Channel Selection					
Underwriting					
Loan Closing					
File Management					
Customer Billing					
Internal Collections					
External Collections					
Employee Hiring					
Recognition					
Document Change					
Compliance Refund					

Table 3.4

	Impact on Strategic Business Objectives	Current Performance 5 = Poor 1 = Excellent	Impact on Resources	Potential Cost Savings	Chance for Success	Total
Idea Creation	5.0	3.0	3.0	4.0	3.0	18.0
Product Design	5.0	4.0	2.0	4.0	2.0	17.0
Supplier Management	4.0	3.0	1.0	5.0	3.0	16.0
Channel Selection	5.0	4.0	4.0	4.0	4.0	21.0
Underwriting	5.0	5.0	5.0	5.0	4.0	24.0
Loan Closing	5.0	5.0	4.0	4.0	4.0	22.0
File Management	5.0	5.0	5.0	5.0	4.0	24.0
Customer Billing	5.0	5.0	5.0	5.0	3.0	23.0
Internal Collections	5.0	5.0	4.0	3.0	4.0	21.0
External Collections	5.0	4.0	4.0	3.0	3.0	19.0
Employee Hiring	5.0	3.0	3.0	4.0	4.0	19.0
Recognition	4.0	4.0	4.0	4.0	3.0	19.0
Document Change	5.0	5.0	5.0	4.0	3.0	22.0
Compliance Refund	5.0	4.0	4.0	5.0	3.0	21.0

group to analyze the results. A rule of thumb I suggested to the group was that with 5 criteria any process with a number of 20 should be strongly considered for a first-wave project. The following partial list reveals that 8 projects were selected using my rule of thumb:

- File Management
- Underwriting
- Customer Billing
- Loan Closing
- Document Change
- Channel Selection
- Internal Collections
- Compliance Refund

The group heartily endorsed these eight as the first-wave Six Sigma projects. The group had also seen how creating the Six Sigma strategy migrated into the beginning steps of the tactics of Six Sigma. Examining the list I noticed that there are no human resources projects. When this occurs (which is common), I make the suggestion that a ninth project be added to the list. I make the point that when done properly we want to convey to the organization that Six Sigma is a way of doing business for everyone, not just the cost savings, defect reduction approach made popular by Motorola. I make the case to include the highest-rated Employee Development process. Two were tied at 19 points each, Employee Hiring and Employee Recognition. After a brief discussion, Employee Hiring is added as the ninth Wave 1 project. The list of selected projects is found in Figure 3.6.

Next Steps-Project crafting

The last activity of the afternoon was to begin the crafting of what the project would look like for each of the targeted processes for Wave 1 projects. I moved to a flip chart stand where I had created a three-column grid with the following:

- Process
- Project Focus
- Project Sponsor (Champion)

- File Management
- Underwriting
- Customer Billing
- Loan Closing
- Document Change
- Channel Selection
- Internal Collections
- Compliance Refund
- Employee Hiring

Figure 3.6   Selected projects

With nine projects the large group was divided into nine teams based on subject matter expertise, and instructed to fill out the three columns. The contents of the first column are obvious. The second column should state the focus of the project. Teams often struggle with what they want to accomplish. I recommend they revisit the process dashboard and form some sentences about the low performing measure(s) of effectiveness and/or efficiency that constitute the process dashboard. Finally, I instruct the teams that each project must have a sponsor called a project champion. I instruct them to assume that the Project Champion should be the process owner unless there is some extraordinary reason (e.g., the process owner is going on maternity leave).

Figure 3.7 shows one example (process underwriting) of project crafting.

The day concludes with a verbal plus/delta session. Virtually all of the comments center around how profitable the four days have been, how much they look forward to the next steps, and how they have been humbled looking at the organization horizontally which explains why they have been having so much trouble meeting their strategic business objectives.

The last step is calendar checking for the next element in our Six Sigma work, Champions training, and preliminary charter creating for the first-wave tactical Six Sigma projects. That becomes the focus of our next chapter, Executing Project Sponsorship, The Six Sigma Champion.

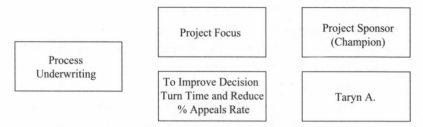

Figure 3.7   Project Crafting—an example

Summary

Chapter 3 addresses the crucial element of actively involving management in the Six Sigma process. The strategy of Six Sigma (called business process management) is the set of activities that align a business by process to better achieve the strategic business objectives. We chronicled the inefficiency of functional management, showing the problems that existed during 9/11 because of the issues associated with "chain of command" style management.

We then took you through the first steps necessary to create the strategy of Six Sigma, showing how ultimately this leads to the selection of first-wave tactical Six Sigma projects that will not only hold the interest of management but their active involvement as well. In our next chapter we address how management successfully sponsors a project from beginning to end.

Key Learnings

- There are three components to a successful Six Sigma execution.
- The first element that obtains management's active involvement is the strategy of Six Sigma, called Business Process Management.
- Business Process Management seeks to link the key processes of an organization with the strategic business objectives of an organization.
- A process-focused organization seeks to create a series of cross-functional, interdepartmental processes that ultimately improve the effectiveness and efficiency of an organization.

- A process-focused approach to air traffic control would have lessened the death toll of 9/11.
- A process-focused approach to intelligence gathering and counterterrorism between the FBI and CIA would have prevented 9/11 altogether.
- Creating the business process management system is done in a set of four formal days of working with business leaders of an organization.
- The first two days of gathering business leaders together focuses on confirming strategic business objectives, identifying key processes, and determining measures of effectiveness and efficiency for each of those processes.
- The last two days of gathering business leaders together focus on reports of measures of effectiveness and efficiency for each key process (called process dashboards), determining project selection criteria, and picking the first Six Sigma projects.

Executing Six Sigma Sponsorship: The Project Champion

Learning is not compulsory.... neither is survival.
—W. Edwards Deming,
www.quotationspage.com/quote/1889.html

Introduction

WHILE W. EDWARDS DEMING was rumored to be curmudgeonly, the quality guru succeeded in transforming postwar Japan into a manufacturing power and was revered in the United States during the 1980s, consulting with such companies as Ford and GM.

I was privileged to have met with Dr. Deming on several occasions, events which cemented my understanding of his methodology. As I chronicle in my previous book, *Six Sigma Revolution,* my first contact with the great man was less than pleasant. When I asked my first question anticipating a font of knowledge to flow forth, I was told to read his books. Humbled, I did. Less than two years later I was fortunate to have a series of breakfasts alone with him when he was neither churlish nor irascible. During those breakfasts he provided insights into his work with management, both from Japan and the United States. In the early 1980s he was not enamored with U.S. management, feeling that they viewed his advice as a quick fix. Deming was smart enough to know what he was preaching to U.S. businesses would not instantly take root and was irritated with management's impatience in the United States.

Of greater import during those breakfasts was his insistence that managers needed to commit to being actively involved in implementation efforts. In Chapter 3 we discussed a vehicle for managing horizontally through processes instead of traditional vertical management. But that is just the beginning of the involvement of management. We have found that a primary cause of project failure is inadequate levels of involvement, what we call poor sponsorship of the team. In Six Sigma parlance, the sponsor of the project team is called the Project Champion. There are a myriad of responsibilities that a Champion must address to achieve the goals and objectives of her assigned project team. In this chapter we will return to one of the financial services projects discussed in Chapter 3 and show how a Champion addresses the tasks that need to be accomplished prior to team training.

Champions Training—The Business Simulation

Champions training should be scheduled once business process management training is completed. In our Champions training at Eckes and Associates, the first two days involve a detailed overview of the tactics of Six Sigma, with a twist. We instill in each Champion a set of questions he should be asking of his team as it migrates through the Define, Measure, Analyze, Improve, and Control sections of DMAIC.

The vehicle we use to assist Champions in learning the tactics of Six Sigma was invented by Rath and Strong. This consulting company created a highly interactive business simulation that allows Champions an opportunity to learn about a broken process that parallels the way most processes in an organization look today.

Over the first two days the Champions get an opportunity to apply the methodology known as DMAIC to improving the process. On Day 3 we begin training those Champions working on first-wave projects.

Day 3 Champions Training—Creating the Preliminary Charter

Day 3 of Champions training is devoted to only those Champions who have first-wave projects. The major deliverable of the third day of training is to work with the Champion to create a preliminary charter for each team. The charter is the collection of documents that helps create purpose and motivation for the team to complete its work over the next six to nine months.

The day is highly interactive, with my team doing quick 10–15 minute lectures on the elements of the charter. Each lecture is followed by an assignment that is expected to be completed in 15–20 minutes and then presented back to the entire group.

The first assignment that Andrea Price, Eckes and Associates' Champions expert, has on her flip chart is a question regarding what transpired during the first two days of Champions training, what they have learned about their roles as Champions, and what they need to be aware of when sponsoring their teams. The answers typically fall into the following categories:

- Jumping to solutions: Champions often encounter team members who want to jump prematurely to the "I" section of DMAIC where solutions are generated and selected.
- Using a facilitator: Having a facilitator forces the team to practice balanced participation, follow an agenda, and utilize ground rules for adaptive behaviors to flourish versus maladaptive behavior where everyone wants their ideas implemented without the benefit of data.
- Not paying attention to data: At their core, Six Sigma and DMAIC are data-based methods, so ignoring the facts at any phase is hazardous to the project.
- Piloting solutions: Testing solutions before their final rollout allows teams to tweak where necessary and introduces the new process to the end users prior to its full deployment.

Appendix B contains the Day 3 breakout activities, including key learnings of the business simulation, responsibilities of the Champion, and elements of a good charter.

Creating the Preliminary Charter

The first task for a Champion is to create a preliminary charter for her project. Establishing, maintaining, and communicating the charter are key responsibilities of the Champion. The project charter includes the following 10 tasks:

1. Selecting the team
2. Choosing a Team Leader
3. Creating a business case
4. Creating the preliminary problem statement
5. Defining the scope of the project
6. Identifying the team's goals and objectives
7. Allocating resources
8. Setting the project time line
9. Communicating the business case to the team
10. Agreeing on decisions that the team can make alone and those that should involve the Champion

The project example we will highlight for the elements in this section is the financial services project of improving the underwriting process.

Team Member Selection

The first of the assignments is to select the team members. The first and most important criterion Champions must consider is to pick those individuals who have the greatest subject matter expertise in the process targeted for improvement. The key to any success for a project team is to populate that team with those who know not only what could be the key problems associated with the process, but those whose theories about root causation and ultimate improvement have the greatest chance of being substantiated with data later in the application of DMAIC.

Another criterion we suggest in the selection of team membership is diversity within the organizational structure. A team comprised of just managers might see the process from a certain lens that would preclude greater creativity in ideas. Individual contributors in addition to a strong manager typically make the best teams.

A final consideration is who should comprise the full-time team members and whether there will be the need for ad hoc membership. We strongly suggest that full-time membership size be between six and eight individuals. At the same time we recognize that during the course of the project some teams will need special expertise that will require an ad hoc team member that could be a part of a team for a meeting, a week, or a month.

Two final considerations need to be thought through by the project Champion. First, in some organizations where projects have been selected that are similar, there might be an issue where the same people are desired by more than one Champion. For example, at Hewlett Packard IPG Americas Consumer Operations, the business process management work resulted in eight projects being selected. Two of them were interconnected. One issue centered on a call center where one project was responsible for the diagnostics of a customer issue, where another project team was responsible for problem resolution. These two teams were part and parcel of the same issue. Thus, the two Champions had to reconcile the fact that only one person can be on one team. If compromise cannot be reached, this issue needs to be brought to the business leader for his determination of where a person goes.

Finally, in some projects a decision should be made about whether a supplier or customer should be made a part of the team. For example, a project that has as an external customer touch point could result in valuable information being shared by the customer. Additionally, including the customer in Six Sigma projects can result in better customer relations. The customer will see the supplier actively trying to meet her needs and improve how the two work together.

With these criteria the underwriting Champion presents her nominees for the project. They are as follows:

- Nikki C.
- Jessie C.
- Christi H.
- Debra H.
- Mackenzie K.
- Bryson K.
- Walt L.
- Vicki L.

Another project team Champion indicates that she also wanted Bryson K. and Mackenzie K. A spirited discussion ensues with a proposed compromise suggested and agreed to that both Bryson and Mackenzie would be ad hoc members of the other team, not to exceed 10 hours of participation each.

Selecting a Team Leader

There are two approaches to selecting a team leader. Both approaches have advantages and disadvantages. Since Mikel Harry's work with Texas Instruments, karate terminology has been utilized for mastery of the technical elements of Six Sigma.

For large companies willing and able to devote resources on a full-time basis, full-time team leaders called black belts are chosen. Black belts typically are responsible for three to four DMAIC projects per year. The advantages of a black belt approach to team leadership is that by the time a black belt has one or two projects completed, her level of expertise has grown sufficiently that projects can be completed quicker and with greater results ensuing. The drawback of the black belt approach is that team members who see the resources committed to black belts see team members' roles as secondary. We have repeatedly seen that organizations that commit to black belts suffer lack of involvement on the part of team members who believe that their involvement is not as important as the black belt's.

This creates both a tactical and cultural problem. The tactical problem that exists is that with less involvement on the part of the entire team, the black belt often takes up the slack, knowing his reputation for leading the team to success ultimately results in his career enhancement. Instead of attempting to gain greater team involvement, the black belt often does a disproportionate amount of the DMAIC work. Culturally, the black belt approach is also a problem as the organization starts to believe there are special resources devoted to Six Sigma and thus the employees believe they don't need to participate as much as they should.

The alternative to the black belt approach is the green belt approach, where the team leader holds a full-time position in the organization and will be the team leader for this specific project and probably will not be a green belt again for years to come. Obviously, the green belt approach helps to integrate Six Sigma as a cultural phenomenon because all team members play a crucial role in the project's success, not just the team leader. Further, the tools and techniques learned in a more balanced team approach practiced by the green belt philosophy help to generate that tool usage in everyday situations once the project is complete. Of course, there are disadvantages to the green belt approach, most notably the extra time it takes to generate project results, particularly for first-time efforts.

Our underwriting case study is an example of the green belt approach. The project Champion asks for our input on what criteria she should use to pick the team leader (i.e., green belt) from her list of eight team members. We stress several key factors in her selection process. First, the team leader should have the respect of those on the team. This doesn't necessarily mean that the team leader should be from management, though this is often the case. Second, the team leader chosen should be someone with some level of project management skills. The team leader's ability to multitask, delegate, and use action plans to achieve the milestones of DMAIC is a key success factor in the ability of the team to achieve its goals and objectives. We further stress to the Champion that the team leader should be someone that the Champion is comfortable with in a working relationship. Most of the Champion's work that occurs during the months a team exists will be through the team leader. A good Champion will meet at a minimum once a week with a team leader and more often as situations arise that call for the Champion's involvement. As such, the working relationship between the two is pivotal to the success of the team, the team leader, and the Champion. With these considerations in mind, the financial services underwriting Champion picks Christi H., who holds all the aforementioned talents.

Creating the Business Case

Once the team and its leader have been chosen, the Champion should begin work on the business case for the project. A business case is a nonquantitative statement about why this project exists and how it impacts the organization. In its final form the business case should create motivation for the team's emotion and behavior, and ultimately establish the focus of the work for the team.

The biggest mistake Champions make in creating the business case is putting too much information into it. The best business case is usually two or three sentences. During the third day of Champions training, we give each Champion a 10-minute period to write out the business case, and then each of the Champions reads and receives feedback from the group and my consulting team.

We tee up each reading of the business cases by telling participants that they should pretend they are on the receiving end of the statement. Does this motivate them if they were chosen by the team to participate? Does the statement possess sufficient clarity so that the purpose of why this was chosen as one of the first-wave projects comes across?

The first reading of the underwriting business case went poorly. Our underwriting Champion had decided to write a book, and the purpose of the team didn't come across. I reminded her of something I had learned in a writing class once that prompted her to edit her original business case.

I shared a story about an assignment I had been given. I was told to write an ad for a picture using my creative writing skills. The picture was a recently caught fish lying on a bed of ice inside a fish store.

Thinking that less is more, I created a two-paragraph marketing pitch using words like succulent, tasty, affordable, and several others. The instructor laughed at my wordy response and simply told me that "Fresh fish sold here" conveyed what I wanted to say. Of course, he wasn't done. He then went on say that it would be obvious that at a fish store, fish was not going to be given away so the "sold here" had to go. Then he reviewed the picture and said it would be obvious that a picture of fish that appeared freshly caught would not require any words at all. I learned that day that less is more when it comes to writing (aren't you glad this book isn't 500 pages long?).

I told this story in an attempt to get our underwriting Champion to keep to the basics. The underwriting project was chosen because of its poor performance on several dashboard measures and its impact to the strategic business objective of growth and operating profits. Thus, I told her to limit her business case that addressed both the performance issues and the impact of underwriting to the strategic business objectives. With her second try she nicely states the business case for the underwriting project:

The Gamma Alpha Company is faced with growing loan demand that strongly contributes to our growth and operating profits business objectives. Excessive loan processing time and maccuracy in loan decisions negatively impact both business objectives, requiring us to initiate this project to improve both cycle time and loan decision accuracy.

The underwriting Champion gets feedback from all those present. They tell her that this revised business case creates the right motivation for the team as well as establishes focus for the group. The issue the team is expected to work on is related to reducing cycle time and improving accuracy of the loan decisions as it affects Gamma Alpha's business objectives of growth and operating profit. Now we want to know what is specifically wrong with cycle time and loan decision accuracy. Our next prework item will begin to clear this up.

Creating the Preliminary Problem Statement

The problem statement is a quantitative statement of the problem that specifies a time frame, describes impact to the organization, is specific and measurable, and most importantly is stated in neutral terms, neither jumping ahead to root causation nor stating an implied solution.

As such, the final problem statement is the domain of the project team once it begins to collect data in the Measure phase of DMAIC. However, it is the responsibility of the Champion to create the *preliminary* problem statement that will give the project team footing as it collects data on the right problem.

After a brief review of the aforementioned criteria that constitute the problem statement, we provide an example from our own DMAIC work. Several years ago we had a large client that was particularly late in payment of our invoices. Knowing firsthand that DMAIC works, we formed our own Six Sigma project team to practice what we preached. The success of that project spawned several other projects where we "practiced what we preached." In 2001 we attempted to create a problem statement about our employee development process and crafted the following statement we used to have each of the first-wave Champions practice his feedback skills to a project team.

Since 1999 Eckes and Associates Inc. has missed the opportunity to bid on large companywide Six Sigma contracts. These large companywide bids required a minimum of 30 fully committed contract laborers from Eckes and Associates. Therefore, we have missed out on a total of 8 potential contracts, which has impacted our revenue business objectives by several million dollars.

As was our pattern earlier during the creation of the business process management system, we begin by having the participants find what they like about our problem statement. We strongly encourage the first-wave Champions to follow the same pattern when they review their teams' work. Project teams are learning a new methodology and directly applying their learnings to real problems. As such they need to learn as much about what they are doing well as their mistakes. It is a great motivator to know what they are doing well and to receive feedback on what they need to improve. Therefore, the team examines our problem statement and provides feedback on what we did well.

Among the positives they note the time frame we have mentioned, the impact to our business objectives, and the specificity of the number of contracts we have missed out on. We then move to how it could be made better (i.e., the deltas). We stress that just criticizing an idea will result in unmotivated project team members. Thus, we strongly suggest that for any item on the problem statement they don't like they provide a suggestion for improvement. Here, they think the statement is not as neutral as it could have been, citing the fact that we are saying the missed opportunity is due to needing 30 fully committed contract laborers from Eckes and Associates. This is valid input until they become aware that we substantiated this claim with data when we were not pursued to place a formal proposal.

With the knowledge of what constitutes a good problem statement, we allow each first-wave Champion an opportunity to craft a preliminary problem statement. We stress to the group that data might be missing so we encourage each Champion to leave a blank for data that is needed and will be required by the project team when they reach the Measure phase of the DMAIC methodology.

Our underwriting Champion does a better job with her preliminary problem statement and shares the following statement with the group:

> **Since fiscal year 2002 Gamma Alpha has spent an average of—— processing loan applications with an accuracy rate of—. This has negatively impacted our labor costs and FTEs (i.e., Full Time Equivalent employees, author's note), growth objectives, and operating profits.**

Overall, the feedback on this statement is positive. It is neutral without reference to the root cause of the cycle time issue or the accuracy problems. Further, it specifies a time frame and describes the impact to the organization both in terms of labor costs and impact to business objectives. Suggestions for improvement centered around fleshing out the impact on FTEs, growth, and operating profits when that data was collected in the Measure and Analysis phase.

Identifying Project Scope

Eckes and Associates Inc. has indicated to clients that failure to scope the project properly and manage that scope is one of the major sources for failure of a DMAIC project team.

Scope refers to the boundaries of the project. Specifically, what the team is expected to work on and more importantly what the team should avoid by way of its work. Scope creep occurs when the team migrates beyond its original boundaries and engages in work that should be devoted to another team's efforts in Wave 2 projects or beyond.

We have investigated why scope creep occurs. Ironically, it comes from two major well-meaning sources. First, a well-intentioned team begins to see where the data leads and finds out that the process in question is in far worse shape than originally suspected. Conscientious to do a good job, the team members erroneously begin to feel their job is to solve *all* problems associated with the process instead of what they have been chartered to accomplish. This situation is exacerbated by the second source of scope creep, aggressive Champions that want to have their teams accomplish too much. The problem with these two sources of scope creep is that either alone or both in combination will result in project failure.

Thus, our tutorial on project scope is done with utmost seriousness. We share several project failures we have encountered that were due to project scope creep and hasten to add that what they begin in the next breakout should be one of their most important managerial responsibilities as their projects move forward.

Several common mistakes occur when scoping a project besides boundaries that are too broad. Champions are coached that scope does not refer to a restatement of goals and objectives. Additionally, scope does not refer simply to stating the boundaries of the process in question. It does refer to the elements of work that a project team is expected to address, and more importantly work on areas that they should avoid. I use several well-known examples of good project scoping that everyone in the room should be familiar with to prove my points. I talk about our eight-year mission during the 1960s to place a man on the moon as excellent scope management and contrast that with our doomed effort in Viet Nam, where our original goal in the early 1960s to train the South Vietnamese turned into actual combat and eventually incursions into Laos and Cambodia.

With these admonitions, we then go to the 15-minute breakout where each Champion is expected to take a first shot at crafting her project scope. Our underwriting Champion crafts and reports out the following for both what is inside of scope and outside of scope:

In	Out
Income Analysis	Unique Applications (e.g., Flood)
Credit Analysis	Pre-Apps
Loan Decisioning	Document Prep
Application Data Transfer	
Appraisal	
Post Decision	
Title Investigation	
Title Transfer	

There are lots of positives with this list. The Champion has done a great job providing guidance for the project team relative to actual work that will be inside of scope rather than falling into the trap of simply restating the goals and objectives or giving the start and end points of the process of underwriting. We are quick to point out this major plus in her breakout work. However, most of the other Champions are swift in their feedback that some of the items on the "in" list are not only too ambitious for the team but happen to be within the scope of two other projects. For example, there is the Loan Closing project whose Champion points out loan decisioning will play a major part in her project. Second, the document change Champion points out Application Data Transfer will be inside his project team's scope. A healthy discussion ensues where eventually the underwriting Champion sees that not only other teams are working on items that she has placed inside of scope but is told that he has "bitten off more than her team can chew" relative to getting that much done during a first-wave project. She reluctantly removes Loan Decisioning and Application Data Transfer from her "in" list and moves it to her "out" list.

One final caution is provided to each Champion at the conclusion of the report outs. I inform each Champion that in the first days of DMAIC the project team will be taught project scope and be given a breakout where they can modify the list with the ultimate approval of the Champion. I tell them no matter how smart they all are, that information provided by a team needs to be reconciled by its Champion (with the Champion getting 51 percent of the vote) before the team can move forward with its project work.

Goals and Objectives

Typical first-wave projects are operating at such a low sigma level, dramatic improvement should be expected. It is accepted by most experts that until data is collected in the Measure phase of DMAIC, setting a target of 50-percent improvement in baseline performance is recommended. It should be noted that this 50-percent improvement is related to the actual measurement in question, not sigma performance. For example, later in the project the underwriting project team determined that loan accuracy rates were operating at an abysmal 6-percent yield. In other words, 94 percent of loans were processed inaccurately. Therefore, we encourage project Champion to adjust the 50-percent improvement goal once actual data is collected. In some cases the 50-percent improvement might be too timid, in other cases too aggressive.

Resource Allocation

The Champion is responsible for providing resources for the team to do its work. There are traditional resources that are seen across all teams and then there are unique resources needed by a team. Among the more traditional resources needed is a work room that some term the "war room." Because the work of DMAIC can be storyboarded using a series of flip charts, a room that can be used for the duration of the project team's existence is recommended. In most cases, some secretarial support is suggested and additionally, a percentage of IT support will be needed. In the case of the underwriting project, there was the concern for geographical diversity among two members who required Internet software support as well as teleconference capabilities.

Establishing the Time Line for the Project

First-wave projects always take longer than subsequent projects. The organization is developing its infrastructure, teams become overly concerned with not making any mistakes during DMAIC, and because they are the organization's Six Sigma pioneers, the time line for first projects will take longer.

Our approach, which will be discussed in great detail in Chapters 5 and 6, is based on action learning where the entire team learns the methodology of DMAIC in small increments through brief lecturettes followed by lengthy breakouts where the team members begin to learn the tool or technique covered in the lecturette as well as begin actual work on their project. However, the bulk of the work is done in intersessions between training modules. Figure 4.1 shows a typical time line for a first-wave project.

This schedule calls for the involvement of the Champion during the Define and Measure report out and the Analysis Report outs (June 9 and August 4). During these morning sessions, each project team's leader gives a status of work done to that date. Each Champion is expected to attend not only to hear his project report out but those of other teams as well. Similar to the report outs from the third day of Business Process Management (see Chapter 3), performance of intersession deliverables tends to be accomplished if a team leader is to give a presentation in front of not only your Champion but other teams and their Champions as well.

Communicating the Business Case to the Team

As part of the prework prior to the team receiving their first training sessions on DMAIC, the Champion needs to develop a communication plan to work with the project team. Initially, our discussion about communication to the team falls on deaf ears. There is the perception that this communication is simply done to inform the project team to block

Define and Measure Training	April 8 – 12
Define and Measure Intersession Work	April 13 – June 9
Define and Measure Report Outs	June 9
Analysis Training	June 9 – 13
Analysis Intersession Work	June 13 – August 4
Analysis Report Outs	August 4
Improve and Control Training	August 4 – 7
Post Session Work	August 7 – November 4

Figure 4.1   First-wave project time line

out the days of training and show up on time. Nothing could be further from what is needed to make this action item successful.

Essentially, the communication of the business case to the team members has as its goal "selling" the project to the team. Most of the time those team members selected for the project have some reporting relationship to the Champion or others in management who report to the Champion. As such, the Champion can make the mistake that participation on the DMAIC team is just another assignment.

To assist the Champion with "selling" the project we ask her to create what General Electric calls the "elevator speech." An elevator speech answers several key questions. Its goal is to create support and involvement among those the elevator speech is aimed at. To create an elevator speech, we ask the Champion to answer several questions in writing, and then instruct him once he has perfected his speech to memorize and deliver it to the team members whether individually or as a group.

Figure 4.2 has the list of questions that the Champion should answer in writing, to assist her in creating the elevator speech.

The Champions spend the next 20 minutes crafting their answers

1. What is the business case for your project (see preactivity number 3)?
2. Briefly describe what Six Sigma is as it relates to your project.
3. Describe why you selected the individuals for the project (skills, insights, perspectives, etc).
4. What do you expect of those on the team?
5. What benefits will be derived by the organization by participating on the team?
6. What benefits will be derived by the participants on the team?

Figure 4.2 Questions for elevator speech

and report out their elevator speeches. Our underwriting Champion does the best job of creating her written elevator speech, which follows:

I have called you all here today to announce the formation of a project that has as its goal the reduction in loan application decision time and simultaneously the reduction of the error rate in loan approval accuracy. For some time now loan approval accuracy has worsened, and at the same time the time it takes to approve those loans has risen dramatically. This has negatively impacted growth and our operating profits.

Gamma Alpha has committed to using a methodology called Six Sigma to improve cycle time and loan decision accuracy. Six Sigma is a proven approach to give those who live in the underwriting process the tools and techniques to make things more effective and efficient.

I have been asked to select the best and brightest people associated with underwriting to learn Six Sigma methodology and apply those tools and your expertise to improve the underwriting process. You will be expected to attend training classes and spend upwards of 25 percent of your time working on this project. I, as your sponsor, will provide you the necessary resources that will lead us to achieving a 50-percent improvement in both accuracy and cycle time reduction.

Six Sigma will become a way of life at Gamma Alpha. Those who expect to enhance their careers and see promotion opportunities will utilize this chance to join one of the first successful teams at our organization.

The feedback was universally positive to this elevator speech. The last thing mentioned to each Champion is to plan delivery of the elevator speech soon enough that all team members would be able to clear their calendars for the DMAIC training that will start in four weeks.

Agreeing on Decisions That the Team Can Make Alone and Those That Should Involve the Champion

We start the lecturette for this final prework element of the Champion training by reminding them that at a minimum the Champion and team leader need to confer at least once a week.

Additionally, we stress that each of the subelements of DMAIC (known as tollgates) need to be formally reviewed and approved by the Champion.

Finally we stress that the Champion should start thinking about the criteria he wants each team to apply to its proposed solutions. In Chapter 6 we will go into more detail about solution criteria. There are two types of solution criteria: must criteria and want criteria. Must criteria are either/or statements that determine whether a solution should be further considered for implementation. Typical must criteria are that a solution must not add to head count and must be implemented in 90 days or less. Must criteria are the sole domain of the Champion, and we stress it is never too early to begin thinking as a Champion about what must solution criteria will be applied to the project team's work.

Summary

A key element in the success of any Six Sigma team is the active involvement of the project sponsor called the Champion. Chapter 4 addressed the specific activities needed to jump-start the project team once they begin their training.

Among the items needed to plan for success is the selection of the best and brightest minds associated with the process targeted for improvement. A team leader who is well versed in project management techniques and is well respected by both the team and the Champion is a crucial success factor in the launch of the team.

Further, the Champion must create both the business case and preliminary problem statement for her team. The business case is a nonquantitative statement of why the project is needed and how it impacts the strategic business objectives of the organization. The preliminary problem statement is quantitative in nature, spelling out how long the problem has existed, specifying the gap between current and desired activity, describing the impact of the problem to the organization, and most importantly, stated in neutral terms with no causes, solutions, or blame.

Project scope is perhaps the most important responsibility of the project Champion. Scope refers to the boundaries of the project, namely what the team needs to work on and where the team should not go in terms of content. First-wave projects should be scoped tightly as the team members are not only learning a new methodology but also applying what they learn to real work.

Goals and objectives need to be established for the team. Typically, 50-percent improvement of the desired goal is the target for a first-wave project. Additionally, the Champion is responsible for the allocation of resources for his team, which can include IT assistance, a specific area of work, and any secretarial assistance.

The milestones and time line for completion of the work is a Champion's responsibility. A first-wave project is typically completed in 9 months with multiple short-term goals along the way.

Prior to the team beginning its training, the Champion is expected to communicate the business case to her team. This is seen more as a selling of the project to those involved rather than just a pronouncement of a training session.

Key Learnings

- The project sponsor for a Six Sigma team is called the project Champion.
- There is a set of responsibilities a Champion has before a Six Sigma team is formed, during the time a Six Sigma team does its work, and after the Six Sigma team disbands.
- The first responsibility a Champion has is to establish his Six Sigma team populated with the best and brightest minds in the process targeted for improvement. One of the team members

must be identified as the team leader called either the green belt or the black belt.

- The second responsibility of a Champion is to create the business case for the Six Sigma project, a nonquantitative statement that explains why this project is important, how it impacts the business, and is stated in a way to create motivation and focus for the team.

- The Champion is also responsible for creating a preliminary problem statement that states what the problem is, how long it has been a problem, what the gap is from current to desired state, and describes the impact to the organization. It should be stated in neutral terms with no blame, perceived causation, or solutions.

- The most important responsibility of the Champion is to identify and manage the project scope, which refers to the boundaries of what the Six Sigma team should work on and more importantly what it should avoid in its work.

- Among other prework of the Champion is to allocate proper resources, and establish the time line for the project as well as the preliminary goals and objectives of the project.

- The Champion must communicate the business case to the project team members with the goal of creating motivation for each to participate in the project.

- Finally, the Champion needs to clarify what decisions can be made by the team alone and which decisions require Champion involvement.

Six Sigma Tactical Execution: Team Dynamics, Define and Measure

Personally, I'm always ready to learn, although I do not always like being taught.

—Winston Churchill

Introduction

THE EXECUTIVE TEAM must create the business process management system (i.e., the strategy of Six Sigma), and select high-profile projects. The team sponsors (called Champions) must be trained, and then the DMAIC project teams can begin their work.

Because of the project Champion's necessary posttraining work, it is common for the DMAIC team members to commence their training approximately one month after Champions training.

This chapter addresses execution of the tactics of Six Sigma process improvement using the DMAIC methodology. But first, let me tell you what this chapter is *not* about. It is not about teaching you the details of DMAIC. This has been addressed in my other books. So if this is your first exposure to Six Sigma, I strongly recommend that you get more exposure to the concepts, tools, and techniques of Six Sigma.

Transferring knowledge on such a heady subject can—and often does—result in failure. My background in psychology allowed me to learn several key concepts of human behavior, one of which was based on *Adult Learning Theory*. I have been a fan of Adult Learning Theory since my early twenties when I began my classroom training as a clinical psychologist at Delta College in Saginaw Michigan. Traditional classroom training is based on the faulty premise that there is an expert (the instructor) who imparts knowledge to a group of participants (the students) who lack the expertise that the instructor possesses (the students). However, in my first year of being an instructor, I was 22 years old and only 2–4 years older than some of the people I was instructing. Granted, I had the advantage of a graduate degree but I knew that I had to develop a different way of training adults who didn't have appreciably less experience than a first-year psychologist.

Far from the "I am the expert and I will impart knowledge" approach, Adult Learning Theory is based on several key distinctions (listed below).

Adults learn best when:

- The instructor uses real-world examples that the student can relate to
- Support is provided by the instructor and other participants through sincere praise
- They participate in small groups, applying what they learned in the large group
- Lectures are less than an hour
- The instructor checks constantly for confirmation of learning, because learning cannot be assumed
- Information is provided through varied media
- They are having fun

The problem with Six Sigma training is that few—if any—of the aforementioned concepts are practiced by Six Sigma trainers. The reasons for this are varied. First, by its very nature, Six Sigma is a combination of tools, techniques, and concepts that can be confusing due to their statistical complexity. Second, because of this statistical complexity, it attracts statisticians with teaching credentials. Sadly, this only compounds the first problem. Statisticians are among the most intelligent people I have come across, but frankly, they don't live in the real world. Therefore, many statisticians relish the role of the "expert" where they dispense answers regarding theory and formulas. Statisticians play to their strength: the mathematics of Six Sigma. However, the math of Six Sigma merely attempts to achieve greater effectiveness and efficiency in processes targeted for improvement. In a statistician's Six Sigma training session, participants often perceive that mathematical complexity is the only key to Six Sigma project success. They then learn to apply three tools when one would suffice. In sum, statisticians make Six Sigma unnecessarily intimidating.

If Adult Learning Theory is based on student participation, then most Six Sigma learning is directly opposite, instead focusing on an "expert" telling others what to do.

I learned this painful lesson firsthand as I first matriculated through some of Mikel Harry's courses. I was struck by his brilliance. At the same time I was also taken aback by his professorial pose. He did not encourage questions, and when he did accept them he was prone to such perplexing answers that I was left with the impression he was less answering the question and more telling the questioner to pay closer attention, and stop interrupting.

Ever stubborn, I continued questioning him, increasingly frustrated by his inability to simplify the complex material. This frustration reached its nadir when I cornered him late one afternoon to explain to me the now infamous, internationally recognized 1.5 sigma shift that explains the conversion charts. (See Appendix D.) At first, I followed his logic as he attempted to explain that all things vary, including process sigma. He continued with talk of sampling and the fact that any measure of sigma is simply a measure of variation at that point in time and true sigma is worse if measured over time.

"But that is not my question, Mr. Harry. My question is the derivative of the 1.5 sigma shift. It stands to reason that in some processes, a 1.5 shift would be too much and in some processes 1.5 would be too little. How can you suggest that 1.5 applies to all processes? In fact, Mr. Harry, if Six Sigma is based on reducing variation in any process, how in good conscience can we recommend a constant that is an average adjustment for long-term variation?"

Sadly, his response went over my head. And therein lies the problem with so much Six Sigma training. If a concept cannot be explained to me, then how can a novice master the technical jargon?

It was at that seminar I vowed to teach Six Sigma in a manner that would take the complex and arcane and make it simple, so that any one of my students would not only understand Six Sigma, but also implement its philosophy into day-to-day operational behavior. Six Sigma should be made accessible, not just something to be flaunted by elitist "experts."

Aware that Six Sigma is complex, I took each of the aforementioned adult learning theory concepts and decided to create both a curriculum and a consulting strategy to ensure that my students would not only understand, but get excited about Six Sigma.

Adults learn best when the instructor uses real-world examples that the student can relate to. My firm has invented a Six Sigma learning model called CPTE. This acronym stands for Concept, Practical Use, Technical, and Example. This implies that instructors of Six Sigma must describe the concept, address the practical use of the concept, appropriately address the technical elements of that concept, and then share an example or story of its application.

Note that you need not always teach CPTE in the same order as the acronym. Either way, I have found that any lecture with all four elements goes a long way to facilitate understanding and generate excitement about the tool or technique.

I have also found out the hard way that the example used in the lecture should be unrelated to the audience members' real work. In my firm's early days of training we always furnished an example central to their business. If we were working with an injection molding firm, we would illustrate a point with a plastics example of warpage or bowing. If we were training a financial services organization, we'd have an underwriting or compliance example for the CPTE lecture. We quickly learned this was a huge mistake. The class participants focused more on the content of the example and less on the tool or technique to be mastered. This is a logical outcome, as another component of adult learning theory asserts that any work done by adults can be divided into two sectors: content and method. Figure 5.1 shows the two sectors.

We tested out new Six Sigma teaching methods that included generic, easy-to-understand examples and then immediately gave the participants an opportunity to apply the tool they learned in a large group in the breakout session. When first learning a difficult subject we have now experienced far greater absorption of the material using a generic example in a large group followed immediately by a breakout where

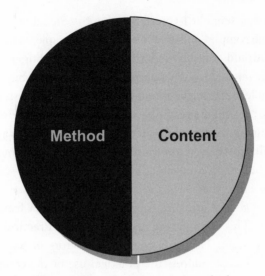

Figure 5.1   Content versus method

they then apply the tool to the participants' real project. For example, when we teach process mapping we compare it to buying a new car.

The beauty of this example is that virtually everyone in the audience has purchased a car and can identify with the experiences in the high-level steps from submitting the first offer to negotiating the price of the final purchase. Universal, generic examples keep students from losing the method in the details.

First introduce the concept of process mapping, the "P" in CPTE. Instructors must explain the need for the new car. We then address the "C" of process mapping using the mnemonic device known as SIPOC, which stands for Suppliers who provide Inputs to the Process that produce Output(s) for Customers.

Now the "T" (technical element) of CPTE is all about the sequence of process mapping. First we start by labeling the process itself. Labeling the process should not be done casually, as the name of the process has impact to the scope of the project. Simultaneously during the "T" part of the lecture, we introduce the "E" of CPTE. We use a variety of generic examples but have found the new car purchase works best. To illustrate that process naming is crucial, we note that the car buying process is different than the car leasing process.

Next is the technical step of labeling the start and stop points of the process. Using the car buying example, we describe the start point as the old car breaking down (or in my case, wanting a new sports car to deal with my midlife crisis). The stop point for the car buying process would be driving it off the lot. (Again, unlike the car leasing process where the stop point would be returning the car. The leasing process takes the lessee through a longer process, which could impact project scope.)

Again utilizing "T" and "E" simultaneously, we assert that the output of the car buying process should be a simple noun, the car. Next we illustrate the concept of the primary and secondary customers of the output. In my case I have two teenage boys who love sports cars. They are my secondary customers and I'm the primary customer.

Next we define the key suppliers and their inputs: the dealer who provides the car, automotive magazines that provide information about different makes and models, and the Internet, which provides information about pricing.

Finally I take the participants through the last technical step of process mapping in this example, identifying the high level steps in the process.

Adults learn best when support is provided by the instructor and other participants through sincere praise. It's common sense; people respond more to praise than criticism. The complexity of Six Sigma tools and techniques can unleash a type of resistance called technical resistance.

Technical resistance occurs when otherwise competent people resist tasks that make them feel incompetent. Like most people, I have attended my fair share of weddings. Wedding receptions often include dancing. Unfortunately, I experience great anxiety around dancing. In the few times I have made it to the dance floor, negative comments about my lack of skills only strengthen my resistance to dancing. The same thing happens to Six Sigma teams. Each team learns a new methodology and applies that methodology to real work. If they are made to feel inadequate, their resistance to Six Sigma will only grow. Therefore, a key component of our training focuses on building on small successes and reinforcing key lessons among participants.

Six Sigma learning must be highly interactive when taking place in a large group. The instructor should constantly ask questions to make sure lessons are sinking in. I often will teach a key point like process mapping and then ask a series of questions to ensure the key points have been absorbed. For correct answers, I am quick to praise. As a sports fan I usually ask the participant for their favorite baseball team and once answered say that they have hit an "upper deck shot."

"Jim, that was a Waveland." (Wrigley Field in Chicago)

"Wanda, that was hit into McCovey Cove." (PacBell Park in San Francisco)

"Tina, that was hit over the Green Monster." (Fenway Park in Boston)

While quirky, you can actually see the pride in their faces for giving a correct answer and getting immediate feedback in front of their peers.

Adults learn best when they participate in small groups, applying what they learned in the large group. While any Six Sigma tool or technique should be learned through a generic example in a large group, it is imperative for the project teams to apply quickly what they have learned to their actual project.

We have divided the DMAIC materials into a series of succinct, small, bite-sized modules where each tool, technique, or concept is then turned into a breakout session. Each team goes into a smaller room to begin applying the tool, technique, or concept to its actual project. The purpose of this breakout is to begin the actual work and—more importantly—have my team gauge whether each team has mastered that day's lesson. My team rotates through the breakout rooms; observes the application of the tool, technique, or concept for each team; answers questions; and generally observes the participants in action. Many participants think that they are expected to complete work on the tool. This is an incorrect assumption. Most implementation work is done outside of both the large training area and the breakout room. So we make sure each group understands that the purpose of small group breakouts is to gain competence in the application of the tool and begin (but not complete) work relative to that module.

Adults learn best when lectures are less than an hour. One of my college professors once told my class that college-age students think about sex once every 10 minutes. So he expected that only about 90 percent of his one-hour lecture would be remembered. While I don't have data to support whether Six Sigma classes are any different, I have learned that adults must stay busy to learn. Sitting more than an hour listening to an instructor can result in missing whatever is covered beyond that hour mark. Thus, we have created the vast majority of our modules to be taught in an hour or less so that most of the learning occurs through the application of the tool in the breakout.

Adults learn best when the instructor checks constantly for confirmation of learning, because learning cannot be assumed. Most traditional training, particularly at the high school and college level, is based on mere test passing. As a result, the majority of students learn the bare minimum to get by. Additionally, it has been shown that most traditional *learning* occurs through reading and note taking rather than what is taught in class. This is not the case with Six Sigma learning. Most of the literature on Six Sigma can often create more misunderstanding rather than true learning. So the instructor of a Six Sigma seminar must constantly validate what is learned. Again, be sure to give positive reinforcement for correct answers.

Adults learn best when information is provided through varied media. No matter how interactive a Six Sigma instructor makes the modules appear, it is crucial to vary the teaching methods to include interactive large-group activities. No one method or venue should be overly relied upon. The following generates the greatest audience participation and interest:

- Large-group team verbal exercises
- Large-group team activities
- Simulations

Large-group team verbal exercises are a way to encourage involvement and gauge the extent of learning. Sometimes these activities take place immediately after a point is made by the instructor. Other times the large-group team verbal exercise is a way for the participants to learn a concept without the need for a teach point. For example, to instruct project scope, a part of the first Define module, I explain that project scope refers to the boundaries inside which the project team must operate. I warn the participants that creeping beyond the scope of the original project is one of the three major reasons behind Six Sigma project failure. These words often fall on deaf ears until we have a large-group verbal exercise. Using the example found in Figure 5.2, I ask each team to describe what its members thought was inside the scope of putting a man on the moon, and more importantly what was outside that scope. After the assignment is given and the teams have a chance to place their answers in the in or out column, I take the first item (space walk) and tell everyone to yell out their answers. Literally every time I have done this large group team verbal exercise, approximately 60 percent of the teams yell out "In" and the other 40 percent yell out "Out."

Group the following items into the Project Scope for NASA in placing a man on the moon:

- Space Walk
- Orbiting the Earth
- Space Station Creation
- Operate a Lunar Module

- Landing a Man on Mars
- Creating Tang
- Circling the Moon

IN   OUT

Figure 5.2 Large-table team exercise—Project scope

We go on to explain that as part of the Gemini program, Ed White did a space walk. In July 1969 we clearly didn't want to have Neil Armstrong get out of the lunar module and vaporize. Therefore, a space walk was inside the scope. However, the team exercise is a better warning than my admonition about limiting project scope. I again warn the participants that this exercise will not be easy, and if they cannot agree then they should add a question mark column for the Champion to resolve.

We also use large-group team exercises so the participants learn through doing. As Confucius said thousands of years ago:

"I hear and forget. I see and remember. I do and I understand."

For example, during the calculating baseline sigma lecture, we introduce the formula of defining a unit, defect, and opportunity. This refers to the "T" of CPTE. We then talk about the importance of carefully and deliberately agreeing on the number of opportunities in calculating baseline sigma because changing the number of opportunities later can affect sigma performance.

At about this time my associate hands out "fun size" packets of M&Ms (and why is something so small called the "fun size"?). We instruct each team to determine what a unit is for M&Ms, what would constitute a defect, and what the number of opportunities are. The exercise is both fun and enlightening, not to mention slightly fattening.

A healthy discussion follows. Everyone lists factors that contribute to the unit and what constitutes a defect. Not all teams report the exact same sigma based on how they determined defects and opportunities. Now we have a better idea of what the customer considers a defect or an opportunity. Participants have not only told me they had fun during this exercise but that they always remember the M&M exercise when they calculate their baseline sigma for their project.

There is a host of highly participative and educational simulations we use to teach Six Sigma. We typically save simulations for more complex Six Sigma tools like Design of Experiments (DOE). Anyone who has sat through a seminar on DOE through traditional instructor training has frustration to vent and at least a few naps to talk about. Hearing some expert drone on about fractional factorials, analysis of variance, and f-ratios would make anyone lose his concentration. After that sort of session, you can't help but have some strong technical resistance.

Two other simulations again prove the wisdom of Confucius. The first simulation occurs on Day 1 of DOE training after a tutorial (one that goes beyond our traditional one-hour limit) about full factorials to establish what process variables (x's) affect the response variable targeted for improvement (the "y"). Knowledge at this point is shaky at best among the brightest in the room. Without some hands-on practice the new concepts and tools of DOE will be forgotten by happy hour. Therefore we finish the day with a 90-minute exercise. Each team conducts an actual experiment. In psychology there is a concept called graduated desensitization. Phobic patients are gradually introduced to the target of their phobia so that they lose their traditional phobic reaction. Our 90-minute exercise is similar in concept because we have set up much of the work of the team. They are given eight plastic cups filled with water and four sticks, four straws, eight brand-name aspirin, and eight store-brand aspirin.

The goal of each team is to conduct eight experiments using a 2^3 full factorial, which necessitates running eight experiments testing three factors (x's) to see their effect (if any) on the quickness of dissolution of aspirin. The three factors are: agitation method (a stick versus a straw), brand of aspirin (Bayer versus store brand), and a catalyst. For purposes of the simulation, four experiments are run with no catalyst, and Calgon water softener acts as the catalyst for the remaining four.

Teams spend 15 minutes setting up the experiment, 60 minutes running the 8 experiments, and 15 minutes analyzing results and discussing key lessons. Prior to running the experiment I ask for any gamblers in the audience and ask them which factor they think affects quicker dissolution time and how much they are willing to bet. While somewhat entertaining, I am also creating the "P" of this exercise. After setting up, running the experiments, and analyzing the results, participants have not only had a good time but have greater confidence in the order of which factors affect dissolution of aspirin. I would tell you the order, but then you would never have to hire me to help you with this simulation.

Another simulation we run is on Days 2 and 3 of DOE training. Again, we practice the concept of gradual desensitization. After we introduce additional tools like the fractional factorial we introduce the Aero-bomb business simulation. This simulation is interspersed through additional lectures that cover concepts of simple and advanced analysis such as effects tables and analysis of variance. During breakouts each team applies the Define, Measure, and Analysis segments of DMAIC as it applies to modifying a balsa wood airplane to hit a target on the last day of DOE training that will be placed 25–50 feet from a launch area in some warehouse area of the organization or a large ballroom in a hotel conference center.

To add further excitement to what can be a dull tool, we offer the winning team a chance at $10,000. This opportunity garners significant discussion over the last days of training, and while no team has ever won $10,000, teams have won a significant amount of money (again, you must hire us to find out what the opportunity is). Teams are given a budget to manage, run a series of experiments, and my team approves experiments, modification to the balsa wood plane, and assists teams with analysis and subsequent designs a team wants to run. Consistently we have received feedback on how this simulation was not only entertaining but very helpful in the quest to learn DOE.

Adults learn best when they are having fun. One aspect of our training we are proud of is the humor we use in our consulting work. As we saw in Chapter 2 with Nigel Andrews of GE, humor can be overdone. However, a key of adult learning theory does stress that people learn more when they are having fun.

The problem with humor is different people find different things funny. Therefore, I strongly suggest that humor meets both the culture of the organization and the personality of the Six Sigma training group. Consultants have virtually the same reputation as attorneys, so self-deprecating humor always works well. With greater experience you can gauge the appropriateness of humor to involve the course participants. But I have seen inexperienced instructors fail miserably with this and caution those who would attempt this prematurely.

Finally, recognize that fun is not all about humor. Include the multitude of participative activities like the M&M exercise and the Aero-bomb business simulation.

Six Sigma Team Dynamics

The aspect of our DMAIC training I am most proud of is our ability to adapt and modify our approach based on feedback of participants and our experiences with what works and what doesn't work.

Given what a client invests on Six Sigma consulting, they should expect to see a significant return on that investment. Fortunately, most of our clients obtain seven-figure ROI in year one of their Six Sigma efforts. Unfortunately, many Six Sigma project teams fail. In years past we began doing failure analysis on our unsuccessful teams. There are technical issues for failure such as project scope creep, poor or nonexistent root cause analysis and the recent development of poor Champion involvement.

However, by far the majority of failed Six Sigma project teams occur due to poor team dynamics. Team dynamics are made up of a variety of elements that contribute to successful completion of DMAIC. These elements include but are not limited to:

- *Creation and utilization of vibrant agendas.* A common complaint of Six Sigma teams is the amount of time it takes to complete a first project. This legitimate issue is compounded by inefficient Six Sigma team meetings. A detailed agenda is imperative if Six Sigma team meetings are to work. It should include the desired outcome for each meeting, the item(s) to be covered in a meeting, the method/tool to address the item, the person(s) responsible for the item, and the amount of time needed to complete the item. Appendix C includes the detailed agendas we use during the DMAIC training breakouts.
- *Agreement on a primary and secondary decision-making method.* Many Six Sigma meetings bog down when there is no standardized decision-making method. We recommend consensus (referenced in detail in Chapter 3) and 2/3 majority as a secondary method when consensus cannot be reached.

- *Established ground rules for meetings.* Good meeting behaviors are nearly assured when operating agreements are established prior to the Six Sigma meeting. In Chapter 3 we addressed several good ground rules that can ensure that a meeting stays on track.
- *Dealing with maladaptive behaviors.* There are a host of maladaptive behaviors that—if allowed to fester—can easily derail a team as they attempt to implement DMAIC. Coming late and leaving early from meetings, one person dominating discussions, and excessive clowning are examples of maladaptive behavior that will cause a team to fail.
- *Dealing with team member resistance.* It can be expected that among the six to eight team members, resistance to Six Sigma will occur. If allowed to continue unabated, the project team is likely to fail. So the team leader and/or Champion must intervene.

Knowing the importance of team dynamics, we have altered our DMAIC training slightly. In previous years we began the first day of DMAIC training with the entire team present and plunged into Define. In the last several years we have been beginning by conducting two days of highly interactive training of team leaders and one or two key team members going through Six Sigma team dynamics training.

The first day begins with a survival exercise. Participants must rank—as a team—the importance of certain items that will determine their chances of survival after a plane crash. We create two arbitrary teams and observe their natural team dynamics for 90 minutes. This exercise helps demonstrate the need for better team dynamics. How? During the debrief each of the two teams reveals how its members utilized their time poorly, mishandled maladaptive behaviors, didn't have an agreed decision-making method to reach agreement, and neglected to use an agenda, which resulted in poor decisions. The remainder of the morning session is directed toward the key ingredients in making Six Sigma meeting more effective and efficient. We divide key lessons into two categories. The first category are those preventive actions that can make Six Sigma teams progress through DMAIC faster and with better results. These include teaching team leaders to create vibrant agendas that include desired outcomes for each meeting or breakout, having a primary and secondary decision-making method, and a set of ground rules for each team member to follow for any given time the team meets.

The second category of key lessons centers around how and when to intervene when meetings are going bad. Team leaders and key team members learn how to enforce ground rules, deal with early or late arrivers, deal with someone who physically or mentally "drops out" of a Six Sigma meeting, or deal with someone who dominates a meeting or shows resistance to the project.

By the time of the first day's lunch, the participants are told the remaining day and a half of training will be in two subgroups of 10–12 individuals. Each person in each subgroup over the next 1½ days will be given the opportunity to run a 45-minute meeting. Each individual is given 10 minutes to set up her breakout room and develop an agenda regarding some generic topic she chooses from a list we provide or an idea of her own. Among the generic topics we have are picking a college for a child or selecting a new home.

While the chosen team leader or key team member preps his room and writes the agenda on a flip chart, my team takes the rest of the group in a hallway and assigns roles to a few selected individuals. The roles they play will reveal maladaptive behaviors that the facilitator of the meeting must deal with. We instruct these role players how to respond if and when the facilitator intervenes.

The advantage of going first or second is you get the anxiety of facilitating over with and then can play a maladaptive role in later sessions. The disadvantage is that each session ends with a thorough debrief where the facilitator evaluates her own performance and then receives the feedback of other participants and the Eckes team. By the middle of our second day, themes emerge around both preventions and interventions. The second day ends with a large group review of key lessons and all are told to get a good night's sleep.

Six Sigma Tactical Training—Define

Eckes and Associates has shaped the DMAIC materials into modules for both teaching and implementation purposes. These modules are based on the concept of the DMAIC "tollgates." Tollgates are the subcategories of activities that teams must master and meet with

Champion approval as they progress through DMAIC. In Define there are three tollgates. The first tollgate is the Project Charter. The second tollgate is Determining Customer, their Needs, and Requirements. The third tollgate is Creating the High Level Process Map. For Define, each of our teaching modules is equivalent to the three tollgates of Define. This equivalency is not always the case for each teaching module. For example, one of the tollgates of Measure constitutes three teaching modules.

Define and Measure tollgates are best explained using two project case studies from our recent work at Hewlett Packard. Since their merger with Compaq, there have been a host of Six Sigma initiatives within different business units of HP, though not the top-down driven approach made popular by AlliedSignal or General Electric.

My first exposure to HP came in June 2003.

Over the course of the next months I was asked to visit several of their facilities and discuss Six Sigma with business leaders. In December 2003 HP IPG Americas Consumer Operations asked me to be part of their all-managers retreat. My one day overview went well and their business leader Mohan Garde shortly contacted me with a multitude of questions about going forward with a launch in his business. In January 2004 we signed a one-year contract.

In January and February we created the business process management system and in March a group of first-wave project Champions that included the likes of Tammy Lockwood, Gail Waller, and Chuck Zelanis helped to create preliminary charters for their first projects.

The assignment of a full-time project quality leader who will be responsible for both strategy and tactics is a crucial contributor to first-year launch success. Mohan chose a bright, energetic, meticulous quality leader, already one of his direct reports, Sean Sanders. Sean dutifully coordinated all aspects of our strategy sessions and the Champions training. When team leaders and key team members congregated at the Hotel Valencia in San Jose in April 2004, I knew Sean had worked well with his management team. I was highly impressed with the caliber of the participants. My senior vice president Susan Ayarbe and I facilitated the team dynamics session and met talented and motivated team leaders like Annie Price, Debbie Gammel, and Gary George.

On the following day nearly 60 team members gathered in the main ballroom of the Hotel Valencia. The Hotel Valencia is located in a swank area of San Jose called Santana Row, reminiscent of Rodeo Drive in Beverly Hills. Upscale restaurants, art gallerys, and drinking establishments that charge $10 for a mojito are prevalent. It was an intoxicating environment and I knew something special was going to happen. Many of the team members were impressed with the selection of the Hotel Valencia and later told us they knew that Mohan was serious about Six Sigma if he was devoting these kinds of resources to the project.

Susan Ayarbe and I know that the first morning of DMAIC training is the most important 3-½ hours of any consulting we do. As my dear mother once said, you only have one opportunity to make a first impression.

The first 45–60 minutes of DMAIC training with such a large group is spent on introductions, a kickoff statement by a key manager, a high-level overview of the DMAIC model, and what each person is expected to accomplish on his project. During the introductions Susan and I obtain the group's expectations. Susan and I establish a set of detailed ground rules that include punctual returns from breakouts and lunches. This is perhaps our most important ground rule when having a group as large as 60 people. Other ground rules imperative for such a large group: only one person can speak at a time, and sidebar conversations at each table should be limited.

Define Tollgate #1—The Preliminary Charter

With these preliminaries out of the way, we begin teaching the first module of Define, the preliminary charter. In less than 45 minutes we cover the key ingredients. Using the CPTE philosophy, we define the concept of a preliminary charter as the collection of documents that establishes purpose and direction for the group. We review the key elements of the charter as:

- *The Business Case.* The nonquantitative statement of purpose that explains why this project should be done and how strategic business objectives of the organization are impacted.
- *The Preliminary Problem Statement.* The quantitative statement of the problem to be solved by the project team. It should state how long the problem has been going on, be specific and measurable,

describe the impact to the organization, and state the gap between current and desired state. Finally, it should be stated in neutral terms with no blame or perceived cause or solution.

- *Project Scope.* The boundaries for the team to work within. It should not only reference what the team needs to work on but what is outside of the boundaries of the project.
- *Goals and Objectives.* What the team is expected to achieve by the end of their DMAIC work.
- *Milestones.* The time line for the teams to complete their work. The HP teams were expected to start D/M training in April and complete implementation of the tollgates of D/M by mid June when Analysis Training began. Analysis was expected to be nearly complete when Improve and Control training commenced in July. From July 16 (the last day of training for the teams at the Hotel Valencia) through Thanksgiving 2004, the teams were expected to complete the project and disband.

Both Susan and I caution the teams about typical preliminary charter pitfalls. First, we explain that it's called the preliminary charter because any work the team does is in an advisory capacity. It is the domain of the Champion to make the final charter decisions.

Second, we emphasize the importance of providing project scope input and reviewing what has been created tentatively by the Champion. Often, Champions expect too much from a first-year team. Thus we advise the project teams to provide candid feedback about the project scope to their Champion.

With regard to goals and objectives, most first-wave projects attempt to achieve a 50-percent improvement in the baseline performance of the targeted problem.

After our lecture, Susan shows a flip chart with the desired outcomes of the first breakout. Figure 5.3 shows the Desired Outcomes, recommended decision-making method, and the agenda for the 75-minute breakout. Unlike many of the breakouts to follow, the decision-making method is consultative because the Champion is to reconcile the team's input and determine the final charter within a week of the D/M training.

This first breakout gives Susan and me an opportunity to observe the facilitative skills of the team leaders. It is one thing to conduct a

Breakout #1—The Project Charter

Desired Outcomes:
- Review and provide input to Champion on the Business Case
- Review and provide input to Champion on the Problem Statement
- Review and provide input to Champion on Project Scope
- Review Team Membership for possible revision

Decision-Making Method
- Consultative

Item	Method	Person	Time
Review Agenda	Discussion	Team Leader	5 minutes
Review Business Case	Discussion	Team Leader and Team	10 minutes
Review Problem Statement	Discussion	Team Leader and Team	15 minutes
Review Project Scope	In/Out/? Tool	Team Leader and Team	30 minutes
Review Team Membership	Discussion	Team Leader and Team	5 minutes
Complete Parking Lot for unfinished items	Parking Lot	Team Leader and Team	5 minutes
Plus Delta of Breakout	Plus/Delta	Team Leader and Team	5 minutes
		TOTAL	75 minutes

Team Roles
- Facilitator_____
- Scribe_____
- Timekeeper_____

Remember to post and review a set of ground rules

Figure 5.3

facilitation working on generic topics like choosing a college for your children. It is completely different when facilitating peers on a real project. We knew by the end of the first breakout we were dealing with very special people. We were particularly impressed with the leadership of the Diagnostics team and the Service Order Status team led by Annie Price and Debbie Gammel respectively.

As the name of the team implies, the Service Order Status (SOS) team had the goal of reducing the number of customer escalations and related contacts for customers who were inquiring about their orders. Just as we did for the strategic component of Six Sigma, Susan and I circulated through the breakout rooms to see which teams were struggling with the charter breakout. As this was the team's first breakout, we took a more active role. Amazingly, each team was doing well. The SOS room was our last stop. I am always struck by the originality of some teams, and that day Debbie's SOS team taught the teachers something new. They took each project scope agenda item and the team brainstormed a series of project scope criteria that they then applied. For example, the SOS team brainstormed criteria like geography, vendors, and customer touch points. Then they decided what was inside of the scope and more importantly what was outside of the scope. For geography the United States was in, Canada out. For customer touch points, emails and Web calls were inside of scope, the proactive phone system was outside of the scope. Susan and I profusely complimented the SOS team on their creativity (in keeping with adult learning theory) and asked the team if they wouldn't mind being highlighted during the large group debrief.

Just prior to the lunch at the Valencia, the eight HP teams returned to the large ballroom. Years ago we would have had each team give what we thought would be a brief status of its breakout work. Susan and I learned from painful experience that teams love to talk about their work and when this type of debrief would take as long as the breakout itself, we dispensed with this approach. Instead, we asked two questions and highlighted one or two teams. The first question was "What went well during the breakout?" This question allows teams not only to exhibit growing confidence with the material but gives Susan and me a chance to confirm impressions we gathered as we did our rounds. The second question was "What did you struggle with?," which allows us a chance to reinforce ideas and reteach actual concepts if warranted. The debrief ends with Debbie Gammel's report of the SOS team's brainstorming technique with project scope. Other team leaders liked the idea and planned to revisit their scope activity with the same technique.

Define Tollgate #2—Determining Customers, their Needs, and Requirements

Later that afternoon Susan gave the lecture on the second tollgate of Define, Determing Customers, their Needs, and Requirements. Using a combination of traditional teaching and interactive techniques, Susan addressed the key lessons of the second tollgate of Define; namely:

- *The definition of the customer.* Susan specified that a customer is the recipient of the product or service in question. As such, a customer could just as likely be another HP employee (the internal customer) as an external customer. Additionally, Susan addressed the fact that some customers are more important to the project than others. The concept of determining primary, secondary, and even tertiary customers through a process called segmentation is addressed in lecture.
- *Distiguishing the difference between a need and a requirement.* Utilizing the "E" of CPTE, Susan shared her coffee drinking habits, explaining the need for a cup of coffee with her requirements of hot, strong, and caffeinated.
- *The CTQ tree.* The major tool to determine customer needs and requirements is the CTQ tree. CTQ stands for Critical to Quality. Figure 5.4 shows a CTQ tree for the underwriting project we discussed in Chapter 4.
- *The methods required to collect information on customer's needs and requirements.* Susan used a large-group team exercise where she introduced six different methods, from focus groups to surveys, to obtain information on customer's needs and requirements. She assigned each of the teams one of the methods after a brief definition and asked each team to be ready to report out the advantages and disadvantages of each method in five minutes. Of course, Susan could share these advantages and disadvantages herself,

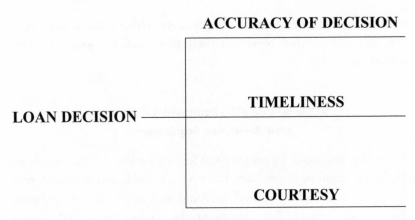

Figure 5.4

but the benefit of team involvement far outweighs getting done sooner. A key lesson is that each method has both advantages and disadvantages. Therefore Susan is quick to point out that when the project teams collect information on their customers' needs and requirements, they should use a minimum of two methods.

- *A review of Kano's model.* Once a project team starts to brainstorm customer requirements through the CTQ tree, they become overwhelmed by the quantity of possible requirements. One tool to reduce the amount of requirements is called Kano's model. This tool separates requirements into must haves and one-dimensional characteristics (nice to haves). For purposes of the project we instruct them to first focus on the must haves using Kano's model.

As we approached the hour mark, Susan was ready to assign the teams their second breakout around the second tollgate of Define. Once again, she showed a flip chart list of expectations: to determine customers of the project and segment if necessary, create a CTQ tree, and apply Kano's model. She was quick to point out that most of the work of determining needs and requirements occurs during intersession work when the teams return to work, and cannot be achieved at the Hotel Valencia. Nonetheless, Susan and I expect them to become familiar with the tools during the breakout. Figure 5.5 shows the detailed agenda for the second breakout.

Breakout #2—Customer Focus

Desired Outcomes:
• Determine Customer(s) of your project
• Determine segmentation of customers if needed
• Create a CTQ tree with brainstormed needs and requirements
• Gain experience applying Kano's Model to potential customer requirements

Decision-Making Method
• Primary—Consensus
• Secondary—2/3 majority vote

Item	Method	Person	Time
Review Agenda	Discussion	Team Leader	5 minutes
Determine Customers of your project and determine segments if needed	Discussion	Team Leader and Team	15 minutes
Create a CTQ tree for the primary customer	CTQ tree	Team Leader and Team	30 minutes
Apply Kano's model for the first level requirements	Kano's Model	Team Leader and Team	10 minutes
Complete Parking Lot for unfinished items	Parking Lot	Team Leader and Team	5 minutes
Plus Delta of Breakout	Plus/Delta	Team Leader and Team	5 minutes
		TOTAL	70 minutes

Team Roles

• Facilitator_____
• Scribe_____
• Timekeeper_____

Remember to post and review
a set of groundrules

Figure 5.5

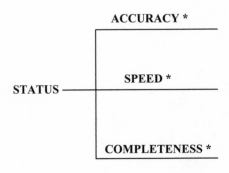

* Must have (Kano's Model)

Figure 5.6

The second breakout went well, with most teams embracing the CTQ tree and Kano's model. A repeated theme both Susan and I echo is that they should not become married to their CTQ tree because during the intersession work they will need to validate the requirements with their customers. Once again we are impressed with the work of the SOS team as they create the CTQ tree highlighted in Figure 5.6, complete with a Kano analysis.

During the large group debrief we addressed several struggles that took place during the breakout. Many mislabeled the CTQ tree. Each branch of the CTQ tree should be a more detailed description of the previous branch of the tree. Some teams labeled these additional branches with new requirements. We use the SOS team to show the proper use of the more detailed branches of a CTQ tree. As seen in Figure 5.7, we could add two additional branches to the initial branch of completeness to make the requirements more detailed.

Another dilemma: some teams in the breakout have created the equivalent of a Redwood. We encourage teams to recognize that during their intersession work they must validate what is important to the customer. As such, they need to apply the Pareto principle to data they collect during the intersession, where 20 percent of their brainstormed requirements will account for 80 percent of responses from customers.

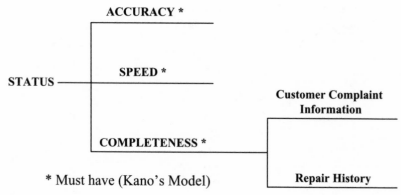

Figure 5.7

Define Tollgate #3—Creating the High-Level Process Map

Earlier we addressed the concept of process mapping. In less than one-half hour of lecture, I took the HP group through the Car Buying Process Map example. Among the key points I make during this example are:

- Sequencing the steps is crucial. You first begin by labeling the process, indicating the start/stop points, labeling the output with nouns, determining and prioritizing customers and suppliers, determining inputs and identifying the five to seven high-level steps in the process as they are currently performed.
- Both Susan and I explain that the process map is the "Work Horse" tool of DMAIC because we use it during the Define, Measure, Analysis, Improve, and Control steps. This is the only tool that is used during the entire phase of the DMAIC application.
- Process mapping is a relatively simple tool. However, teams often make mistakes with this tool. Therefore, to avoid these mistakes we share the two major mistakes teams make in creating the high-level map. First, they tend to create the map the way they would like it to be. This map is called the should-be map and is part of the Improve phase of DMAIC. Second, teams go into too much detail creating the high-level map. A more detailed subprocess map is created in the Analysis phase.

Process Name: CSO (Customer Service Order) Status Checking Process

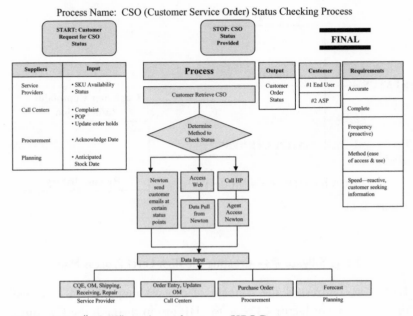

Figure 5.8   "AS-IS" service order status SIPOC

During the breakouts Susan and I had to remind several teams of the two aforementioned mistakes, but overall the HP teams were responding well to the lecture. Figure 5.8 shows the SOS team's process map.

Six Sigma Tactical Training—Measure

Measure Tollgate #1—The Data Collection Plan

> Everything you can measure you should measure. Everything you can't measure you should make measurable
> —Galileo

Most teams exhibit a sense of dread as the second element of DMAIC is introduced. Remembering their math courses from high school or college usually results in some sense of phobia and resentment among our Six Sigma participants, particularly if they have no engineering or technology background. Our first order of business when we begin teaching the Measure section of DMAIC is to start with encouragement to the audience. Many times we have heard from clients how much they dreaded the Measure section of their project only to find out later that it was one of the relatively easier steps in implementing their projects.

There are several reasons behind our confidence in easing their fears. First, we stress to the participants that we will not be discussing the theory of Measurement. I have taken Six Sigma courses where a disproportionate time has been spent on such topics as the central limit theorem, a review of the Gaussian and Poisson distributions, and tests of statistical significance. While riveting, it is not necessary to understand all the theory behind Measure. It does virtually nothing to help teams calculate their baseline sigma. So our teaching approach to Measure is much like the difference between learning how to drive the car versus learning the intricacies of how a carburetor works or how intake valves affect the RPMs in your car.

Second, we address the fact that through the business process management activities, low-performing processes were targeted for improvement. We explain that if minor mistakes are made in how baseline sigma is calculated and the real sigma of their project is 1.4 and they calculate 1.6, there is no harm to the project.

With these admonitions we proceed to the rationale behind measure. One aspect of good DMAIC execution is assuring that those who teach it carefully link each of the steps of DMAIC with each other. To begin this, we return to our initial discussion of what Six Sigma is trying to achieve at its highest level. Each project team is attempting to improve the effectiveness and efficiency of the targeted process. Figure 5.9 shows the three areas where measures must take place.

There are three areas we want to collect data. First and foremost are the measures important to the customer. In Figure 5.9 this would be the output measures. Because these measures affect the customer, we refer to them as the customer measures of effectiveness. Next, we need to be concerned with inputs to the process. These are referred to as measures of effectiveness emanating from the supplier. As the saying goes, garbage in, garbage out. Finally, there are measures of efficiency within the process whether they are cost, time, labor, or value. We ask participants what Figure 5.9 looks like, and invariably we hear someone say it resembles the SIPOC model of process mapping. We reinforce the fact that the third tollgate of Define assists us in the first tollgate of Measure.

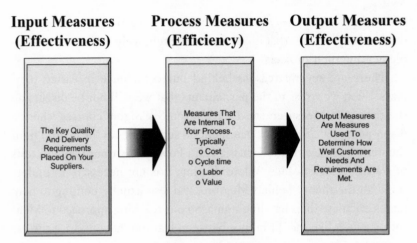

Figure 5.9 Input, process, and output measures

We then introduce the participants to the data collection plan. This nine-column chart is usually flip charted by Susan or myself prior to our lecture using three or four flip charts taped to a wall visible to all participants. This is reflected in Table 5.1.

Measure Tollgate #1—Creating the Data Collection Plan.
Module #1—The first four columns

While there are two major tollgates in Measure (Creating the Data Collection Plan and Implementing the Data Collection Plan), we divide the teaching modules into three.

Our first teaching module addresses the first four columns of the Data Collection Plan.

They include:

- *What to measure.* The measures that the project team will use to calculate baseline sigma.
- *The type of measure.* There are three types of measures: output, input, or process measures. Typically, there are two to three output measures, one or two input measures, and one process measure.
- *Type of data.* There are two types of data. Discrete data is categorized as either/or data whether it's on/off or good/bad type measures,

Table 5.1 Data Collection Plan

Measure	Type Measure	Type Data	Operational Definition	Specification	Target	Data Collection Form	Sampling	Baseline 6 Sigma

while continuous data is data that occurs within a continuum like miles, time, or height.

- *Operational Definitions.* Operational Defintion is a description of something where those affected by the measure have a common understanding of what is being described.

I proceeded to label the first column "What to Measure," utilizing the generic example of ordering a meal at a a TGIF's, Applebee's, or Olive Garden.

First we brainstormed a list of customer requirements regarding my dining experience. Within minutes we had generated more than 10 requirements through interaction with the participants. It was at this point I told everyone that typically two mistakes are made on a Six Sigma project. The first is not measuring enough of the key requirements important to the customer. The second mistake is measuring everything. Through this example I then asked them to vote for which requirements were more important to them than the others. Through this application of the Pareto principle we found that the top three account for over 80 percent of the responses. Those become what we term the validated customer requirements and necessitate measurement. In our case the top three requirements were food quality, delivery speed, and menu variety. Table 5.2 reflects the first column of the data collection plan filled out.

Again, I returned to the concept of too little or too much measurement to explain the second column of the data collection plan. Referencing the slide of Figure 5.9, I explained that a measure can be an output measure, an input measure, or a process measure. Using the Pareto principle we could see that we had three output measures that had been validated with the class participants. It is common that there will be one to three measures after potential output measures are validated with the customer. I further instructed the group that there should be one or two input measures of effectiveness, but the number is determined by the team because it is the customer to its suppliers. Next, we only needed one process measure because the most common measures of process efficiency (cost, time, labor, and/or value) so strongly correlate with one another. For example, if return on assets is strongly correlated with inventory turns, it is wasteful to measure both. For Six Sigma projects, time and cost to collect data are always at a premium. Therefore it is only necessary to measure one aspect of process efficiency.

Table 5.2 Data Collection Plan

Measure	Type Measure	Type Data	Operational Definition	Specification	Target	Data Collection Form	Sampling	Baseline 6 Sigma
Food Quality								
Delivery Speed								
Menu Variety								

One measure can do more than one thing for the team, as I showed with our generic class example. I first wrote down in the second column how food quality is an output measure and placed an "O." But then I explained that food quality is determined by suppliers, whether that supplier was the food prep process or the food distributors that provide the restaurant. Thus I place an "I" next to the "O" for food quality. I proceeded to delivery speed, which has been validated as the second output measure validated by the customers. Next I asked if it could be any other measure. Class participants quickly responded that it is a process measure of efficiency. Therefore I placed a "P" next to delivery speed. Sometimes class participants indicate delivery speed could be a result of the food prep process and say we could put an "I" next to delivery speed.

We continue to Menu variety, where an "O" is placed because of its validation of importance to the customer. Menus at restaurants like TGIF's and Applebee's come from a corporate source so an "I" is placed there as well.

I instructed the participants that these three measures constituted the amount of data needed if this were to be a Six Sigma project. I further explained that if there were no "P" or "I" measures in the second column the team would need to return to the first column and find appropriate measures until there were one or two input measures, one process measure, and two or three output measures.

The aforementioned large-group activity took less than 15 minutes. I explained that two of the nine columns had been completed in virtually no time at all to reinforce the concept that Measure is not as difficult as initially thought. This is reflected in Table 5.3.

We then defined the two types of data, discrete and continuous. Again trying to use easy-to-understand examples, I asked the participants if they ever watched the Ebert and Roeper movie review program on TV. Most responded affirmatively. I asked how they rate a movie and a volunteer offered the now famous "Thumbs up or Thumbs Down" rating system made popular years ago by Roger Ebert and Gene Siskel. I used this simple example of discrete data also to show its limitations. I asked how Ebert and Roeper rated a movie when they *really* liked a movie, and hear the answer "Thumbs way up." Thus, we had created through this simple example how continuous data reveals more information when data is measured on a continuum. A movie rated as a 9 on a 1–10 scale would tell us more about the movie than one rated a 7.

Table 5.3 Data Collection Plan

Measure	Type Measure	Type Data	Operational Definition	Specification	Target	Data Collection Form	Sampling	Baseline 6 Sigma
Food Quality	0, I							
Delivery Speed	0, P							
Menu Variety	0, I							

We then moved to the wall where our dining example was located. For Food Quality we could simply ask whether they liked the meal, yes or no. This closed-ended question will result in discrete data that doesn't tell us as much as continuous data. However, what if we asked the diner how she would rate the meal on a scale from 1–10 or 1–5. Through this primitive form of "data transformation," we can learn much more about the food quality requirement. We decided to use the now famous Likert Scale of 1–5 named after a University of Michigan statistician who found that scales from 1–5 or 1–7 are used more evenly than scales of 1–10.

Going on to our other two measures we could see that delivery speed can be measured easily with continuous data in terms of the amount of minutes that elapse from food order to food arrival. Finally, we once again used a Likert scale for how well the customer perceives menu variety. This is reflected in Table 5.4.

Once again I pointed out the relative ease of filling out the data collection plan, indicating that 3 of the 9 columns are filled out, and we hadn't spent more than 30 minutes on it.

We had saved the remaining teach time for the fourth and last column in this module, operational definitions. Operational definitions are a description of something where those affected have a common understanding such that all parties involved experience no ambiguity over what is being described. We cautioned the participants that when data collected is counter to what their beliefs tell them, they attack the data rather than challenge their beliefs.

We start with the "E" and "P" of CPTE by revisiting the 2000 presidential election in Florida.

"Without sharing your political beliefs, can you see the controversy engendered in 2000 when there wasn't a clear operational definition of what constituted a vote in Florida?" I queried. "We were exposed to more than we ever wanted to know about hanging chads, dimpled chads, pregnant chads, and perforated chads." With knowing glances from the participants, Susan and I put them into large-group teams and assigned them the task of operationally defining departure time for an airline flight. The group is given 10 minutes to come to a decision and give a rationale to support it.

Among the answers provided were push back from gate and "wheels up." During the debrief we saw that without agreement, different numbers are generated for push back from gate versus "wheels up." We

Table 5.4 Data Collection Plan

Measure	Type Measure	Type Data	Operational Definition	Specification	Target	Data Collection Form	Sampling	Baseline 6 Sigma
Food Quality	0, I	Continuous						
Delivery Speed	0, P	Continuous						
Menu Variety	0, I	Continuous						

stressed that neither answer was right or wrong. We simply informed the teams that without resolving the different operational definitions, their data could be challenged by those who don't agree with the definitions. Finally, using the airplane example we pointed out that the rationale for selecting an operational definition should bias the customer. With this in mind, the discussion focused on the fact that push back from gate often can result in delays, while "wheels up" means you are on to your destination.

The amount of time on operational definitions was the longest of the first four columns. A disproportionate amount of time should be spent as well on operational definitions during the next breakout. Susan showed a detailed agenda for the first Data Collection breakout and the teams disbanded to return later. The completed data collection plan for the first four columns is found in Table 5.5.

Figure 5.10 shows the detailed breakout for the first data collection plan breakout.

During the breakout we cautioned the teams not to cling to the CTQs they brainstormed during the second breakout of Define. They might change after validating them with customers during their intersession work. So during this breakout we dissuaded the teams from emotional discussions of operational definitions. During our rounds, Susan and I saw more than one spirited discussion regarding operational definitions, but we told teams that this kind of discussion should only get heated once they were tackling real CTQs validated by the customer.

During the large-group debrief, we heard most teams struggle with the operational definition. While this is normal, the decision on the ultimate operational definition should reflect the impressions of the customer. We once again called on the SOS team to share one of its operational definitions. The team chose response speed and explained that the operational definition was first contact with HP to final resolution.

Measure Tollgate #1—Creating the Data Collection Plan.
Module #2—Columns 5–8

In most cases Susan and I alternate teaching modules, and at the Hotel Valencia she took over the teaching of the next four columns on the data collection plan. They include:

Table 5.5 Data Collection Plan

Measure	Type Measure	Type Data	Operational Definition	Specification	Target	Data Collection Form	Sampling	Baseline 6 Sigma
Food Quality	0, I	Continuous	From end of order to arrival of food					
Delivery Speed	0, P	Continuous	Likert scale 1–5 rating from customer					
Menu Variety	0, I	Continuous	Likert scale 1–5 rating from customer					

Breakout #4—Creating the Data Collection Plan (Pt.1)

Desired Outcomes:
- Determine the potential measures for your project
- Determine the type of measures and types of data
- Determine operational definitions for all potential measures

Decision-Making Method
- Primary—Consensus
- Secondary—2/3 majority vote

Item	Method	Person	Time
Review Agenda	Discussion	Team Leader	5 minutes
List the potential CTQ's of the project's customers	Discussion	Team Leader and Team	5 minutes
Determine type of measures and types of data	Discussion	Team Leader and Team	15 minutes
Determine operational definitions for all potential measures	Discussion	Team Leader and Team	30 minutes
Complete Parking Lot for unfinished items	Parking Lot	Team Leader and Team	5 minutes
Plus Delta of Breakout	Plus/Delta	Team Leader and Team	5 minutes
		TOTAL	65 minutes

Team Roles
- Facilitator _____
- Scribe _____
- Timekeeper _____

Remember to post and review a set of groundrules

Figure 5.10

- *Determining the Target.* The target measure is the customer's ideal performance of the product or service.
- *Determining the Specification.* A specification is the least acceptable measure of performance for the product or service in the eyes of the customer.
- *Data Collection Forms.* There are two types of data. Therefore there are two basic types of data collection forms. A defect checksheet used for discrete data and a frequency distribution checksheet used for continuous data.
- *Sampling.* Most projects cannot look at the entire population of events whether they are products or services. Therefore sampling is imperative to save time and money. Sampling is the process of taking only a few products or services from a larger pool of events. Unfortunately, when a team samples, there is the tendency to make a mistake about what is sampled (called bias).

The teach points for educating the teams on targets and specifications are straightforward. Using the dining experience we indicated that when ordering our meal the target would be the meal appearing as soon as possible and depending on the restaurant, 30 minutes would be the specification.

Next, Susan proceeded to go back to the third column of the data collection plan and reinforced the previous learning that there are two types of data, discrete and continuous. Thus, there are basically two types of data collection forms, one for discrete data and one for continuous data.

Susan took the Food Quality measure to show how a discrete data collection check sheet would work even though we had transformed the data into continuous data through the Likert scale. She asked the participants to temporarily turn Food Quality into discrete data, that you either liked or disliked the meal. For this type of discrete data, reason codes for why the meal was disliked have to be created and put into the check sheet. Then, when a disliked meal is recorded the reason code should be recorded in the appropriate area of the check sheet. At the end of the data collection period, the data should then be transformed into a Pareto chart or pie chart. The check sheet, Pareto, and pie chart are all shown in Figure 5.11.

Reason Disliked	Frequency
Meal Overcooked	ЖЖ ЖЖ ЖЖ ЖЖ III
Incorrect Order	ЖЖ ЖЖ ЖЖ II
Appearance of Meal	ЖЖ ЖЖ II
Meal Undercooked	ЖЖ IIII
Tasted "Funny"	IIII
Too Salty	III
Miscellaneous	I

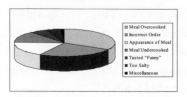

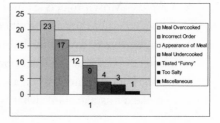

Figure 5.11

Susan then took the delivery-speed measure and introduced the data collection form for continuous data. This is called the frequency distribution chart. The majority of frequency distribution charts have measurement "cells" of 5–7. We see in Figure 5.12 the actual times from the moment a meal is ordered to the time it is received—collected in groups of 10-minute cells.

Susan then approached the sensitive topic of sampling by asking which question she hears most often about sampling. Right away she was told that it is "How large should the sample size be?" There are three questions that should be asked about sample size, and she explained that this question should be third in order of asking.

The first question: "What has the team done to ensure that the sample is a representative sample?" and the second is: "What has the team done to ensure that the sample is taken in a random manner?"

As we detailed at the beginning of this chapter, when teaching more complex topics the "E" should come first. She told the story of the 1932 presidential election where one week prior to the election between Hoover and FDR a telephone poll was taken. Over 50,000 potential voters were asked who they would vote for. Over 65 percent said they would vote for Hoover, and he lost—by a lot—that next week. Susan

		X		
		X		
X	X	X		
X	X	X		
X	X	X	X	X

| 0-10 | 11-20 | 21-30 | 31-40 | 41-50 | 51-60 |

Figure 5.12

pointed out the sample was large but not representative of the potential voters that year since in 1932 having a phone was a sign of affluence and the affluent tended to vote more for Republicans (Hoover). Therefore, each team must first use their expertise in the subject matter to brainstorm and agree to a set of factors that would determine how representative the sample was when it was drawn from the larger population.

To reinforce this concept, Susan conducted a large-team exercise. Everyone was told to imagine they work at a high-rise large-city hotel, and they must draw a sample of room service deliveries to determine speed of delivery. Susan then flip charted the most common responses from each team. The following themes about ensuring a representative sample emerged:

- Multiple floors from the hotel, not just floors closest to the food prep area
- Samples taken over several days not just their busiest or slowest time
- Samples taken from breakfast, lunch, and dinner
- Different types of meals ordered, not just quick orders like salads
- Samples that avoid holidays when the hotel might not be that busy

Next, Susan talked about sample randomness. A random sample is when any one event has an equal likelihood of being taken. The random button on your stereo indicates that song 7 has an equal likelihood of being played first as song 2 or song 9. In our hotel example Susan pointed out that a random number generator (like the random button on your CD player) could determine the floor of the hotel where our room service delivery sample would be taken. If the random number generator turned up 8, the first sample would be the first room service order request from the 8th floor that matched the previous representative criteria.

In her final comments Susan discussed the two types of formulas that determine sample size. One is for discrete data and the other for continuous data. In previous years we would spend more large-group time teaching the intricacies, but now show an example that simply illuminates two key teach points. One is that when using discrete data, sample sizes are usually larger than when using continuous data because we are measuring defects and we need to collect enough samples for defects to reveal themselves. The second key point in each of the sample size formulas is for the team to determine the desired magnitude of change it wishes the sample to reveal. Susan shared with them that her colleague (namely me) lost 35 lbs in 2003 (yes, the divorce diet worked quite well for me). One of our clients who hadn't seen me in months quickly noticed my weight loss. His "sample size" of observation to observe such a large change in the data (my before and after weight) was a glance. But if he wanted to know if I had lost 5 lbs, he might have to observe me more closely, over time (a larger sample size).

At that point we were ready for the second data collection breakout. Susan reviewed that the teams should be brainstorming targets and specifications, discussing data collection methods, and brainstorming criteria that would ensure that their samples would be both random and representative. Figure 5.13 shows the detailed breakout agenda.

Measure Tollgate #2—Creating the Data Collection Plan.
Module #3—Column 9

The first week of D and M training is nearly complete. The last column on the creation of the data collection plan remains. It is the all-important formula for calculating the project team's baseline sigma.

The key teach points of this lecture focus on two key areas:

- *Understanding the concept of the standard deviation.* Before any formulas are shared with the participants, we address the concept of the standard deviation. We also explain why we use sigma language to measure distance from the average performance in a process to the point at which a customer is dissatisfied.
- *Understanding the discrete method of calculating baseline sigma performance.* Because all first-wave project teams anticipate poor baseline sigma performance, we universally teach the easier discrete method of

Breakout #5—Creating the Data Collection Plan (Pt. 2)

Desired Outcomes:
- Determine the targets and specifications of the potential measures for the project
- Determine the type of data collection forms necessary to collect your team's data
- Determine factors that will contribute to ensuring your sampling will be representative and random

Decision-Making Method
- Primary—Consensus
- Secondary—2/3 majority vote

Item	Method	Person	Time
Review Agenda	Discussion	Team Leader	5 minutes
Determine the targets and specifications for your potential measures	Discussion	Team Leader and Team	10 minutes
Determine the types of data collection forms necessary to collect data	Discussion	Team Leader and Team	15 minutes
Determine how the sampling for the project will be both representative and random	Discussion	Team Leader and Team	20 minutes
Complete Parking Lot for unfinished items	Parking Lot	Team Leader and Team	5 minutes
Plus Delta of Breakout	Plus/Delta	Team Leader and Team	5 minutes
		TOTAL	60 minutes

Team Roles

- Facilitator _____
- Scribe _____
- Timekeeper _____

Remember to post and review a set of groundrules

Figure 5.13

calculating baseline sigma based on determining what a defect, unit, and opportunity are.

A crucial element to appreciate Six Sigma is to understand that your customers feel every variation in a process, not the average performance.

To begin the lecture on the last teaching module of M, I showed a set of data points as follows: 4, 9, 14, 9, 3, 10, 20, 4, 9, 18. I asked someone with a calculator to determine the average of the 10 data points and I quickly got the answer of 10.

I asked the participants to imagine these are wait times. I asked them to imagine them as wait times in a fast food drive through, the grocery store checkout line, the hotel checkout line, or even the wait to check in for their return flights at an airport.

An interactive discussion ensued where participants described the frustration of variation they experience in processes like these. I informed the participants that the calculation of their project's baseline sigma performance was nothing more than capturing the amount of variation in their processes as it compared to their customers' requirements.

This is shown in Figure 5.14, as the distribution of performance extends past the upper specification desired by the customer. I explained that the peak of the curve was the process performance average, but the participants already knew that they didn't feel the average but instead felt the variation in this process, which extends past the upper specification.

I then showed that the distribution they were observing can be divided up into a series of segments. Each segment is divided evenly like cutting wedges in a pie. I instructed them that each segment is called the standard deviation of performance from the mean. It is represented by the Greek term sigma and represented accordingly as σ.

Telling the participants to not worry about the math for the time being, I asked them to judge how many standard deviations (or sigmas) did it visually look like existed from the average of the distribution to the point our customer was unhappy with performance. From this "ocular" test we got answers around 2.0, and that indicated that they then understood the concept of determining baseline sigma.

I further explained that their teams had to calculate their baseline sigma performance and then, over time, they could improve the performance by either shifting the mean of the distribution away from the customer's specification, reducing the variation around the current

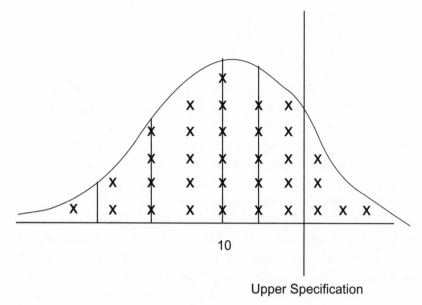

10

Upper Specification

Figure 5.14

mean, or ideally doing both simultaneously. I explained that in our later training in June and July we would tell them how to do that. At that point we then wanted to turn our attention to how to calculate their baseline sigma performance mathematically.

There are two ways to calculate baseline sigma. The more sophisticated and accurate method is based on determining the actual mean and standard deviation for performance and comparing the data to the customer's specification. I then informed the participants that there is a quick and dirty method to calculate baseline sigma that is much easier. I asked which method they wished me to teach them. After the laughter died down, I proceeded to teach them the formula for the easy method of calculating baseline sigma. Our formula for calculating baseline sigma is found below.

Baseline Sigma (Defects per Million Opportunities (DPMO))

$$\frac{\text{Number of Defects}}{\text{Units} \times \text{Opportunities}} \times 1,000,000$$

There are three questions to answer to determine your baseline sigma:

- What is the unit?
- How can a defect be created?
- How many opportunities exist for a defect to occur?

For the last time we returned to our generic example that we had used throughout Measure training, the food dining example. After a brief review of the flip-charted eight columns, I asked what they thought the unit was, knowing its equivalent to the customer's need. Quickly we established the unit for our generic example: the meal.

Next we revisited the measure, target, and specification columns to determine how a defect can be created. We know that Food Quality, speed of delivery, and menu variety can result in defects. Therefore two of the three questions have been answered. For the third and final question I explained that the vast majority of times the number of opportunities will equal the number of validated customer CTQs. In our example that would equal three representing food quality, delivery speed, and menu variety.

We were then ready to take them through an example. I asked what if this project team had determined that an adequate sample size is 150 meals to measure, complete with a brief questionnaire asking selected diners to fill out regarding food quality and menu variety, knowing we can record delivery speed without the input of the customer. A common question we hear at this point is how to ensure we can get a customer to fill out a questionnaire. I explained that some type of incentive (e.g., free dessert or a discount on their next meal) can readily improve questionnaire return rates.

I then showed them the following data and asked participants to walk with me through my calculations. For the 150 meals measured there were 3 meals where the Likert scale was below 3 (the customer's lower specification) and 4 meals were delivered late. Therefore we would take the 7 defects and divide by the number of units, times the number of opportunities.

Our Defects per Million Opportunities equals 15,555. If Six Sigma is 3.4 defects per million, we obviously have a problem. The extent of the problem measured in baseline sigma was then determined by referencing a conversion chart found in the back of their DMAIC work materials (your conversion chart is found in Appendix D). Examining the conversion chart I told them that the long-term sigma between 13,903 and

17,864 would equate to a baseline sigma performance between 3.6 and 3.7. Usually I immediately receive a question about the difference between long-term and short-term sigma performance. This is where most statisticians would begin a tutorial about the now infamous 1.5 sigma shift. Instead I simply explain that the short-term sigma is a snapshot of what sigma is, and all processes vary over time. The long-term sigma is a more accurate picture of what your defect level would look like over time. If I get questions about the statistics behind each, I am quick to explain to that person we can have a talk about the derivative of the different metrics offline.

The final issue to be addressed centers around calculating defects per million opportunities versus defects per million units. To highlight this point I ask for a volunteer who would give credit for good food quality taken from an impressive menu where the meal arrived late. Invariably, a hand is raised. I then ask for someone where the late arrival would ruin their dining experience. Likewise, I have no problems finding a volunteer. Our final teach point is that if the customers in a team's project are like our first respondent, the team should calculate Defects per Million Opportunity. If the customers are more like our second respondent (all or nothing), we need to calculate Defects per Million Units (DPMU). We take our same example and calculate defects per million units by simply dividing 7 by 150 and multiplying by 1,000,000, which would give us 46,666 defects. Again using the conversion chart, we see that would result in a baseline sigma of between 3.1 and 3.2. Clearly, from these two volunteers we can see that sigma performance is influenced by the number of opportunities. If your customer has an all-or-nothing perspective, you have only one opportunity to please or displease, and sigma performance will likely be worse.

To give the participants an opportunity to become comfortable with the concept of calculating baseline sigma, Susan handed out the fun size M&Ms for the exercise we discussed earlier in this chapter. This confidence-boosting exercise was debriefed with the focus on differences in baseline sigma being either teams deciding on different CTQs or calculating a DPMO or a DPMU.

The aforementioned lecture and large-group M&M activity usually takes place on the morning of the last training day. By then, team leaders and key team members had been in training for nearly five days. With mental and physical fatigue palpable (as well as late nights partying in

Santana Row), the teams were ready for their last breakout, which we usually do in the large ballroom to save time. I asked them to brainstorm for their project what is a unit, how a defect can be created, and what they anticipate will be the number of opportunities should they be calculating DPMO.

After a high-level debrief we left for our last lunch together before our last planning session that afternoon. The completed data collection plan is found in Table 5.6.

Planning for the Intersession Work

The HP teams had put in a lot of work during that third week of April. While Mohan Garde explained through Sean Sanders that some work would be offset for these teams to do their Six Sigma project, invariably the pressures of being on a Six Sigma team lead to a cautious few approaching Susan and me at lunch in the Hotel Valencia's courtyard to determine whether it was safe to catch an earlier flight.

Both Susan and I had 4:30 flights back to Reno and Denver, our respective homes. We informed those wanting to leave early that the afternoon would be spent mostly in breakout, but it might be the most important breakout of the week. With a forlorn look, they retreated to their lunch tables without contacting the HP airline desk.

Susan started the afternoon out by showing six bullets on a PowerPoint presentation that talked about what needed to be done for each project team between that third week of April and our return in mid-June.

With emphasis placed on the fact that the past week had been a chance to learn about the Define and Measure steps of DMAIC, she explained that successful teams spend Friday afternoon putting together a detailed action plan to implement in full the tollgates of Define and Measure.

The six major intersession deliverables are:

- Confirm project charter
- Validate customer needs/requirements
- Validate high-level process map
- Complete data collection plan
- Implement data collection plan
- Create 10-minute presentation for 6:14 a.m.

Table 5.6 Data Collection Plan

Measure	Type Measure	Type Data	Operational Definition	Specification	Target	Data Collection Form	Sampling	Baseline 6 Sigma
Food Quality	0, I	Continuous	From end of order to arrival of food	30 min.	ASAP	Freq. dist. checksheet	The sample will be based on the continuous formula ensuring representativeness and randomness	DPMO between 3.6 and 3.7
Delivery Speed	0, P	Continuous	Likert scale 1–5 rating from customer	3 on 1–5 Likert scale	5 on 1–5 Likert scale	Freq. dist. checksheet		
Menu Variety	0, I	Continuous	Likert scale 1–5 rating from customer	3 on 1–5 Likert scale	5 on 1–5 Likert scale	Freq. dist. checksheet		

- Confirm Project Charter

- Validate Customer Needs/Requirements

- Validate High-Level Process Map

- Complete Data Collection Plan

- Implement Data Collection Plan

- Create 10-minute presentation for 6-14 a.m.

Figure 5.15 Intersession deliverables

This is reflected in Figure 5.15.

Confirm Project Charter

Susan pointed out that during the first breakout, the teams had brainstormed alterations to the project charter. Again, reinforcing the concept that the charter is the purview of the Champion, teams were reminded to have at least one meeting to complete anything associated with their input to the charter. This includes alterations made to the business case, input to the preliminary problem statement, and particularly suggestions or questions the team had generated relative to the project scope. While the project Champions had also assembled top-notch teams—as evidenced by that past week—any alterations to the team membership should also be communicated to the project Champion.

Susan explained that many teams had little left to do as a result of the productive breakouts regarding the project charter. At most, one additional meeting should suffice to clear up any of these questions. However, because of its importance, Susan explained that once the team had given all their charter input, the team leader should schedule a meeting with the team Champion no later than one week hence (April 30) to finalize the charter.

Determining Customers, their Needs, and Requirements

While most of the project team's work for the charter was consultative and thus wouldn't take much time to complete, the second tollgate of

Define was the area where teams would see that they had just started the tollgate in the breakout.

As detailed in the intersession handout found in Appendix C, project teams were expected to determine a primary and secondary customer, complete their CTQ tree, come to agreement on at least two methods to validate their customer's requirements, and validate those requirements. Susan hastened to remind them that they should not be surprised to find a requirement not brainstormed in the breakout to make the final list. This is common and has been a litmus test Susan and I use two months later to determine if teams had indeed done validation with their customers. We explained that these activities should have a hard deadline of May 14th.

Validating the High-Level Process Map

Susan informed the participants to complete the process map the way they thought it was. Next they must create a plan to validate the high-level "As is" map. This is usually conducted through two venues. One is to follow the product or service from the start point of the process to it completion. In our food service example, it would be from the time the order is placed to the time the wait person places the meal on the table. Direct, firsthand observation can be one method to validate the high-level steps in the process. The second method is to interview those people who live in the process.

For this third tollgate, Susan informed the HP teams they should complete their action items no later than May 31st.

Completion of the Data Collection Plan

Susan explained that work on the data collection plan could not begin until customers' needs and requirements had been validated, which should be completed by May 14th. Once these customer requirements had been validated, the remaining columns of the data collection plan could be finished and implemented, resulting in baseline sigma being calculated. Specifically, the teams should confirm operational definitions, identify targets and specifications, determine and/or create their data collection forms, work to determine their sampling techniques, and calculate baseline sigma for their project no later than June 11th.

The June 14th Ten-Minute Presentation

The teams were expected to return the week of June 14th for Analysis training. Just as we did for the second portion of Business Process Management consulting, each team was expected to make a presentation showing the other teams and Champions their Define and Measure work. As we explained in Chapter 3, when you are expected to make a presentation to upwards of 70 people, work tends to be completed. We provided each team leader with a set of templates (which are found in Appendix C) that they could use if they liked, with the admonition that no tollgate should be more than two slides and that their entire presentation should be complete in 10 minutes or less. Susan and I both have experienced presentations that last more than 10 minutes, and we find that invariably the presentation is more sizzle than steak.

After Susan's comments and a few questions, in less than half an hour we instructed each of the HP teams to return to their breakout rooms to complete a detailed action plan for the intersession work. We did a series of rounds to instruct on basic project management tools like action planning, gantt charts, and work breakdown analysis should any team lack the basics of project management understanding.

As we circulated for the last times among the breakout rooms at the Hotel Valencia, Susan and I exchanged our opinions of the group. We felt the team leaders and key team members were among the best in recent memory and we expected positive results from these teams. With minor exception, the teams stayed past 3:00 p.m. working on their intersession planning, and the action plans generated were impressive.

Susan and I retreated to the Hotel Valencia bar for a celebratory drink before heading to the airport, expecting good things when we returned to San Jose in June.

Summary

This chapter has instructed how to execute Six Sigma training in a more effective and efficient manner. We first addressed the special challenges that teaching Six Sigma can provide to a potential instructor.

We addressed key elements of adult learning theory, which are essential elements of transferring knowledge regarding Six Sigma. Some of the key lessons of adult learning theory that must be practiced by Six

Sigma instructors include relating to adult experiences, using generic examples in large group so that the concept is understood, giving participants immediate opportunity to apply lessons to their project, limiting large group lectures to an hour or less, providing constant reinforcement, ensuring that multiple venues for learning occurs in large group, and by far remembering to have fun.

Next we addressed how to instruct and consult on the first two elements of the DMAIC improvement methodology, Define and Measure. At Eckes and Associates Inc. we have taken the subtasks of Define and Measure (called tollgates) and created a series of teach modules. Each module is taught to the large group of Six Sigma team participants followed by an immediate opportunity to apply what is learned.

Key Lessons

- Six Sigma is a complex topic to teach.
- Traditional instruction (I am the expert, you will receive my knowledge) often fails when applied to Six Sigma.
- Adult learning theory is the key ingredient for transfer of knowledge of Six Sigma.
- Among the key theories behind adult learning is knowledge must be linked to real-world experience when generic examples are first taught, when participants are given an immediate opportunity to apply what is learned to their real project, when they are constantly reinforced for their learning, when large-group lectures are limited to an hour, when the instructor constantly checks for confirmation of learning, when multiple venues of teaching occurs, and when class participants are having fun.
- The DMAIC subtasks are called tollgates.
- The Define element of DMAIC has three tollgates: the project charter, determining customers' needs and requirements, and creating the high-level process map.
- The Measure element of DMAIC has two tollgates: creating the data collection plan and implementing that plan.
- Each of the elements of DMAIC can be subdivided into teaching modules.

Six Sigma Tactical Execution—Analysis, Improve, and Control

> Our remedies oft in ourselves do lie.
> —William Shakespeare, *All's Well That Ends Well*
> Act 1, Scene 1.

Introduction

THIS CHAPTER COMPLETES the journey through the elements of DMAIC, Analysis, Improve, and Control. Once again, I will provide tollgates and teaching modules, showing how the HP IPG Americas Consumer Ops group applied them.

Six Sigma Tactical Execution: Analysis

More than 60 people showed up on the morning of June 14 for Analysis training. The morning was devoted to project report outs. Each of the eight HP teams shared their Define and Measure work from the previous two months. Participants trickled in between 8:00 and 8:30 and warmly greeted Susan and me. We were appreciative of the fact that Sean had made up new name tags for everyone. This group was special to us, and we made it a point to remember names, but Sean's detailed effort certainly didn't hurt. As I kicked things off promptly at 8:30 I sensed excitement in the audience. People were actually happy to be back.

The audience was mostly made up of team members, but we also extended invitations to each project Champion. Most Champions are in management, so project teams generally work harder on their presentation knowing they will have 10–15 minutes of their supervisors' undivided attention. Champion attendance is a great motivator because a great report out could potentially lead to future career opportunities.

As with other steps, Susan and I try to limit each presentation to 10 minutes followed by questions and comments. Suggestions are welcomed from Champions and other teams, and then Susan and I give our feedback. Susan and I didn't expect any surprises because two days of intersession consulting are built into each contract.

Susan handled the bulk of intersession consulting days, while I traveled to Ft. Collins to work with Marilu DeLeon and the Entitlement Team. I was very impressed with their work during my visit in early May. The Entitlement team was expected to improve the current warranty status performance. Their problem statement focused on the distribution of inaccurate and inconsistent first-time warranty status information to the customer. During my May visit, modifications were made to their sampling quantity and method of calculating baseline sigma.

But a pattern emerged in May that was echoed several times during the June 14th Analysis presentations. Teams had spent much time actually researching customers' perceived CTQs (variables that are "Critical to Quality"). Time and again they found that the CTQs the team listed during April's breakout were different than the actual priorities of the customer.

Led by Champion Gail Waller, the Entitlement team, had wisely decided to scale back the scope of their project to increase their chances for success. Larger organizations often have several improvement activities going on simultaneously. As it turned out, that was the situation at HP. While this would present a special problem late in the summer, when debates rose over which project was responsible for the project's success, at this session in May I liberally commended the team's efforts to reduce scope and make the Entitlement project more manageable.

All eight teams were highly impressive, but the SOS team led by Debbie Gammel and the Diagnostics Team led by Annie Price did exceptionally well. The SOS team had let "Data lead the way" and deferred to the data rather than allowing their own preconceptions and opinions dictate the direction of the project.

The first example of this was their treatment of the CTQs. They collected data on more than 9,000 actual customer comments and concluded that customers in need of a status order are more concerned with the frequency of status rather than how fast the status is provided. Second, they discovered two other customer requirements: 1. detailed repair information during their status requests, and 2. confirmation that their complaint data was entered into the system. Meeting this second requirement was part of the new should-be process. This could take place immediately as part of a "quick hit," though the entire should-be process wasn't finalized until after the team was in the Improve section of DMAIC. Debbie's preliminary assessment of a $1,200,000 annual cost opportunity caught the attention of all project Champions. Amazingly, the Diagnostics team's preliminary cost opportunity was even larger.

As psychologists, Susan and I recognize the toll of seeing baseline sigma. By now teams are aware of the difference between a two or three sigma performing process and a four or five sigma process. Despite our encouragement that these processes were targeted because they were low performing, people get discouraged or embarrassed that the systems were so broken.

Time and again our HP team leaders gave confident presentations until it was time to provide baseline sigma. With rare exception, most sheepishly reported baseline sigma below two. In our feedback we emphasized that it showed that management had chosen the right processes to improve. We said again that extremely low-performing processes stand the greatest chance of improvement.

With that encouraging message we were then ready to tackle the most important element of DMAIC: Analysis.

Six Sigma Tactical Execution—Analysis

The problem with many teams is they like to jump over Analysis. To them it's the old proverb, Why let data interfere with a good opinion.
—Dave Schulenberg

Many of the Champions wanted to stay for the remaining part of the day and I was happy to encourage this. During my opening comments about Analysis I pointed out that Analysis is the most important step in the process of DMAIC. I referred them to the quote at the beginning of this section.

Along with scope creep, poor team dynamics, and poor Champion involvement, the lack of good analysis is the downfall of many well-intentioned teams. There are a variety of reasons behind poor analysis. Some teams see their poor baseline sigma and want to solve the problem immediately. This is foolish because they don't yet know the root cause of the poor performance. True improvement comes about through determining and validating root causation, which is the crucial desired outcome of Analysis. Another reason people skip or rush through Analysis is that theories must be generated by the project team's subject matter experts and then tested empirically. It's hard work, and it takes time. It's one thing to talk around the water cooler about why you think things are broken. It's a completely different thing to be certain of your problems and solutions after a rigorous test.

There are three major tollgates in the Analysis phase. First, the data collected during the Measure phase must be analyzed. Second, the process itself should be analyzed. Finally, and most importantly, Root Cause analysis must be conducted.

Analysis Tollgate #1—Data Analysis

I introduced the idea of Analysis with a metaphor. Analysis is a house we want to enter; more specifically, it's the root cause house. There are two doors to enter the root cause house, the data door and the process door. For projects that directly improve effectiveness measures (i.e., customer issues like accuracy or customer satisfaction), the data door is the predominant source of analysis. For projects that have a greater influence upon efficiency measures (i.e., reducing cycle time, reducing labor or cost) the process door is the predominant source of analysis.

The highlights of the Data Analysis Tollgate are as follows:

There are two types of data analysis tools. There are tools like Pareto charts and pie charts for discrete data and histograms and run charts for continuous data.

The goal of any data analysis tool is to create a series of microproblem statements. A microproblem statement is a more detailed statement of the problem based on analysis of data or the process itself.

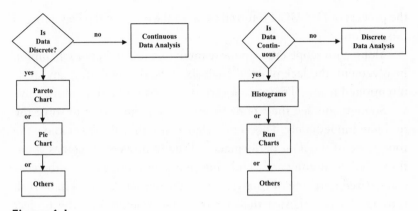

Figure 6.1

The data door represents taking data collected during their Measure work and creating various statistical pictures of the variation in the process. I proceeded to teach the participants an adage told to me by W. Edwards Deming, the famous quality guru.

Variation is the enemy in any process. It is far easier to fight an enemy you can see.

I showed two flow charts to suggest possible visual aids, depending on whether their data is discrete or continuous. Figure 6.1 shows the two flow charts and the recommended tools for each category of data. I stressed in my lecture that there are many tools for either types of data. These are just the most commonly used tools, and if their project necessitated it, we would teach alternative tools during their breakouts or analysis intersession.

For discrete data we recommend the Pareto chart or pie chart. These easy-to-read visual charts alert the project team to the more predominant reason codes for the discrete defect that was collected in the last two months.

We again used a generic example to create a pie chart and what the team needs to do with the Pareto chart during the analysis phase of DMAIC.

We used the generic example CTQ of billing accuracy for invoices at a major credit card company. A review of 120 inaccurate invoices revealed a pie chart that looked like the one in Figure 6.2.

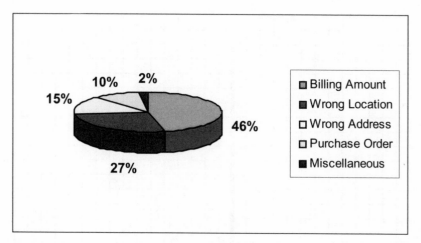

10% 2%
15%
46%
27%

☐ Billing Amount
■ Wrong Location
☐ Wrong Address
☐ Purchase Order
■ Miscellaneous

Figure 6.2

This visual display of the reasons behind inaccurate invoices led us to the key deliverable for both data and process analysis, the micro-problem statement.

Successful Six Sigma teams become focused on the details and minutae of their work. Microproblem statements become the "key" to getting into the root cause house.

A microproblem statement is the vehicle for the Six Sigma project team to become more detail focused. In the billing project, the Define stage problem statement dealt with outstanding payments from their primary customer. A review of the pie chart led this particular team to create the following microproblem question:

"Why are there so many billing amount inaccuracies on our invoices?"

I also showed the two major tools used for continuous data analysis, the histogram and the run chart. A histogram is a bar graph that is created from the frequency distribution checksheet in the Measure phase of their project. The beauty of the histogram is that it allows the project team to determine whether the process is exhibiting common cause or special cause variation. Returning to our restaurant dining example, we can see in Figure 6.3 that most of the values in the histogram are located in the middle and fewer values tail out in either direction. The histogram tells us that no one family of factors (machines, methods, materials, mother nature/environment, measurement, and people) has

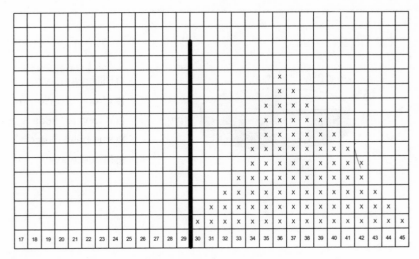

Figure 6.3 Restaurant dining example

undue influence on the process. Yet we also see unhappy customers who are receiving meals past their desired wait time of 30 minutes or less. With unhappy customers a traditional manager would have to perform some management intervention. A common mistake of traditional managers is to focus first on the people in a process. Common cause variation is evidence that there is a system problem. In service projects, methods solutions are more successful. In fact, data shows that in this process focusing incorrectly on workers' errors would probably worsen performance as they drop trays in their haste, deliver the meal incorrectly, or cook the meal faster than required.

As a large table team exercise, we had the participants examine a series of histograms to determine if they could use continuous data analysis like Columbo can examine a crime scene and see things that occurred even though he wasn't there when the crime was committed.

In Figure 6.4 we see two examples taken from the large-group table team exercise. Each team was expected to determine whether their assigned histogram was exhibiting common versus special cause variation, whether the process was capable of meeting the customer's specifications, and what the distribution told them, even though they weren't present when the data was collected.

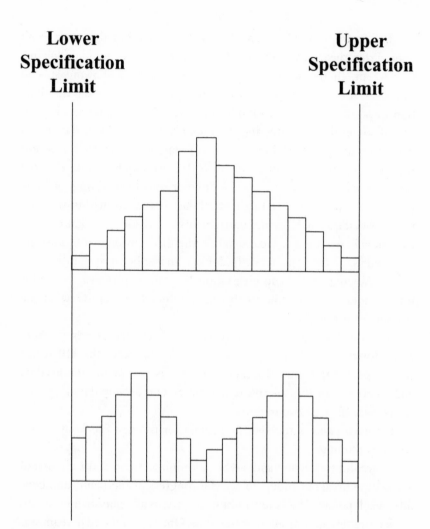

Figure 6.4

In the first example the process is exhibiting common cause variation because most of the values are in the middle and tail off in either direction. The process is capable but barely. When we teach histogram analysis we instruct our participants that the specifications are the "voice of the customer" and the histogram is the "voice of the process." We use the metaphor to think of the histogram as a car and specifications as a garage. We ask, "Can the car fit in the garage?" Clearly in the first example the car can fit into the garage but the doors can't open. From this analysis we see that the process is a candidate for improvement. In the second example, the process is showing special cause variation. This type of distribution is called a bimodal distribution because there are two modes or "peaks." This is indicative that two of something are affecting the process, whether this is data taken from two different machines, two different methods, two different suppliers, or even two different shifts. We are quick to note that the raw data would not tell us there is "two of something" going on. The raw data simply would tell us that all data points are within the customer specification. Here the participants can readily see that the histogram is better than raw data. While the distribution can fit into the customer specifications, it really doesn't matter because the distribution is showing special cause variation. This process is a candidate for improvement. The people in this process need to identify what the two modes represent.

Because all HP project teams had some effectiveness goals, we were ready for the first Analysis breakout. In this breakout the HP teams were expected to review whether they had discrete or continuous data and create one or two microproblem statements around data they collected over the past two months.

Figure 6.5 shows the specific agenda for the first breakout of our Analysis training.

As we did for Define and Measure training, Susan and I circulated among the breakout rooms to see the progress of the teams and conduct teach points. The latter is not necessary, as all teams had mastered the lecture on microproblem statements. Once again the SOS team was doing a great job of applying the concept to their project. With regard to status accuracy, they segmented their data by reason codes and created pie charts around such factors as commit date failures, airbill failures, and address failures. As a result of their detailed segmentation of status order inaccuracies, they generated three superb, detailed microproblem statements:

1. Why are so many "in air bills" inaccurate?
2. Why are failures highly concentrated in five service types for accuracy?
3. Why do so many orders have multiple accuracy errors?

Breakout #1—Data Analysis Breakout

Desired Outcomes:
• Review Discrete or Continuous Data Collected to Date
• Create 1-2 Micro Problem Statements

Decision-Making Method:
• Consensus with ⅔s majority vote as fallback

ITEM	METHOD	PERSON	TIME
Review agenda/assign roles	Discussion	Team Leader	5 minutes
Review Discrete or Continuous Data Collected to Date	Discussion	Team	30 minutes
Create 1-2 Micro Problem Statements	Discussion	Team	45 minutes
Plus/Deltas		Team	5 minutes
		TOTAL	1hr 25 minutes

Figure 6.5

Analysis Tollgate #2—Process Analysis

Susan began the second tollgate lecture of Analysis by briefly reviewing the key teach points:

- *Subprocess mapping.* The process map is the workhorse tool of
  DMAIC. The subprocess map is a more detailed accounting of
  the high-level map created in the Define portion of their project.
- *Nature of work analysis.* Once the subprocess map has been created
  and validated, it needs to be analyzed to see which steps add
  value and which steps do not. In order for a step to add value, the
  step must be important to the customer, be done right the first
  time, and the product or service must be physically transformed.
- *Flow of work analysis.* Because many teams list "reducing cycle
  time" as a project goal, flow of work is taught. Flow of work is estimating how long each step in the process takes to complete.
- *Moments of Truth analysis.* Of particular importance in service-
  related processes is identification of those steps in the process
  where either a positive or negative impression of the supplier can
  be formed in the eyes of the customer.
- *The Process Summary Analysis Worksheet.* This worksheet is a summary
  of the steps in the process that add value and those that don't. The
  most common types of nonvalue categories include re-work, delays,
  waits, botched moments of truth (external failures) and bottlenecks.
  These are listed and categorized on the process summary worksheet.

Susan revisited the process mapping activities each team conducted
in the Define training and during their intersession. She stressed that
work done in the Define phase was to create the high-level process map
as it currently is conducted. She reminded the audience of one of my
famous "Eckesisms." Eckesisms are phrases that try to embody some
key truth to assist the team during its project work. Eckesism #2, stated
during the Define training, was "Stay as high as you can as long as you
can," referring to a common mistake teams make—too quickly getting
into too much detail on the process maps.

Then the project teams drilled down into their process maps. Again,
using our adult learning theory concept of CPTE, we reintroduced our
process mapping concept of dining at TGIF.

Susan used a prepared SIPOC model she had put on the wall at

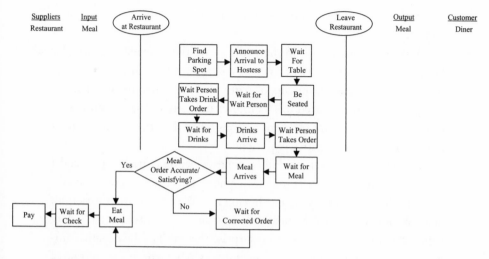

Figure 6.6 Restaurant dining process

lunch to walk the participants through subprocess mapping. As seen in Figure 6.6. Susan had captured the detailed steps of ordering the meal from the time she is seated to the time she leaves. She was quick to point out that when doing subprocess mapping the participants needed to capture the "invisible" steps in the process as opposed to the high-level process map where only the more visible steps are captured. Included in these invisible steps are all the waits in this process, from waiting for the staff, the wait for food, and waiting for the bill to be processed.

Susan also pointed out that our generic example was simple and direct, certainly more simple and direct than many of the complex processes represented by the HP project teams. She indicated that if their process was a simple one, the entire high-level process should be subprocess mapped. If the process was particularly detailed, the team needs to make a decision to take one or two of the higher-level validated steps and subprocess map them, not the entire process.

At this point, Susan indicated that the subprocess map needed to be analyzed for moments of truth, the nature of work, and the flow of work. Beginning with moments of truth, Susan provided criteria that determine whether a moment of truth would be considered a positive or negative moment. Among the criteria were when a service provider consciously makes up for a previously botched moment of truth, resolves an issue in favor of the most profitable impact to the customer, or employs a "whatever it takes" approach to ensuring customer satisfaction.

With the criteria fresh in their minds, we then turned to a popular large-group team exercise. Susan instructed each team to share both positive and negative moments of truth from each team's personal experiences and be prepared in 10 minutes not only to share their team's best positive or negative moment but reference the criteria that made it either a positive or negative experience.

This large-team exercise can be time-consuming. Both Susan and I enjoy the stories as much as the participants. This exercise clearly meets the adult learning theory goal of having fun. We have heard a variety of negative moments of truth, most coming from our clients, that truly defy logic. Of course, it will come as no surprise that most of the negative moments of truth come from the airline industry. My favorite was the tale of a newlywed couple on their way to Europe for their honeymoon who were separated into different seats by a flight attendant for *kissing*.

Despite the enjoyment of the exercise, both Susan and I attempted to link the stories to the moment of truth criteria, and most importantly we asked those in the class to recognize where their customers might experience similar frustrations at the hands of HP.

Susan continued to the second element of process analysis. In order to analyze the process for the nature of work, it is important to know what steps add value to the process and which steps don't. Value add is defined as meeting three criteria:

- The customer considers the step important.
- There is some physical change to the product or service.
- It's done right the first time.

Susan took the participants back to the subprocess map she created for the restaurant dining experience to highlight some of the challenges the teams would encounter when doing this on their subprocess map.

Each of the steps must meet all three criteria. Susan indicated that we had seen teams get bogged down attempting to reach consensus when team members disagree whether a step meets all three criteria. She used one of the steps in the restaurant dining experience to prove her point. Does waiting for the meal to arrive add value or not? Some say that waiting for food might allow the diners to talk and anticipate the meal, which would be a value add. Others feel that an excessive wait (more than 30 minutes) would make it a non-value add. Susan pointed out that there might be actually two steps (a reasonable wait and then a post-30-minute wait, the latter of which would be nonvalue added). The key is to recognize that some steps in the process will not lend themselves to consensus. Therefore, she encouraged teams to have brief, albeit spirited discussion, but quickly move to the backup decision-making method of a two-thirds majority vote if consensus cannot be reached.

Susan proceeded to define the flow of work relative to the restaurant dining experience. She reviewed timing each of the detailed steps, both visible and invisible steps, and stressed that they should strive for estimates if actual times cannot be determined.

Finally she introduced the Process Summary Analysis worksheet. This takes each of the subprocess steps and provides the estimated time of each step, determines whether that step adds value or not, and then categorizes the non-value-added steps. Figure 6.7 shows the steps in the

Process	Value Add/ Non-Value Add	Time
Find Parking Spot	Value Add	5 Minutes
Announce arrival to Hostess	Value Add	2 Minutes
Wait for Table	Non-Value Add	10 Minutes
Be Seated	Value Add	1 Minute
Wait for Wait Person	Non-Value Add	5 Minutes
Wait Person Takes Drink Order	Value Add	2 Minutes
Wait for Drinks	Non-Value Add	10 Minutes
Drinks Arrive	Value Add	1 Minute
Wait Person Takes Order	Value Add	2 Minutes
Wait for Meal	Non-Value Add	35 Minutes
Meal Arrives	Value Add	1 Minute
Wait for Corrected Order	Non-Value Add	10 Minutes
Eat Meal	Value Add	30 Minutes
Wait for Check	Non-Value Add	10 Minutes
Pay	Value Add	5 Minutes

Figure 6.7

subprocess map detailing which steps add value and which don't, while time estimates of the work flow are documented.

Just as the last step of Data Analysis is the creation of key microproblem statements, so too is the last step of process analysis. Once the Process Summary Analysis is complete, the project team must use it to create key microproblem statements. A review of Figure 6.7 shows that over 60 percent of the subprocess steps do not add value and all non-value-added minutes are waits. Therefore, if reduced customer satisfaction is the macroproblem statement of this restaurant, logically the microproblem statement could be:

"Why are there so many delays (waits) in our process?"

Susan then moved to the flip chart stand, where she prepared the teams for their Process Summary breakouts.

Again, each project team present had efficiency goals. Therefore, each team should know that most of the work associated with process analysis must be done during the next intersession. The deliverables include taking a first pass at subprocess mapping, conducting a nature-of-work analysis to determine which steps add value and which do not, and estimating the time associated with each subprocess step. Finally, teams were expected to brainstorm a short list of possible microproblem statements. Figure 6.8 shows the detailed agenda for the process analysis breakout.

The breakout session was a lengthy one as teams spent a great deal of their time subprocess mapping. As Susan and I made our rounds, we stressed to the participants that, like the high-level process map, the subprocess map must be validated. Not surprisingly, the SOS team again impressed us during the breakout. Because of the complexity of their high-level process referenced in Chapter 5, they decided to take one high-level process step and drill down in that process step as opposed to doing the entire high-level process. Figure 6.9 shows the high-level process and the targeted area for subprocess mapping for the SOS team.

The SOS team created a subprocess with 56 steps. Most of the time the ratio of value to non-value-added steps is 20-80. This turned out to be the case for the SOS team as they determined 82 percent of the subprocess steps didn't add value (this was later verified during their intersession work).

The SOS team's Process Summary Analysis work led to the following two microproblem statements:

"Why do we have so many moves and setup steps?"

Breakout #2—Process Analysis

Desired Outcomes:
- Develop preliminary subprocess map for one high level process
- Perform value analysis on subprocess map
- Complete summary matrix
- Identify 1-2 microproblem statements

Decision-Making Method
- Consensus with 2/3 majority vote as fallback

ITEM	METHOD	PERSON	TIME
Review Agenda/assign roles	Discussion	Team Leader	5 minutes
Subprocess map	Select one key high-level step from the SIPOC. Brainstorm subprocess steps on Post-it notes.	Team	40 minutes
Value Analysis/Summary Matrix	Identify each step as value add or non-value add. Record decision on the summary matrix. Calculate percentage of VA to NVA steps	Team	40 minutes
Microproblem statement	Analyze summary matrix and brainstorm list of microproblem statements. Narrow to your top 1-2.	Team	15 minutes
Plus/Deltas		Team	5 minutes
		TOTAL	1hr 45 minutes

Figure 6.8

Process Name: CSO (Customer Service Order) Status-Checking Process

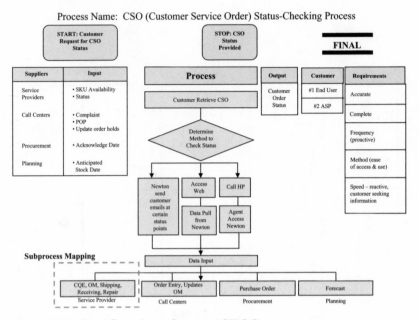

Figure 6.9 "As-is" service order status SIPOC

"Why do we have so many exceptions and rework processes?"

Two of the three tollgates of Analysis had now been completed. From data analysis and process analysis a series of microproblem statements had been generated. Although not uncommon, teams have generated five, six, and even eight microproblem statements. During our debrief we stressed that some type of prioritization scheme be implemented so that two or three microproblem statements exist after both data and process analysis has completed.

Using the metaphor of an airline boarding pass, I informed the HP teams that their microproblem statements are passes that allow them to enter the third and most important tollgate of Analysis, Root Cause Analysis.

Analysis Tollgate #3—Root Cause Analysis

If Analysis is the most important step in DMAIC, then Root Cause Analysis is the most important tollgate in Analysis. With the team's microproblem statements in hand, they were about to enter a tollgate that we believe ultimately determines the success or failure of the project team.

Because of the amount of the material and the importance of this tollgate, we divided Root Cause Analysis into three lectures. I started our first lecture with an overview of the key learnings of the Root Cause Analysis tollgate:

- *The concept of Y=f(x)*. The formula $Y=f(x)$ must be solved before a team enters the Improve element of DMAIC. Y equals the output measure the project team is expected to improve. Small f stands for a function of and x represents the process factors that explain Y. A variation of this formula is $y=f(x)$ where small y represents the microproblem statement(s).
- *The concept of Open, Narrow, and Close.* The process of determining which x's explain Y or y is achieved by using a set of tools divided into three stages. In the first or Open stage, teams are expected to utilize their project team's subject matter expertise to brainstorm as many possible x's that could explain Y/y. During the Narrow stage, teams are expected to use their subject matter expertise to choose the most likely x's that explain Y/y. Finally, during the Close stage of Root Cause Analysis, teams are expected to empirically validate their theories (or hypotheses) as to which x's explain Y/y.

After a review of $Y=f(x)$ I stressed the importance of the Open-Narrow-Close concept and how it applies, going from the project team using its subject matter expertise to generate as many possible x's in Open, to using that same expertise to narrow the list and finally to use empirical data to prove which x's account for the largest proportion of Y.

We have used many generic examples to teach the Open and Narrow portions of root causation. In previous years we had fun solving my invoice delay problems with this tool. To keep things fresh we have recently generated a new example. All people relate to eating (particularly at Six Sigma conferences). In my first book I discussed my ex-mother-in-law's lasagna and her secret ingredient that improved taste (and just for the record, hers was never as good as my mother's).

We went to a large wall in the ballroom where Susan had created a Cause Effect Diagram. The Cause Effect Diagram, also known as the Fishbone (or "Fishhead" to cynics like *Dilbert* creator Scott Adams) Diagram, is where we placed our microproblem statement in the box to the far right. Extending to the left is the spine of the fish and extending

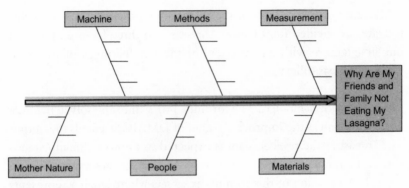

Figure 6.10 The cause-effect diagram

out are six bones that represent the major components of variation in any process, the five Ms and one P.

As seen in Figure 6.10 we had created a Cause Effect Diagram with the microproblem statement of "Why are my friends and family not eating my lasagna?"

We then requested table teams to brainstorm a list of "x's" that could explain why my friends and family are not eating my lasagna. Using Post-It notes, they contributed ideas and posted them on the large Cause Effect Diagram on the wall. We cautioned that the People stem of the diagram should only be used as a last resort. Best-practice learning teaches us that the predominant number of "x"s in manufacturing are machine related, while method dominates in the service arena.

After five minutes of brainstorming, each table team designated a courier, and they posted their ideas on the large diagram on the wall. I stated that for purposes of this exercise the "Open" phase had finished.

I indicated there are four action items as part of the "Narrow" phase of root causation. They are:

- Clarification
- Duplication
- Multivote
- The 5 Why Diagram

I began the Narrowing function by reading each Post-It note aloud. I stressed that the clarification function was solely meant to have everyone on the team understand the Post It. We warned that during the actual application of the tool, people would want to debate or disagree with ideas that are posted. This should not occur.

Simultaneously, we gathered the duplicate ideas and placed those Post-It notes on top of each other. If the idea was similar but not identical, we grouped them close to one another. In this way, the first two steps of narrowing the Cause Effect Diagram are similar to the affinity diagram.

Once the clarification and duplication steps were conducted, the Cause Effect Diagram on the wall looked leaner. Lots of duplicate ideas (overcooking, wrong cheese) had been grouped together so fewer "x"s are present on the wall.

At that point, similar to the affinity diagram, we gave each team five votes (small round dot stickers) and had them determine the most likely "x"s that explain my bad lasagna.

After a five-minute table team discussion, the courier from each team placed her sticky dots on the appropriate x's. Again, in a page taken from doing an affinity diagram, I utilized the Pareto principle to take the more voted upon x's and construct the hypothesis that explained y (lack of consumption of lasagna). The hypothesis is located below:

Y (bad lasagna)=function of $x1$ (cooking time) and/or $x2$ (type of cheese) and/or $x3$ (amount of cheese) and/or $x4$ (freshness of ingredients) and/or $x5$ (amount of tomato sauce) and/or $x6$ (cooking temperature).

The final narrowing tool is the 5 Why diagram. After nearly an hour of interactive teaching, I turned the seminar over to Susan, who described her generic example of using the 5 Why diagram to make one or more of the x's more detailed.

She began with the E of CPTE describing her home in Reno, Nevada, where she lives with her son Ryan and daughter Jacqueline. When she first moved in, she found her backyard full of holes. Determining root cause she found out her dog was digging the holes. If she were to jump to solutions, she would get rid of the dog. But as she is an animal lover, she digs deeper—so to speak—and asks the next question.

"Why is my dog digging holes?"

With this second Why question Susan found out that there are rodents called voles eating a certain weed in the yard. Of course solving this problem would be costly and not totally effective, so Susan asked her third Why.

"Why are there voles in my yard when there haven't been voles in the yard before?

A brainstorming session with a neighbor who is a gardening expert led to the discovery she was using a different fertilizer. Of course at this stage she changed fertilizer and the voles do not return. Technically she could have asked yet another Why question and determined that she changed to a cheaper fertilizer based on our original problem—Eckes and Associates invoices not being paid in a timely manner.

This led to a question and a comment from the participants. One participant asked, "When do you stop drilling down on the 5 Why diagram?" Susan said that one must use common sense. The purpose of the 5 Why diagram is to make a larger x more detailed. Sometimes that may mean asking Why three times and other times asking Why six times; the 5 is just a suggestion. Susan also points out that the 5 Why diagram can be done vertically or horizontally, and sometimes you look for repeated answers or other x's not associated with the 5 Why's as further evidence of an x.

In our cooking example, all of the x's are clear and direct, devoid of the need for a 5 Why except x_4, where a 5 Why diagram could be applied to the hypothesis that freshness of ingredients could be made more detailed. The greatest use of a 5 Why diagram is to make an "X" more granular. Freshness of ingredients are replaced with two more detailed x's, saving cost and being too lazy to go to the store. Therefore, the revised hypothesis for our generic example is:

Y (bad lasagna) = function of $x1$ (cooking time) and/or $x2$ (type of cheese) and/or $x3$ (amount of cheese) and/or $x4$ (amount of tomato sauce) and/or $x5$ (cooking temperature) and/or $x6$ (saving cost) and/or $x7$ (being too lazy to go to the store).

We stressed that having between 5–15 x's is a standard expectation, leaving Narrow and entering the Close phase of Root Causation. With the extent of the material covered, we were then ready to go into a very important breakout. During this breakout teams were expected to develop a preliminary Cause and Effect Diagram, identify preliminary x's, use the narrowing tools to generate a hypothesis on at least one microproblem statement, and become familiar with the 5 Why diagram.

Figure 6.11 shows the detailed agenda for the root cause breakout.

The extended (2 hour, 5 minute) breakout went well until teams began applying the 5 Why diagram. Among my Eckesisms is, "You use the quality tool; don't let the quality tool use you." Sadly, we find that if one team

Breakout #3—Root Cause Analysis

Desired Outcomes:
• Develop preliminary Cause and Effect Diagram
• Identify preliminary suspect Xs
• Perform Five Why's

Decision-Making Method:
• Consensus with 2/3 majority vote as fallback

ITEM	METHOD	PERSON	TIME
Review agenda/assign roles	Discussion	Team Leader	5 minutes
Cause and Effect Diagram	Choose one micro-problem statement. Complete a preliminary C&E diagram.	Team	60 minutes
Suspect Xs	Use multivoting to identify the 3-5 preliminary suspect Xs. Put into a Pareto chart	Team	10 minutes
Five Why's	Choose one suspect X and perform a 5 Why Analysis.	Team	15 minutes
Additional C&E analysis	Time permitting, select another microproblem statement and create another C&E diagram	Team	30 minutes
Plus/Deltas		Team	5 minutes
		TOTAL	2hrs 5 minutes

Figure 6.11

is having problems with a tool, many others do as well. As we went into breakout rooms, we experienced positive results from the Cause Effect Diagram, the concept of clarifying and duplicating and multivoting. The SOS team tackled its air bill noncompletion microproblem statement and generated a series of method-related theories that led to a good hypothesis.

The only problem was late in the breakout when teams were having the 5 Why diagram use them rather than vice versa. Susan and I went into reteach mode when this happened. It was imperative that we didn't do the work for the team despite both our temptation and the desire of many teams to be told what to do. Ultimately, after frustration that lasted through the end of the breakout and beyond, the teams mastered the 5 Why's during their intersession work.

The Open, Narrow, Close concept. The Close of Root Causation

After a debrief where even I said I was getting confused about the 5 Why diagram, I began the second of the three lectures on Root Causation, the ever-important section on the Close of Open Narrow Close. I began by indicating that if Analysis is the most important element of DMAIC and Root Cause Analysis is the most important tollgate of Analysis, then testing the hypothesis they created in the Close of Root Causation might be the most important phase of their project.

Closing root causation is all about the word validation. I showed them the Likert Scale found in Figure 6.12 that provides the validation techniques available to them.

Susan and I quickly dismissed numbers one and two on the likert scale as quality validation methods. The first method, "doing nothing," is self-explanatory as a poor method of root cause validation. As Susan says, "Because I told you" is good enough if you are a parent but weak as a validation method. Because someone else tells you is in essence an interview method and would be a poor validation method as well.

Far better is number three. Here basic data collection might already exist that would validate (or invalidate for that matter) a potential x. For example, at Eckes and Associates we actually conducted a DMAIC project on late payment from a client. One factor was dissatisfaction with performance. Data collection available to us through course evaluations showed us as their highest rated consultant and this x was dismissed from the hypothesis.

1- Doing Nothing
2- Because I Said So
3- Basic Data Collection
4- Scatter Analysis or Regression
5- Design of Experiments

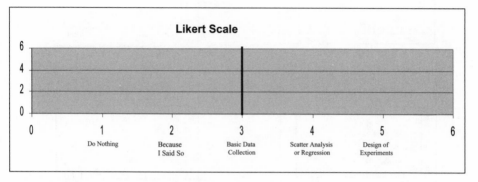

Figure 6.12   Root cause validation methods

We continued with level four of the Likert Scale and introduced scatter plots to the participants. We reviewed the four scatter plots found in Figure 6.13 defining what a positive and negative correlation means, no correlation, and unusual patterns. Again, using generic examples we gave an example of pressure on the accelerator pedal and speed of the car (positive correlation), number of innings pitched, and velocity of the fastball (negative correlation), and educational level and managerial ability (no correlation). For the unusual pattern where y is initially high as x is low then y is low and then high again as x rises, we gave another example: chronological age and diaper use.

We cautioned participants about using continuous data and the infamous third variable effect where there might be a third variable affecting x and y (shark attacks and ice cream sales; the third variable is seasonality).

Because there are no breakouts associated with the aforementioned, we had a large table team exercise to ensure the adult learning theory concept of testing mastery of what is taught. We asked table teams to come up with potential positive, negative, and unusual patterns of correlation in their business and determine whether reteach points are necessary based on report outs. The HP groups did well.

Finally we discussed regression and how to determine mathematically

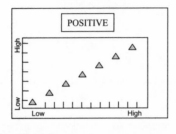

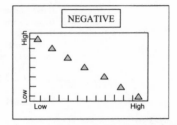

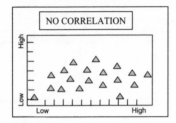

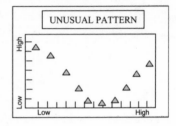

Figure 6.13

the strength of how much of y is explained by a given x. We reviewed a perfectly positive correlation (+1.00) through to a perfectly negative correlation (−1.00) and asked what a correlation coefficient of zero would indicate (no correlation).

Every Six Sigma consultant has his biases. For me, the tool of Design of Experiments (DOE) is a preferred tool. Its power has been displayed with a variety of project teams time and again. While primarily used in manufacturing, I have been fortunate to see its application in the service arena in recent years.

We teach DOE in an unorthodox fashion. First, we alerted the participants that they will be given a 2½ day project "holiday" where they are instructed to forget their projects as they learn DOE. As we mentioned in Chapter 5, DOE training still follows the tenets of Adult Learning theory with emphasis on two highly interactive business simulations.

The first half-day was spent in more traditional teaching of the three components of DOE (Design Setup, Design Execution, Design Analysis). Most DOE courses I have attended are taught by statisticians who spend a disproportionate time teaching design analysis. Yet our experience teaches us that setup and execution are the areas where most teams fail. So we focus on these areas.

By the end of the first day we had had large team exercises. However, the last 90 minutes of day one were devoted to the first business simulation. The participants ran a simple 2^3 full factorial (where we are testing three factors at two levels) determining the effects on dissolution of aspirin where we told them the three factors to test. (Brand of aspirin, a catalyst, and agitation method.) They gained experience in design execution and simple analysis. The biggest desired outcome was gaining confidence with the concept of DOE.

By the second day we introduced the power of fractional factorials. For the remaining day and half of DOE training, they were in the Aero-Bomb business simulation designing, running, and analyzing a series of experiments. The goal was to take a balsa wood airplane and modify it through a series of experiments where the plane can go farther and with greater accuracy by the last day of training. Susan and I went room to room, approving experiments, teaching them analysis techniques and how to screen factors (x's) and utilize DOE as an optimization technique by the third day.

At midday on the third day of DOE training, the 8 teams congregated in the ballroom of the Hotel Valencia with only one table present. All others had been removed by the hotel staff for the final launches of each team's three attempts to hit a target from a distance of 30 feet from the launch table located at one end of the ballroom. By then, teams had run a series of screening and optimization experiments that resulted in the modification of their original balsa wood airplanes that less than three days before had had poor accuracy and could come nowhere near 30 feet in terms of launch distance.

Teams put on a marketing presentation for extra credit points, which could have been the deciding factor if no team was able to hit the target (one of my son's, Temo's, first cuddly bear). The presentations were incredibly funny, which included taking shots at the instructors in a highly humorous fashion. Susan, Andrea (who had joined us for DOE training), and myself see it as a sign of bonding with the Eckes team if they feel comfortable enough to make fun of the instructors during the DOE presentations. Each team was aware that the winning team had an opportunity to win $10,000. While several teams performed well, it was no surprise when the SOS team hit the target twice out of three attempts and walked off with their $10,000 opportunity.

The beauty of such an interactive simulation is that all desired goals

- Complete D/M Work

- Create and Agree on 1–3 Micro Problem Statements

- Complete the Initial Work of Root Causation

- Begin Work on the Validation of Root Causation

- Determine Financial Opportunity for your Project

Figure 6.14 Intersession deliverables analysis

had been met. The teams had set up, executed, and analyzed numerous experiments. They both understood the concept and had become excited toward the tool, which immediately translated into more enthusiasm toward their project.

With one afternoon left in Analysis training, we gathered the team leaders and key team members to go over the ever-important intersession deliverables for their Analysis work.

Figure 6.14 indicates what the teams had to accomplish between the close of day June 18 and, depending on their root cause validation method, no later than Labor Day.

All but one of the teams were done with their D/M work. One team had difficulty acquiring data and its members were told bluntly to finish quickly with the Define and Measure work.

The second intersession deliverable was to come to agreement on no more than three microproblem statements after their data and process analysis. This presented a challenge to several of the HP teams because they had done such a thorough job in the breakouts some teams had upward of 10 to choose from. Susan and I recommended consolidation or prioritization of others based on the goals and objectives found in their charter. We also indicated that, once they completed their subprocess mapping activities, validated the subprocess maps, and completed their process summary analysis worksheets, consolidation of the microproblem statements could occur. We recommended the agreement to these statements be completed by the first week of July.

Because of a scheduling quirk we needed to begin work on the Improve and Control training with HP mid-July. We stressed to them they would not be completed with Analysis work but should plan to complete both the Open and Narrow phases of root causation by the morning of July 13th, the next time a 10-minute presentation was expected by each team leader. There was significant concern about starting Improve and Control training without first finishing Analysis intersession work. I apologized profusely, explaining that it was not Sean Sanders's or HP's fault. I decided to fall on my sword and tell them that the Eckes team had prior engagements with other clients the entire month of August.

During the brief intersession teams were progressing nicely. While all teams save one was right on target, it came as no surprise to either Susan or myself that the SOS team was excelling. They narrowed their list of microproblem statements to the following precise and detailed y's.

> Why are failures so highly concentrated in five service areas?
> Why do we not provide the customer problem information with their status?
> Why do we have so many moves and setup steps in providing status?
> Why do we have so many exceptions and rework steps in the process?

By early July the SOS team was deep into the Open and Narrow steps of root causation. They had generated over 50 x's to explain their major y's. Susan and I were impressed with the focus and detail of their x's. We find that the more detailed the x the easier it is to test whether that x has an impact on y. For example, among their x's was whether the service center manually keyed in the air bill. Validation of this x would be easily accomplished through validation method number three (basic data collection). Other x's, like the air bill field not being long enough for all types of air bills, were perfect to test in an experiment.

July 13th was another bright and sunny day in San Jose as the teams met at the Hotel Valencia for the last four days of training. Project report outs again were highlighted by most of the teams being on target for what was expected of their Analysis intersession work. No team is complete, having just four weeks to work on the most important element of DMAIC. Susan and I stressed the logistics of having to move forward with training, yet the groups were universally apologetic despite our encouragement that they were not expected to complete Analysis by the morning of July 13. Most groups had completed their subprocess mapping and data analysis work, begun the open and narrow phase of root causation, and two groups were planning to conduct a DOE. Yet this hard-charging, bright group of HP employees had wanted to do more by July 13th.

This raised the question about how to set the intersession time period. Unfortunately, this is more art than science. There were teams like the HP group that truly wanted to achieve all of the Analysis work before starting Improve training. Sometimes, though, too much time can be provided for a team. Our only client that dismissed us was one where they requested over three months for intersession work. Reluctantly I agreed. Amazingly, no one of the teams completed their intersession work. I learned there that if you are to err, err on the side of giving too little time for intersession work rather than too much. While the HP team gave us legitimate negative feedback for the scheduling of Improve and Control training too soon, they even accomplished more in one month by way of intersession work than most groups.

The other major development during the intersession for the HP DMAIC sessions was the loss of one team. This is not uncommon. Typically, two or three project teams exceed goals and requirements, two or three meet their requirements, and one or two teams either produce substandard results or (as was the case with one HP team) decide not to move forward. There is always a myriad of reasons behind team failure. In the case of the drop of this HP team, there was a lack of data, and there was a transfer of key personnel into another division of HP that was not on board with Six Sigma yet. To the credit of the remaining members of the team, they attended the Improve and Control training.

We had asked each remaining team to work with the finance office to conduct a more thorough investigation of cost opportunity. By the end of the morning teams had reported a total of 18 million dollars in cost opportunity. Teams that achieved a 50-percent improvement in goals and objectives meant that these first-wave projects had a potential $9 million in cost savings. This figure was not lost on Mohan Garde, who attended the first morning report outs. At the close of the morning session he gave a spirited speech both thanking the participants for their hard work and encouraging them to complete their tasks.

As the afternoon began Susan and I were ready to begin the Improve lectures. There are two tollgates to Improve. We have found that teams that do a good job in the D/M/A segments of the project spend little time in the first tollgate of Improve and actually report it as one of the easier elements of the DMAIC model.

The key teach points of the first tollgate of Improve include:

- *Understanding the concept of the Affinity Diagram as it relates to generating and selecting solutions.* In previous chapters we have addressed the concept of the affinity diagram. It is the job of the project team to generate and agree on a set of solutions for their project. The affinity diagram is used to achieve this goal.
- *Understanding and applying must and want criteria to their selected solutions.* Each solution must be compared to two types of criteria. Must criteria are applied to a solution where either the solution is discarded or is still considered for implementation. Want criteria helps a project team determine the prioritization of the solutions that get through the must critieria.
- *Understanding the importance of piloting a solution.* The last element of the first tollgate of Improve is communicating to the participants the importance of piloting their solutions.

Because by this point teams are familiar and experienced with the concept of affinity diagrams, Susan and I don't spend much time on the topic. We go through a generic example to refresh their memory.

Once a team has generated a list of solutions using their affinity diagram, they are anxious to implement a variety of solutions. However, before we do, we must pass the solutions against two types of solution criteria. Must criteria are questions that are applied to the solutions where the solution either passes or fails the criteria. If it fails, the solution cannot be considered further by the team. In the case of our project teams, must criteria are created by the champion and communicated to the team. Typical must criteria for a first-wave project include:

- Must not add to head count
- Must not be outside of budget constraints
- Must be implemented in 90 days or less

The problem experienced by so many Six Sigma project teams is they want to implement an array of solutions they now hold near and dear to their hearts. Susan and I stress that, particularly for first-wave projects, management is anxiously awaiting results. Therefore, they should front end their easy, high-impact solutions first, and pass other solutions to the Champion for "next generation" consideration. In this way, longer projects are not abandoned but management gets what they want by way of quicker results from their first-year investment in Six Sigma.

Once must criteria have been addressed, the solutions should be weighted against a set of want criteria. Want criteria are typically formed as open-ended questions such as, "Impact on…" Common want criteria are:

- Impact on root causes (the more impact, the higher that solution is raised in terms of importance).
- Impact to stakeholders (stakeholders are those affected by the solution). If a solution has less impact on fewer people, the chances of implementation rise for that solution.
- Impact on cost to implement (obviously, less-expensive solutions are better to implement than more-expensive ones).

Finally, in our lecture we stress the importance of piloting a solution. We return to my lasagna example. I want to test out my new solutions on a close friend or two before going into a full implementation of my lasagna for a fancy party.

The good news is that this lecture is straightforward, direct, and with little confusion on the part of the participants. Most groups are anxious to get into breakout. Therefore Susan and I don't belabor the ease of the improvement tools and get them into the breakout as quickly as possible. Figure 6.15 shows the detailed agenda for the first Improve breakout.

We stress that if they have not already done so, they should call their Champion to get their must criteria to accomplish the first deliverable of the breakout, clarifying and understanding the must criteria.

One aspect of this breakout that always amuses Susan and me is the agenda item for brainstorming, clarifying, and duplicating a set of potential solutions. The HP group had been no different than any other group we had worked with from the perspective of wanting to jump to solutions during the Define, Measure, and Analysis phases of their work. Now was their first opportunity to begin solution generation. Like so many of our clients, they balked. As Susan and I visited breakout room after breakout room; the teams felt they weren't ready to begin

Improve and Control—Breakout Session #1

Desired Outcomes:
- Clarify and Gain Understanding of the "Must" Criteria Issued By Your Project Champion
- Brainstorm and Gain Agreement of the "Want" Criteria For Your Project
- Brainstorm, Clarify, and Duplicate a Set of Potential Solutions That Address Your Potential Root Causes

Decision-Making Method
- Consultative/Consensus (Back-up 2/3 Majority)

Item	Method	Person	Time
Review Agenda	Discussion	Team Leader and Team	5 minutes
Clarify and Gain Understanding "Must" Criteria	Discussion	Team Leader and Team	10 minutes
Brainstorm and Gain Agreement on the "Want" Criteria	Affinity Diagram	Team Leader and Team	1 Hour
Brainstorm, Clarify, and Duplicate a Set of Potential Solutions	Affinity Diagram	Team Leader and Team	1 Hour
Review "Parking Lot"	Discussion	Team Leader and Team	5 minutes
Plus/Delta	Discussion	Team Leader and Team	5 minutes
		TOTAL	2 Hours 25 minutes

Figure 6.15

this step, or wanted to return to Analysis for review of work already done. Both Susan and I gently prodded team members to brainstorm some solutions even though they hadn't finished Analysis, indicating to them to assume their hypothesis has been verified, knowing later they can dismiss a solution if parts of their hypothesis have not been validated.

Upon the completion of the large-group debrief, Susan was ready to tackle the second tollgate of Improve, gaining buy-in to the solutions of key stakeholders. Among the highlighted teach points for this second tollgate are:

- *The definition of a stakeholder.* Often confused with the definition of a customer, the stakeholder is someone affected by the project team's solutions or someone needed to implement a solution.
- *The concept of the stakeholder analysis chart.* A stakeholder analysis chart graphs who the key stakeholders are and rates both current commitment to the solution set and where those same stakeholders need to be in order for the team to implement their solutions successfully.
- *Types of resistance.* There are four major types of resistance to Six Sigma solutions. The first type is technical, where the resistor sees change as fear of the unknown. The second type of resistance is political, where change equals loss, real or perceived. The third type of resistance is organizational, where the change is resisted based on loss of control. The fourth type of resistance is individual resistance where a person might be experiencing personal stress in his life such that taking on Six Sigma implementation responsibilities causes further emotional paralysis.

Susan addressed the first item around the second tollgate of Improve by defining a stakeholder. She continued with the introduction of the stakeholder analysis chart and its six columns. As seen in Figure 6.16 the first column has the list of key stakeholders. We don't list every possible stakeholder since that list could be in the hundreds for some projects. Instead, a key stakeholder is one that has influence over other stakeholders.

She then reviewed the other five columns of the chart starting at the far right and moving to the left. The far-right column is labeled Strongly Supportive. Susan operationally defines a stakeholder as someone who

Key Stakeholder	Strongly Against	Moderately Against	Neutral	Moderately Supportive	Strongly Supportive

Figure 6.16   Stakeholder analysis

is strongly supportive, who not only does what is asked of her but will take on additional assignments in Six Sigma implementation as well as assist others with their assignments. She describes this type of person as a "Make it Happen" stakeholder.

The next column is described as the Moderately Supportive stakeholder. This person does what is asked of him competently but no more. She finished with the description of this type of stakeholder as the "Help it Happen" individual.

Next, comes the column labeled Neutral. This "Let it Happen" stakeholder is neither for nor against the proposed solutions. She won't help implement, but on the other hand won't get in the way of the project team.

The next column is the Moderately Against stakeholder. This type of stakeholder will either resist doing what is asked or be passively compliant. Susan indicated that the latter is more dangerous because at first, the project team might initially believe the stakeholder is on board with its solutions.

Finally, she addressed the last column, the Strongly Against, who is a stakeholder who will not only not do what is asked but try to sabotage the entire solution set by enlisting other stakeholders against their action items.

Susan shared a generic example that was highly engaging and appealing to the participants. As a certified and licensed Ph.D. psychologist who still has a private practice, she revealed how once she used the stakeholder analysis chart for a family contemplating a move to another city. The mother had been offered her dream job outside of the state and

Key Stakeholder	Strongly Against	Moderately Against	Neutral	Moderately Supportive	Strongly Supportive
Mother					⊗
Father		X———————————→◯			
Child #1		X————————→◯			
Child #2		X————————→◯			
Child #3		X————————→◯			

Figure 6.17   Stakeholder analysis

then did a stakeholder analysis on her husband and three children. Figure 6.17 shows their current and desired state of commitment to the move involving the mother.

An interesting discussion ensued about what kinds of resistance would be exhibited by each family member. The husband's resistance is more organizational. His male ego has been bruised and if he had been asked to move for a job, he would have been Strongly Supportive. However, the move will result in his wife making more money than he will and thus he is experiencing what is sometimes described as NIH (Not invented here), meaning it wasn't his idea.

Meanwhile the children are resistant primarily over losing friends and having to make new ones. The nuances of these losses were shared by certain class participants as they told of their experiences with having to make a move for either themselves or their spouses. At this point we were ready to begin our second breakout around conducting a stakeholder analysis chart. Figure 6.18 shows the detailed agenda for the stakeholder analysis breakout.

Susan and I stressed during our rounds that while there is nothing sophisticated or mathematical about the stakeholder analysis tool, it sometimes can prove difficult to use. DOEs might be complex, but they affect a process, whereas doing a stakeholder analysis affects a person.

One common mistake we see during our rounds is teams indicating a key stakeholder as a department. We emphasize that this ultimately is a meaningless exercise because there often is significant stakeholder variation within a department. We stress to the groups to select a specific person (or people) within that department as key stakeholder(s)

Improve and Control—Breakout Session #2

Desired Outcomes:
• Identify and Agree on a Set of Key Stakeholders for Your Project
• Conduct a Stakeholder Analysis Chart

Decision-Making Method
• Consensus (Back-up 2/3 Majority)

Item	Method	Person	Time
Review Agenda	Discussion	Team Leader and Team	5 minutes
Identify and Agree on Key Stakeholders	Brainstorming & Discussion	Team Leader and Team	45 minutes
Conduct a Stakeholder Analysis Chart	Stakeholder Analysis Chart	Team Leader and Team	1 Hour
Address "Parking Lot"	Discussion	Team Leader and Team	5 minutes
Plus/Deltas	Discussion	Team Leader and Team	5 minutes
		TOTAL	2 Hours

Figure 6.18

and conduct the analysis.

The good news, once this change occurred, was that most of the stakeholders showed either support or were only moderately resistant. There was only one case where someone was targeted as being strongly against a proposed solution, and later it was determined that their resistance was overestimated.

After our debrief, Susan continued with stakeholder analysis, indicating that any gap between current and desired support to a solution is indicative of resistance. She returned to her generic example of the family move and used each family member to highlight the major types of resistance, their underlying issues, and development of strategies to move them to desired levels of support.

She tackled the husband first. The husband's type of resistance is organizational, so labeled because of the "Not Invented Here" issue. The wife knows that the husband's ego is bruised. The strategy with the NIH concept is to stress the advantages to the change and provide empowerment to the resistor. In this case she negotiates with the husband the opportunity for the husband to choose a new home closer to city centers where he would stand the greatest chance of getting a more presitigious job than the one he currently holds.

The children exhibit technical or political resistance where they see the loss of friends and familiarity. She arranges for quick visits to the new location, arranges to meet several new children, and promises frequent visits back to their old home area.

Susan then assigned the group their final Improve breakout, asking each team member to determine which stakeholders were resistant to potential solutions, and having her create an influence strategy to move the stakeholder to her desired state of support.

Figure 6.19 reveals the details of the resistance breakout.

There were now two days left in formal training. The day of July 15, 2004 was our last full day of introducing new material. Experience has taught us that the Control element of DMAIC is best completed during the postsession work with project teams once their solutions are implemented and they are ready to enter the Control phase of their projects.

Nonetheless, it is important to cover the two tollgates of Control. The first tollgate centers around technical monitoring of the newly improved process. The second tollgate centers around how the team dis-

Improve and Control—Breakout Session #3

Desired Outcomes:
· Determine Key Stakeholders Who Could Be Potentially Resistant to Your Solutions
· Create a Planning for Influence Chart For Each Potential Resistor

Decision-Making Method
· Consensus (Back-up 2/3 Majority)

Item	Method	Person	Time
Review Agenda	Discussion	Team Leader and Team	5 minutes
Determine Key Stakeholders Who Could Be Resistant	Discussion	Team Leader and Team	30 minutes
Create a Planning for Influence Chart for Each Potential Resistor	Discussion	Team Leader and Team	1 Hour
Review "Parking Lot"	Discussion	Team Leader and Team	5 minutes
Plus/Deltas	Discussion	Team Leader and Team	5 minutes
		TOTAL	1 Hour 45 minutes

Figure 6.19

bands and the last Six Sigma tool, the project team's Response Plan. I began the lecture on the first tollgate by highlighting the key learnings of Technical Control:

- *Mastery of the two concepts that determine technical control, process throughput and process standardization.* Process throughput represents the amount of product or service going through the new process. Process standardization refers to how consistent the new process steps are after the completion of the Improve stage of DMAIC.
- *The four major categories of control methods depending on process throughput and process standardization.* There are four major types of control methods. The first and most rare is when there is low standardization and low throughput. Self-inspection is the control method. For high throughput and low standardization after the fact, data collection methods like pie charts and bar graphs are the control method. For high standardization and low throughput, checklists are the control method of choice. Finally, for the majority of processes, high standardization and high throughput statistical control charts are the preferred method of control.

In my lecture I reviewed the definitions of process standardization and throughput showing a matrix (what kind of consultant would I be if

High Standardization Low Throughput Nonstatistical Controls ▪ Checklists ▪ Schedules	High Standardization High Throughput Statistical Controls ▪ X Bar and R Charts ▪ Individual and R charts ▪ X Bar and S Charts ▪ CUSUM ▪ Others
Low Standardization Low Throughput Nonstatistical Controls ▪ Periodic Status Reviews	Low Standardization High Throughput Other Statistical Controls ▪ Bar Charts ▪ Pie Charts ▪ Pareto Charts

Figure 6.20   Throughput standardization matrix

I didn't show at least one matrix?) as shown in Figure 6.20.

I asked the participants for examples of something that would have low standardization and low throughput. Most sessions are slow to answer this query, and I posed that this quadrant is reserved for those craftsman and artisans like Michelangelo painting the Sistine Chapel one day (Ok, it took a little longer) and sculpting David or the Pieta the next. Susan and I were quick to point out that this rarely, if ever, applies to any Six Sigma project. We indicated we have never seen a Six Sigma project indicate this as their quadrant of choice. We went on to low standardization and high throughput using a short-order cook as our example. We pointed out how frustrating a job like this can be and hope that project teams don't end up in this quadrant either. Some teams make a mistake and they did. Usually this is a result of the team thinking of the pre-Improve level of standardization in its processes. After the Improve stage of work for project teams, they should have created a more standardized process.

We migrated to the upper-left quadrant of the matrix and shared the example of high standardization and low throughput with an airline pilot's takeoffs and landing per day. Clearly, if we are his/her customer, we want high standardization and low throughput. The choice of using a checklist as a control method was clearly evident to the participants.

Finally, we indicated that the majority of Six Sigma teams will have high standardization (after the improve phase of DMAIC) and high throughput. Thus, their preferred method of control will be some form of statistical control charting.

Susan and I teed up the first Control breakout. Again, most teams will be some distance from implementing technical controls on their project, so our focus is simply to get them thinking about where on the standardization/throughput matrix they will be.

As seen in Figure 6.21, the breakout was not scheduled to be long. We expected them to place their initial projections about their position on the matrix and with any additional time left on their agenda, they could loop back to unfinished analysis work on their projects.

During our rounds Susan and I encountered a typical problem. While we had emphasized that standardization of the process should be evaluated post-Improvement, some teams were struggling with what went through the process rather than the process steps. One of the HP

Improve and Control—Breakout Session #5

Desired Outcomes:
• Determine Throughput and Standardization of Your "New" Process
• Determine Your Method of Control for Your New Process

Decision-Making Method
• Consensus (Back-up 2/3 Majority)

Item	Method	Person	Time
Review Agenda	Discussion	Team Leader and Team Members	5 minutes
Determine Throughput & Standardization of New Process	Discussion	Team Leader and Team Members	30 minutes
Determine Method of Control	Discussion	Team Leader and Team Members*	30 minutes
Review "Parking Lot"	Discussion	Team Leader and Team Members	5 minutes
Plus/Deltas	Discussion	Team Leader and Team	5 minutes
		TOTAL	1 Hour 15 minutes

* with Eckes Team

Figure 6.21

teams mistakenly assumed they had a nonstandardized process based on the varied types of customer calls they got at their call center. Susan and I stressed that they should reflect on the process steps, not what goes into each step. I used the example of one of Eckes and Associates' key processes, our course development process. Each course we develop is different, but the steps in creating a new course are virtually identical, thus making the process highly standardized.

We held a large-group debrief where we told participants not to worry about the type of control method until they are in the C phase of DMAIC. Then we are ready to embark on our last tollgate of DMAIC, disbanding the team and creating the handoff tool back to the Champion, also called the Response Plan.

Susan addressed the key learnings of the last tollgate of Control:

- *Disbanding the team.* The Six Sigma team is disbanded when all initial solutions are implemented and the Response Plan has been created and handed off to the project Champion.
- *The Response Plan.* The Response or Control Plan is a document similar in appearance to the data collection plan. It contains the new "should be" map, the measures crucial to the new process, and their associated targets and specifications. Additionally, the Response Plan contains the data collection forms used in the new process, the control methods, and a list of the process improvements.

Susan reviewed the Response Plan, noting that it is similar in appearance to the data collection, as several of the columns are identical. She walked through the generic example of an Eckes and Associates DMAIC project on invoice processing. She revealed the newly created should-be map that includes *adding* two steps that ultimately ended in reducing multiple rework loops in the original as-is map.

Susan continued through the Eckes and Associates example. She showed the revised set of measures for the new should-be map including targets and specifications. She reviewed the data collection forms and control methods, which include control charts and check sheets that confirm the newly added steps in the should-be map. The last column reinforces the solutions that were added that include verification of the invoice into the client's system and penalty fee invocation if needed. The process improvements are always listed because this is the area the process owner should first address if the process begins to show deterioration in performance. It might take months before these new solutions are embedded in the organization. Therefore, this is the first place for corrective action if the process starts to falter. Figure 6.22 shows a blank response plan.

Because the project teams were nowhere near disbanding, we did not have a breakout for this last tollgate of C, instead instructing team leaders to be aware of the need to schedule time for postsession consulting with the Eckes' team for this tollgate to be implemented.

The day had been long and the fatigue of working projects for several months began to show on our new friends at HP. We always let the group out early, indicating that our last day together will focus on general issues with projects and the all important postsession planning because formal training is not ready to be completed.

Process Improvement Handoff
The Response Plan

Process Map "Should be"	Measures	Specifications & Targets	Data Collection Method	Control Methods	Process Improvement

Eckes & Associates, Inc   4/12/2005

Figure 6.22

During the 15-minute debrief of the day with team leaders, key team members (Sean and his staff of master black belt trainees, Chad Fuller, Ron Sandretti, and Teresa Buckley), Susan, and I were invited to dinner. Both Susan and I usually duck these invitations. Susan usually helps her children with homework via her cell phone. I, on the other hand, am painfully aware I can only appear intelligent for brief spurts of time. Yet this group was different to us. We gladly accepted the offer to eat sushi, and July 15 ended up my favorite evening ever involved in DMAIC training.

DMAIC Postsession Execution

The morning of July 16th began early. While formal training of the DMAIC modules was now complete, it was imperative that the HP teams spend the day in detailed action planning for their postsession.

Susan and I spent part of the morning reviewing key tollgates that remained to be implemented by the teams. We then slowly reviewed what was expected of the teams after they left that afternoon. Specifically, teams would be required to accomplish the following:

Technical Improvement

- Complete the analysis phase of their projects, with the focus being on validating their root causes through solving their $y=f(x)$ formula.
- Once root causation has been established, the teams should generate a list of brainstormed solutions.
- A finalized list of must criteria from the Champion should be confirmed and the want criteria agreed by the team and confirmed by the Champion.
- All proposed solutions should be screened against the must criteria.
- Those solutions passing through the must criteria must be prioritized through the want criteria and finalized.

Cultural Improvement

- Develop a list of key stakeholders.
- Conduct stakeholder analysis.
- Develop an influence strategy for stakeholders that are not in their desired level of support.

- Implement the influence strategy.

Solution Implementation

- Confirm the new "should-be" map for the process.
- Identify the list of resources needed for implementation (people, resources, budget).
- Develop a detailed list of tasks, people responsible for implementation, and due dates for the rollout of the Solutions pilot and full implementation.
- Identify time line for implementation.
- Execute the plan.

The Control Plan

- Identify the process owner if different than the Champion.
- Gain agreement on the type of control method.
- Complete the Response Plan.
- Formalize the handoff of the Response Plan to the Champion and ultimate process owner.

Summary

Chapter 6 addresses execution of the Analysis, Improve, and Control portions of DMAIC. Taking our HP Wave 1 project teams, we focused on the tollgates of Analysis, Improve, and Control. Special focus was placed on the Analysis tollgate, as this is the key element of most successful project teams. Data and Process analysis leads to making the Six Sigma project teams become more granular about the problem statements and their hypotheses behind current poor sigma performance.

Solving the $y=f(x)$ formula becomes the passport into the Improve phase of the Six Sigma team's project.

Key Learnings

- Analysis is the most important element of DMAIC.
- Analysis is made up of Data Analysis, Process Analysis and Root Cause Analysis.

- Improve is made up of two tollgates, Generating/Selecting Solutions and Gaining buy-in to those solutions.
- Improve can be the easiest element of DMAIC if teams do a good job in Analysis, particularly Root Cause Analysis.
- Gaining buy-in to solutions is more difficult than generating and selecting solutions.
- Every team must find a technical control tool to monitor the new process.
- The type of control tool is determined by the standardization of the new process and the amount of throughput of services or products going through the process.
- The Response Plan is the final product of the Six Sigma team.

Six Sigma Cultural Execution

There are risks and costs to a program of action. But they are far less than the long-range risks and costs of comfortable inaction.

—JFK speech prepared to be delivered on November 22nd, 1963

Introduction

As WE STATED earlier, there are three components to Six Sigma execution: strategic, tactical, and cultural. In this chapter we address how to manage and maintain Six Sigma to make it a cultural phenomenon in your organization.

The cultural element of Six Sigma includes a host of changes to the organization:

- Closing the loop of the completed DMAIC project
- Managing process dashboards from completed projects
- Expanding the first-wave projects into Wave 2 projects and beyond
- Creating a more detailed second-year deployment plan that includes a strong communication vehicle and "yellow belt" training
- Weaning yourself off your external consultant and becoming self-sufficient (not only in terms of DMAIC training but project coaching)
- Expanding beyond process improvement projects and into process design projects (DMADV) and Lean Six Sigma projects

- Altering your systems and structures to make Six Sigma a way of doing business in the organization.
- Making the concept of Six Sigma an everyday event for employees.
- Managing the resistance to Six Sigma as a management philosophy.

Closing the Loop of the Completed DMAIC Project

The HP teams worked through the fall of 2004 to achieve their project goals. On December 13th team leaders, Sean Sanders and his group, my team of Susan and Andrea, and Mohan's staff congregated at the Rancho Bernardo Inn in San Diego. It was a full year after we had launched Six Sigma within HP Consumer Operations at Mohan's All Manager's meeting in December 2003.

The purpose of the two-day retreat was twofold. First, each of the project team leaders were giving their final reports on results and handing the project back to the Champion and ultimate process owner. Second, the next-wave projects were to be selected for work in 2005.

While we had intersession report outs where management had been present, these final report outs brought unique pressures to the team leaders. They were about to show the final results from months of work. I had instructed Sean to start and end these presentations with the best results. I had been briefed that not all projects were successful. From the beginning I had informed Mohan that the first-year launch would more than pay for itself with ROI being at least 10-1 and probably higher, though I warned him that not every project would be successful. Instead, one to three projects would account disproportionately for the ROI and he should be prepared for projects that have failed. To his credit, he was prepared and managed those failures superbly.

I was still unsure as to who would lead off the presentations. I assumed the SOS team and Debbie Gammel might be first. Instead, Annie Price of the Diagnostic team was our lead hitter. Simply put, over the next 25 minutes we were treated to an "Upper Deck Shot." Annie began with a review of the problem: incorrect diagnoses of customer problems on support calls and the resultant customer dissatisfaction ratings. She progressed through the Define, Measure, and Analysis steps providing sufficient detail into the tools and techniques her team used. She got management's full attention with projected annual cost savings of 12 million dollars. The project could potentially achieve that result through improved diagnosis, better agent communication, and overall customer satisfaction. This could occur through the next generation of solutions anticipated to be implemented in 2005.

While we hope for a 50-percent improvement in baseline performance, the 22-percent improvement in the aforementioned metrics resulted in a $3.37 million dollar cost savings to HP Consumer Ops. Most impressive was yet another service-related Design of Experiments that was conducted in their Belleville Canada facility. This effort was spearheaded by Craig Hoyt (a talented man but under the delusion that he resembles Robert Redford), Debra Hisaw-Keating, Walt Johns, Ron Sandretti, Brad Nolen, and Annie Price. Showing the power of DOE as both an analysis and improve tool, the Diagnostic team found 4 "x's" that helped propel diagnosis accuracy from 31 percent to 67 percent.

Management rewarded Annie's team with significant praise and genuine applause. The clapping grew louder when I pointed out that the average cost savings of a successful Six Sigma team is approximately $200,000. Put another way, a year ago during the Six Sigma overview at Mohan's management retreat I had indicated our recent clients were generating a 10-1 ROI for their first-year launch. After our first report out I indicated that the 10-1 ROI had been accomplished with *one team.*

I thought for sure the second presenter would be SOS team leader Debbie Gammel. Instead I was pleasantly surprised when Marianne Ozuna took center stage. I had been very impressed with the latter session breakout visits to Marianne's team. Nicknamed the HEROS team (Helping Endusers Reach Outstanding Solutions), Marianne and her cohorts were chartered with improving agent access to solutions during customer calls. Their agents had become frustrated with difficulty in navigation, cumbersome searches, lack of ability to locate proper documentation, and the prevalence of inaccurate solutions. During our Analysis training we stressed the importance of becoming granular with the problem, and the HEROS team had accomplished this granularity nicely by focusing on abandonment rates in customer complaint calls, the amount of rework, and insufficient information. This led to a set of specific root causes around the lack of existing solutions as well as profile settings that were not user friendly.

A series of vibrant modifications made the average resolution time drop from nearly seven minutes to less than two. The improvements in customer satisfaction rates and the reduction in time per call resulted in our second straight seven-figure ROI project. So far, we were batting 1,000.

As I watched Debbie Gammel approach the podium, I become keenly aware that we were about to go three for three in the ROI department. Debbie reviewed the steps leading to a set of five solutions that positively impacted customer satisfaction rates, thereby resulting in an annualized saving of over $500,000. Team champion Tammy Lockwood proudly shared a set of next-generation solutions to improve customer satisfaction and process efficiency through 2005. Together, these solutions would give this project a 7-figure ROI.

While several of the other project teams reported failures in terms of ROI, all of the remaining teams reported validated measures of effectiveness and efficiency for each targeted problem. In my closing comments, I told them that each process owner could now manage the process with facts and data. This is how the tactics of Six Sigma lead to better management of the organization.

During the presentations with less impressive ROI, the mood of the group did not change dramatically. Mohan provided encouragement to those that did not achieve dramatic results without sounding patronizing. At the same time other managers in attendance discussed the continuation of some projects on a more limited basis. This became a small yet important step in making Six Sigma a cultural reality within HP Consumer Ops. Through the more successful projects presented earlier, management now sees the power of creating a culture of process improvement throughout the organization.

I always stress to clients that this science fair and report out is the surest way to achieve results, and that these presentations begin the journey to making Six Sigma a cultural and strategic phenomenon.

Beginning to Manage Process Dashboards
from Completed Projects

HP Consumer Ops began executing Six Sigma in December 2003 with a managerial overview. However, the real work started in January 2004 with the creation of HP Consumer Ops Six Sigma strategy. In January

Figure 7.1

and February the business process management system was launched as eight projects were selected for first-wave tactical activities. For nearly a year the focus of their Six Sigma execution was on these first projects.

If these projects had unfavorable outcomes, Six Sigma would have died within the organization. However, with the great results and renewed enthusiasm of management, it was time to close the loop and make Six Sigma more strategic. This is visually represented in Figure 7.1. Without management involvement at the strategic level, Six Sigma will continue within the organization at nothing more than the tactical level. This would mean several waves of projects that continue to drive out cost in the organization. When businesses proceed in that manner, Six Sigma eventually loses momentum and dies. Employees begin to see Six Sigma as a burden. Complaints about Six Sigma's time consumption become rampant. Eventually, projects are done without the enthusiasm or rigor and cost savings are minimal at best, nonexistent at worse.

Therefore I stress to the clients that they have several responsibilities in bringing tactics back to the strategic level. The first order of business: process owners must begin managing the process dashboard. The process dashboard includes those key measures of effectiveness and efficiency from Wave 1 projects. Even projects that did not achieve their goals will now be validated.

A perfect example would be the Entitlement project. Marilu DeLeon led the team from Ft. Collins in efforts to improve Customer Warranty Verification. Sadly, the team's baseline sigma worsened during the course of the project. I joked that their failure to improve sigma performance could possibly be blamed upon their intersession consultant, namely me.

While clearly disappointed, the team did succeed in other ways. The validated process dashboard showed a new customer-focused measure that was initially overlooked. They learned that the first point of contact with the customer was more important than agent courtesy. While they continued to track and value courtesy, further steps were taken to ensure that at least one point of contact was measured.

Of course, there are other key measures that also drive sigma improvement and therefore need close monitoring. This is the case with the Diagnostics, HEROS, and SOS teams.

Expanding the First-Wave Projects into Wave-2 Projects and Beyond

The first-wave projects take much longer than later waves. When selecting Wave-2 projects, teams should also start to train new people in the methodology. This facilitates more efficient goal achievement throughout an organization. It is very tempting to expand/modify Wave-1 projects using the same people who already have Six Sigma knowledge.

This approach saves training time, so projects are completed much faster. However, the second wave of training must spread the wealth of learning to make Six Sigma practice a part of everyday behavior. Widening the scope of education and involvement is imperative.

Creating a More Detailed Second-Year Deployment Plan

Candidly speaking, the first year of deployment is a test of will. While we insist that the first weeks of deployment are spent with management,

the rest of the first year is spent on Wave-1 tactical training and implementation in lower tiers. These projects end up being what we term
"Show-me" projects. Failure to generate Wave-1 results will likely
mean the Six Sigma initiative will die a quick death.

As such, most management has a wait-and-see approach to a formal,
high-profile, organizationwide Six Sigma launch. Obviously, this directly contradicts the type of launch made famous by Jack Welch at GE.
There, after a thorough review and discussions with Lawrence Bossidy,
Welch made formal his commitment before a single project derived results for the large Connecticut-based conglomerate. Unlike today's organizations that want to "try out" Six Sigma like wading in the shallow
end of the pool, Welch dove in head first, creating the infrastructure and
the communication to Six Sigma. Welch gathered together key managers and conveyed his full commitment to Six Sigma. He then informed financial analysts, thereby boosting GE's stock ratings.

Most organizations are similar to companies like Household Consumer Lending, an Eckes and Associates client since 2002. Household
Consumer Lending is now a division of HSBC. HSBC, headquartered
in London, is one of the largest banking and financial services organizations in the world. HSBC's international network includes more than
9,500 offices in 79 countries and territories in Europe, the Asia-Pacific
region, the Americas, the Middle East, and Africa.

Unlike GE, Household Consumer Lending (now HSBC) made a
commitment to Six Sigma during trying times. Following an October,
2002 landmark settlement with state attorneys general and regulators
nationwide, Household Consumer Lending was ready for Six Sigma.
To their credit, business leader Tom Detelich kicked off the Business
Process Management session with a very clear message. He stated that
there is no good time to launch Six Sigma, and this was the time they
were committing to Six Sigma. The extent of their implementation
would be based on the results of the first-wave "Show me" projects.
They didn't have to worry. Brian Zempel, the most effective Six Sigma
quality leader I have had the pleasure to work with in 20+ years of Six
Sigma implementation, worked the same magic at Consumer Lending
as he did at Retail Services. Therefore, Zempel and Detelich assembled a group of over 100 top executives and performers to launch
Wave-1. Together they set out to tackle 10 projects. The forecast and realized benefits combined from Wave-1 totaled 29.5 million dollars. They

were primed to take Six Sigma to the next level of widespread implementation.

By the time Wave 1 projects were closing, Brian had moved into a senior-line position responsible for all-important Underwriting function. In essence this proved to be a job in which the new quality leader was the former Underwriting director, Mike Dougherty. Dougherty was a key team leader in Consumer Lending's first-wave projects. After his Six Sigma work there and at Conseco, Mike was a natural for the quality-leader position.

An experienced and optimistic leader, Dougherty (nicknamed "Doc") went on to create a cultural implementation of Six Sigma through a vehicle called the Business Performance Group. This group combined the Project Management group and the Six Sigma master black belts to integrate process improvement throughout the organization.

HSBC Household Consumer Lending exemplifies what needs to be done to make Six Sigma a cultural phenomenon in an organization. Doc developed a set of goals and objectives that far exceeded cost-saving DMAIC projects. His Business Performance Group is chartered to make the organization more customer focused in everything it does as well as develop future business leaders. They made five major changes in their first year of deployment:

1. *Business Process Management.* The Business Performance Group works with management to create high-level process flow maps of the entire organization, helps identify process owners, and works with them to validate and manage customer-focused process dashboards.

2. *Full DMAIC Projects.* In their third-wave projects and beyond, the Business Performance Group works with management to select fewer, but more high-profile DMAIC projects. These full DMAIC projects usually tap into previously trained employees, so less time is spent in the classroom and more in the team's war room. The methodology is applied in 6 months or less. One criterion for the projects is an anticipated minimum $500,000 cost savings, twice what is usually expected of a DMAIC project.

3. *Pay It Forward Program.* The Pay It Forward program is a combination of efforts around smaller, yellow- and green-belt project work. It involves "Quick Hit" and "Lean Six Sigma" activities to increase

process efficiency, but these only take a fraction of the time a DMAIC project does.

4. *Six Sigma 101.* Having shown the power of Six Sigma in their first two waves of formal DMAIC projects, Black Belt Steve Trubich created Six Sigma 101 as a communication and indoctrination device. It provides general awareness training to all employees, and Six Sigma is included as a part of new employee orientation.

5. *Modifying their Systems and Structures.* This included modifying rewards and recognition and making Six Sigma activities a part of everyone's job description. This included Yellow Belt, Green Belt, and Black Belt certification.

The Business Performance Group included the development of "site" belts, specially trained by Doc. This core team of master black belts coordinated the myriad types of improvement efforts. They did everything from generating project ideas to tracking ROI to ensuring that all Response plans remain intact and process owners are managing process dashboards.

Doc commented on his efforts to make Six Sigma a cultural phenomenon. "A lot of what we did in year one was focused on Wave-1 projects. The thing we tried to work on in year two was incorporating Six Sigma into listening to the customer and better execution at making Six Sigma a way of doing business."

One tool that HSBC Consumer Lending took from my second book, *Making Six Sigma Last* is the $Q \times A = E$ templates. Q refers to the quality of the strategy and tactics of Six Sigma while A refers to the acceptance of Q, which then equals the excellence of results and the ultimate cultural implementation of Six Sigma. Using 11 templates for both Q and A, organizations in the midst of year-two implementation can mathematically evaluate their current adoption of Six Sigma and identify gaps. Those gaps can then be formulated into their second-year deployment strategies.

HSBC Consumer Lending had two gaps in the 11 areas. One was a need for improvement in their Business Process Management activities and the other called for modification of the systems and structures (e.g., reward and recognition efforts) for employees to embrace Six Sigma more readily as a way of life. According to Doc, "The only way to use Six Sigma as a cultural-change agent within our organization was to use the $Qx A = E$ process. As a result we revamped our BPM activities as part of our second-year deployment as well as addressing gaps in our systems and structures. Additionally, we began our site-belt program getting more localized projects with local ownership. We have five master black belts at corporate headquarters, but we have more than 4000 employees across the United States. We needed to make sure there was someone that was carrying the flag for fact-based decision making with a bias toward speed. That's where we came up with the concept of the local site-belt concept and our Pay It Forward initiative. The site belts were all team members from the first two waves of DMAIC project work."

Weaning Yourself Off Your External Consultant

It is virtually impossible to launch a Six Sigma initiative in year one without some external assistance. Unfortunately and ironically, with the success of a year-one launch, some organizations become dependent on their external consultants throughout the duration of their implementation efforts. To make matters worse, some ethically unsound consultants embed themselves with an organization, creating reasons for their continued involvement with the client (and continued consultation fees). At Eckes and Associates we believe nothing builds a consultant's reputation faster than creating value for the client in year one and then building self-sufficient internal capabilities in year two. It is rare for us to spend any billable time with a client in year three.

This weaning of the external consultant begins first with development of internal resources. Consultants must conduct formal training and more importantly act as coaches to teams (for tactical purposes) and management (for strategic purposes). To accelerate this process, we encourage teams to take our Master Black Belt Train the Trainer course. In 12 days spread out over 3 months, master black belt candidates who have been through Wave-1 training are taught Adult learning theory, methods of training, and then are assigned the teaching modules we addressed in Chapters 5 and 6. During the 12 days, each potential trainer presents an assigned module. After her presentation she receives detailed feedback from my team regarding both content, teaching style, and the ability to master Adult learning theory.

Invariably, one or two of the three to five candidates who matriculate through the program begin to stand out. When working with the quality leader we disproportionately assign future modules so these people are given lead instructor positions for Wave 2 and beyond. At the same time, the other master black belts in training hone their consulting and coaching skills as they receive detailed lectures on training in DMAIC and team coaching.

The train-the-trainer program has received highly positive client feedback. Typically, by the time Wave-2 formal training occurs, the client has identified at least two trainers who end up conducting the bulk of the DMAIC training. Usually, the client will hire one Eckes consultant to do Wave-2 coaching, provide feedback to the primary internal trainers, and do spot training of the more difficult modules as necessary.

Another way to make your company less dependant on the consultant is to create a certification program. Certification works to reinforce the cultural implementation of Six Sigma in several ways. There are three criteria to become certified:

- Completion of an approved DMAIC training program
- Generating results from participation on a Six Sigma project team
- Successful completion of a competency examination

There are multiple levels of Certification. There's the Master Black Belt certification, which entails completion of the DMAIC training program, coupled with train-the-trainer activities and a more detailed competency examination. The traditional black belt certification is bestowed with a slightly less statistical test, and more focus on facilitation and team dynamics skills. Finally, there are green belt certifications. The exam contains even less statistics and requires participation on the project team and completion of the approved DMAIC training program.

The certification program works because it becomes an expectation for current job performance. It then affects annual performance appraisals, and—in more aggressive organizations—becomes a requirement of advancement.

Expanding Beyond Process Improvement Projects

Under the umbrella of tactics are three major approaches. In year one of Six Sigma execution we strongly recommend that the client utilize only the DMAIC process improvement methodology. However, as the client moves into year two and beyond, we encourage our clients to utilize the other two tactical methodologies, DMADV and Lean Six Sigma.

DMADV (Define, Measure, Analyze, Design, Verify) is the acronym used to describe Process or Product Design efforts. There are three conditions when DMADV should be used. If there is not a current process that is needed to achieve a strategic business objective, then DMADV is needed. Second, if a process is irreparably broken, DMADV is needed. Finally, when a process has reached entitlement, which indicates after improvement it still does not achieve customer requirements, then DMADV is needed.

This was the case when I assisted Molex Incorporated in implementing a DMADV project in 2003. Molex is the world's second largest manufacturer of electronic, electrical, fiber optic, and interconnect products and systems. They operate on six continents with more than 16,000 employees. Jay Williamson is their Vice President of Quality. I have had the pleasure of knowing Jay since his days managing the quality operation at Emerson Electric. Jay is a highly knowledgeable, hardworking strategic and tactical thinker who embraced process improvement before it was fashionable.

Long involved in Total Quality Management efforts, Molex began to use Six Sigma at the strategic level. They identified a series of core processes, one of which (Demand Creation) strongly impacted their strategic goal. Thinking this process qualified for a DMADV project, we began using the tools and techniques to create a single global process to identify sales opportunities and turn them into backlog. Jay said that the Demand Creation DMADV project was a problem in search of a process. We created a pilot Demand Creation process in their North America division, which was then duplicated in the other three regions globally. The key to the new process was uniformity at the lower level, where subprocesses such as Market Development, Opportunity Management, and Order Management became methods to increase sales and impact growth.

The second tactical tool that should be expanded in year two of the Six Sigma launch is the use of Lean Six Sigma. At Eckes and Associates we have always taken a very broad definition of Six Sigma. We have been doing lean Six Sigma under our term "Quick Hits" for years.

Quick Hits is our program aimed at exclusively improving the efficiency of a process. To qualify for a Quick Hits project, current sigma performance should be very low (usually less than 2). Teams should target a process within the confines of one department or function and anticipate removing steps in the process to improve efficiency rather than adding steps to create a new process. Finally, a candidate for a Quick Hits project should not be data driven. If facts and data about the process are not already available or obvious, it won't work. Quick Hits does not include extensive data gathering. If these criteria are properly met, a Quick Hits project can call for 3–4 days of work followed by 30–45 days of implementation.

There are several reasons we strongly urge our clients to wait until year two of their launch to begin Quick Hit projects. First, our goal with a Six Sigma initiative is to get the organization to start managing with facts and data. If a Quick Hits program starts first, not only are we focused exclusively on cost savings, but also we neglect the ever-important strategic element of Six Sigma, thus excluding management's active involvement in the launch. Second, first-wave projects take much more time than subsequent waves. We saw this in the HP Consumer Ops examples. Before later projects are completed quicker and the methodology is embedded in the employees, imagine being asked to decide between a year-one DMAIC project that will take up to 9 months, or one that will take a few days of actual training and work followed by 30–45 days of actual implementation. I know which of these two I would prefer. Quick Hit projects should become part of your tactical execution strategy in year two, but typically not before then.

Many businesses are cursed with highly inefficient processes where band-aid solutions only cause later complications. That was the case at the Courage Center Rehabilitation facility in Minneapolis Minnesota in 2003. Their Patient Registration process had been broken for a long time. Conscientious employees had developed unique methods to try to bring patients into treatment processes only to be hampered by the registration process. After spending one day with project Champions chartering two teams, a core project team spent three days analyzing the current process and taking out unnecessary steps. They created a "value chain" of patient registration steps that decreased the wait-time between first point of contact to treatment from 20+ days into near single digits.

Altering Your Systems and Structures to Make
Six Sigma a Way of Doing Business

At the HP Consumer Ops Six Sigma Showcase Event, a question was raised by a manager who had not been actively involved with Wave 1. His question centered on the fact that the Eckes team had estimated that 20 percent of the team members' time would be devoted to the project if participants had good project management skills, and up to 10 percent more time could be expected of the team leader.

The questioner had heard correctly that some teams spent up to 80 percent of their time on the Wave-1 Six Sigma projects. Clearly, that was not as he said, "the advertised amount of time the team should have spent." I was ready to reply that a 20-percent effort would probably have resulted in an average of $200,000 ROI, and these teams should be complimented for giving such a Herculean effort that produced so many seven-figure ROIs.

But before I could interject, Mohan quickly gave his perspective. He focused on the fact that process improvement at HP Consumer Ops was to become an expectation of work there. Mohan sent a dramatic message to his management team and employees in attendance. Improving a process is a job expectation. Those who had been a part of those first projects saw the power of improving a process, but those from afar were still to be convinced.

What this does in an organization is set up the proverbial chicken versus egg dilemma. Until a project participant experiences a new process that operates more effectively and efficiently, management will have to set the expectation that process improvement is part of the job description.

There is the adage that what gets measured gets done. Therefore, another system and structure change we recommend to clients is to put Six Sigma expectations into everyone's performance appraisal expectations. Finally, changing the reward and recognition systems at an organization goes a long way toward creating a culture where Six Sigma is a way of life.

We have seen some unique applications of rewards and recognition that work. They all must be complimentary of the organization's current culture. At WMC Mortgage in Woodland Hills, they have a culture of bonuses for great performance. Therefore, they issued a standard bonus for participation on Six Sigma projects and doubled the amount for meeting the goals and objectives of the project. At GE, it has been well known that Jack Welch mandated that 40 percent of any manager's bonus was tied to Six Sigma efforts. In the ever-competitive health care arena we saw Park Nicollet Health Care in Minneapolis, Minnesota pay physicians to participate on Six Sigma teams (to offset their billable time loss). This went a long way toward shaping more productive projects that directly affected the efficiency and effectiveness of the health care system. This was a vast improvement over simply focusing on transactional quality issues like patient registration or third-party billing and collections.

Another system and structure that is easily neglected is the area of communication. HSBC Consumer Lending instituted a host of different Six Sigma communication vehicles in year two of their launch. This included highlighting projects on their Web site, putting together a Six Sigma newsletter with common questions and answers, and gaining access into the companywide newsletter, the Newslink.

Managing the Resistance in an Organization Toward Adopting Six Sigma

As we wrote in *Making Six Sigma Last*, people abhor change. They associate change with loss. As such, resistance to anything new, even something that will make their professional lives easier through improving the efficiency of a process, will likely be resisted.

The key behind managing resistance is finding out the real issues behind their resistance. This is easier said than done because most individuals will not reveal the true root cause behind their resistance. Sometimes they don't even know why they are so resistant. Instead, they create bogus complaints that hide their fear of doing something out of their comfort zone.

We addressed the four major types of resistance and their underlying issues in *Making Six Sigma Last* and in this book. Also covered were the common strategies to overcome the resistances. Sadly, I have come to see that overcoming resistance is one of the least embraced concepts of executing Six Sigma. It is also one of the most important responsibilities of a business leader relative to Six Sigma's cultural element.

While it is rare for executives to handle resistance with boldness, I have seen exceptions. One of the most famous involved an otherwise productive vice president who felt Six Sigma was bureaucratic and countered their entrepreneurial culture. I had been working with the CEO for the better part of a year on their strategy and tactics with reasonable but not overpowering success. Unlike many business leaders who take a wait and see attitude through the "show me" first-wave projects, this CEO would call me often to get updates on how his organization was embracing Six Sigma. The vice president in question had indirectly been placing obstacles in the way of one team, feeling the time devoted to the Six Sigma project was negatively impacting revenue. While not dramatic in his stubbornness, the vice president's influence over other individuals in the organization was a key factor in ultimately making Six Sigma work as more than a cost-savings tool.

To his credit, the business leader took a keen interest when I told him that there was a major resistor among his direct reports. I coached him on the four major resistances to Six Sigma and to be alert that issues raised by a resistor often are "Iceberg" issues where there are deeper issues of concern than what is raised verbally. While the vice president was raising the issue of bureaucracy and culture, the real issue was this vice president saw Six Sigma as a threat to his more autocratic, authoritarian management style.

The first series of interventions by the business leader proved fruitless. To shift a resistor to a more accepting position toward Six Sigma, the true root cause of the resistance must be uncovered. Clearly, the issue for this vice president wasn't the perceived bureaucracy behind Six Sigma. In order for the business leader to have an impact he had to have the vice president acknowledge his fear at changing his management style from one that was authoritarian to one based on greater collaboration and managing with facts and data.

If verbal interventions don't work, do not give up. Business leaders must continually try to get the resistor to discuss the real issues. Sometimes this occurs best in a nonbusiness situation over dinner or a sporting event. Again, to this business leader's credit he repeatedly attempted these strategies. At the same time the vice president's behavior worsened. I received reports that he was badmouthing Six Sigma and the diverted resources consumed by the first wave of projects.

Our Six Sigma team dynamics course teaches clients that interventions must escalate when lower-level interventions don't work. In the case of this resistor we recommended giving the vice president Six

Sigma assignments to complete. Particularly in the case of overachiev-
ers (as this vice president was), sometimes resistance can be overcome
by easing the resistor into activities that negate the root cause behind
the resistance. Therefore, we made this vice president a project Champion for a Wave-2 project. While I have seen this strategy work in the
past, it proved disastrous for his team as they floundered through D and
M work without input on such crucial matters as project scope and
providing the necessary resources for the team to complete its work.

At the end of the first year launch, the business leader adopted a set
of systems and structures to incorporate Six Sigma culturally. This included making Six Sigma efforts a part of the management bonus program. At the time of the vice president's review his poor performance
as a Champion resulted in a lower bonus. By this time I had coached
the business leader that the vice president was likely a lost cause but he
could be used to send a message to the rest of the organization. Ultimately, this vice president left the company of his own accord, but the
rest of the organization got the message. The business leader was serious about Six Sigma.

Making the Concept of Six Sigma
an Everyday Event for Employees

Lela Gorski was a member of the Urgent Support Email Notification
Team at HP Consumer Ops led by Gary George. During her December 2004 Six Sigma Showcase Event presentation, one of her slides
simply said "Let Data Lead the Way." This phrase had been used repeatedly by Susan and me throughout DMAIC training and consulting.

One aspect of Six Sigma taking hold culturally in an organization is
managing with facts and data. Lela went on in her presentation to say
she now examines data to make decisions rather than making decisions
through gut feeling. She was not alone. Brad Nolen of the Diagnostics
team reveals how being a part of a Six Sigma team has changed his approach to work.

> I have become a pain in the butt . . . I mean, I tend to question
> quick solutions that don't seem to be thought out or don't ad-
> dress the real problem. I crave more structure in my projects and
> try to define the core issue and goal early on. I always thought

that I worked well in ambiguous situations and now I tend to push the team for more of a structured and data-driven approach.

Tim Betsch, the HP champion for the Diagnostics team, detailed how he has made Six Sigma a part of his everyday work:

I'm thinking much more about managing process and structuring the measurements of the process based upon the customer. I am always aware of the effectiveness and efficiency of any process I come into contact with at HP.

Michael Pisias of the SOS team concurs.

It's all oriented to measurements. Six Sigma replaces the concept that people are paid to have an opinion. With Six Sigma, strong opinions and aggressive behavior to push to adopt those opinions loses out to having 'data lead the way.' In effect, Six Sigma removes the frustration that employees experience when opinions dominate and facts are in the way.

Craig Hoyt agrees.

I insist on data to drive decisions. If the data is not conclusive, then I push for further data and don't give up until the data is presented. This becomes infectious, then everyone is insisting on data.

Six Sigma becomes infectious when project team members spread the word and act in a different manner when their team disbands and they return to their day-to-day work. In essence, these individuals become missionaries for the new way to conduct their work. Therefore, we encourage that second, third, and even fourth-wave projects are populated with new people other than previous team members so the word is spread as quickly as possible.

Summary

In this chapter we addressed the pragmatic steps an organization must take to expand Six Sigma into a cultural phenomenon in the organization.

This includes making sure that Wave-1 projects are closed out correctly by properly handing the response plan to the process owner. It also means having the process owner begin to manage the process dashboard measures of effectiveness and efficiency.

In the second year of Six Sigma, a more detailed deployment plan should be created that expands the communication vehicle of Six Sigma to all employees, as well as selecting future projects. It is also in year two of your launch that you should be developing a plan to make yourself less dependent upon your external consultants through a certification and train-the-trainer program.

Additionally, in year two and beyond the tactics of Six Sigma need to be expanded into DMADV (process design) and Lean Six Sigma work (what at Eckes and Associates we call Quick Hits). To move the organization forward into adopting Six Sigma as more than defect reduction work. Systems and Structures must be altered to encourage the work force into compliance. Changing how rewards and recognition are provided, how performance appraisals are conducted, and modifying job descriptions to include Six Sigma are just several ways to execute Six Sigma culturally.

Finally, to ensure a cultural transformation to Six Sigma, business leaders must constantly manage the resistance, which is sure to be part of any launch, as well as use Wave participants as the Six Sigma pioneers to ensure that Six Sigma becomes a way to practice everyday work using facts and data.

Key Learnings

To make Six Sigma a cultural phenomenon in the organization, the following must occur:

- Closing the loop of the completed DMAIC project
- Beginning to manage process dashboards from completed projects
- Expanding the first-wave projects into Wave-2 projects and beyond
- Creating a more detailed second-year deployment plan that includes a strong communication vehicle and "yellow belt" training
- Weaning yourself off your external consultant and becoming self-sufficient not only in terms of DMAIC training but project coaching as well

- Expanding beyond process improvement projects and into process design projects (DMADV) and Lean Six Sigma projects
- Altering your systems and structures to make Six Sigma a way of doing day-to-day business in the organization
- Managing the resistance against Six Sigma as a management philosophy
- Making the concept of Six Sigma an everyday event for employees, tied into rewards and reviews

Pitfalls to Avoid in Executing Six Sigma

> If I had to live my life again, I'd make the same mistakes, only sooner.
>
> —Tallulah Bankhead

Introduction

THIS CHAPTER COVERS some of the pitfalls you might encounter when executing Six Sigma initiatives. These include:

- Learned helplessness
- Making cost reduction your primary Six Sigma goal
- Trying to be a popular Quality Leader
- Consensus management
- Waiting until the last minute
- Neglecting common sense
- Stretching your Six Sigma infrastructure after Wave 1
- Keeping the Six Sigma group in the Quality Department
- Forgetting that Six Sigma is a management philosophy
- Whining

Pitfall #1—Learned Helplessness

I have spent lots of time with rats in my life. I was thinking of this odd fact recently while having Sunday dinner with a good friend and her children, Bryson and Mackenzie. As dinner concluded, Mackenzie brought out her pet rat, Maggie. Ever the gracious guest, I got to hold

Maggie. This brought back 30-year-old memories from when I was an undergraduate assistant at Notre Dame. I ran designed experiments on learned helplessness in the Psychology department.

In one experiment we would time rats as they ran on a narrow path toward their favorite food, crunchy peanut butter. In these experiments, baseline measures of hunger and traverse times were collected, then we would electrify the runway with a shock to cause pain (never death). We then rereleased the rats into the runway so we could time their run over the grid that just shocked them. Amazingly, many of the rats refused to move. Some simply starved. One of the jobs of the undergraduate assistant was to take care of the rats, feed, and clean up after them. One rat in particular caught my eye and I even nicknamed him Byblos (or possibly her, I didn't take care of them that carefully). Byblos was shocked and then placed on the grid. He didn't move. "Come on Byblos, I urged, run to the peanut butter." Time and again I placed Byblos on the grid and he refused to budge. He began to starve.

In any event, the learned helplessness of the rat experiment has materialized time and again in my business experiences. I have seen project teams empowered to improve a process and not want to take the steps necessary to implement DMAIC. This is particularly the case in large organizations (HP Consumer Ops being a dramatic exception to this point).

I have only been dismissed by a client once. It was a large organization that asked for three months of intersession time to get their work done. That was more time than I have ever given for time between sessions, but instead of accomplishing their goals, the morning report outs contained a litany of excuses for why they didn't reach their desired outcomes. One project team had the temerity to blame the CEO for their failure! During that report out, I thought that the team had experienced the same learned helplessness of my rat friends.

The concept of learned helplessness is not limited to project teams. Many executives, particularly at the middle management levels, feel pinched between strategic objectives and the day-to-day grind of task assignments. They become addicted to the adrenaline rush of meetings, eagerly talking about an issue. But when it comes down to it, they don't utilize Six Sigma concepts and tools to do something about their plight.

When done properly, Six Sigma is a potent enabler for change in an organization. But people must make the decision to act. No quality initiative can replace bold action and decisiveness. A culture must overcome any feelings of helplessness in order for Six Sigma to work.

Pitfall #2—Making Cost Reduction Your Primary Six Sigma Goal

There is no industry more broken than the airlines. Six Sigma could be of tremendous benefit to the airline industry, yet if the airlines decided to implement Six Sigma I believe the chances of success would be low.

My pessimism is a result of the airline industry business model. It's based primarily on cost containment. If the airlines decided to implement Six Sigma without changing their model, they would focus their efforts on projects to drive out cost. While cost reduction is a wonderful by-product of successful Six Sigma implementation, it should not be the primary goal of your efforts. As Mike Dougherty indicated at HSBC Consumer Lending, their focus in years two and three of the launch was to use Six Sigma to achieve greater customer satisfaction, increased productivity, and leadership development. This is the true purpose of a Six Sigma launch. The airlines simply don't focus on their customers. They focus almost exclusively on seeing their services as a commodity.

Take the case of RyanAir. A Wall Street article published in the summer of 2004[1] revealed their main cost-cutting measure is never refunding the cost of a ticket, even if the airline cancels a flight. RyanAir employees are required to pay for their own training and uniforms and are told to cut stationery costs by pilfering hotel notepads. They have remodeled planes to remove window shades so that staff need not open them and affect the timing of takeoff preparations. They removed seatback magazine pockets to cut cleaning time. New seats don't recline, thereby reducing repair costs. Excess baggage costs were raised to 17 percent. As RyanAir CEO Michael O'Leary said, "Stop bringing so much old rubbish with you." Certainly a customer-focused leader don't you think?

If Mr. O'Leary had any interest in Six Sigma, it would be only to continue the pattern shown by so many business leaders I encounter. When used exclusively as a cost-reduction tool, Six Sigma dies an ugly death. Sadly, too many business leaders see Six Sigma as a quick fix to trim costs and impact the bottom line. On some level I sympathize with business leaders who are under much financial pressure, like those in the airline industry. However, as we saw in earlier chapters, done properly, Six Sigma transforms the whole business environment to be more customer and process focused, using facts and data to make decisions.

Keep reminding yourself that Six Sigma is a driver to become more customer focused. This is clearly not the case today in the airline industry. The airline industry gives only lip service to customer satisfaction. As a lifelong United passenger (note that we aren't even called customers) I recall receiving my new Red Carpet Club card that claims that it would provide greater service to me. The new card had to be swiped by the Red Carpet Club representative as opposed to my old card which I simply had to show to gain access to the club. "How could having to remove the card and have it swiped provide better service to me?" I asked rhetorically. It later proved prescient. I now wait in longer lines while people's cards have to be repeatedly swiped. On at least one occasion I have bypassed the club altogether after seeing the line to gain admittance to the club.

Avoid the temptation to simply drive out cost with a Six Sigma initiative. If Six Sigma is used as a mere cost-reduction program, then it will die a quick and ugly death. In such cases, employees will view it as yet another veiled attempt by management to drive more work out of employees.

Pitfall #3—Trying to Be a Popular Quality Leader

Too many Quality Leaders do not understand some of the tough decisions they must make in the first year of deployment. Without a strong presence and active involvement of the Quality Leader in the first wave of projects, it is unlikely that success can be generated.

We chronicled the work of Brian Zempel at HSBC Household Retail Services and Consumer Lending elsewhere. One of his notable achievements is leading Retail Services' first wave of nine projects. For the first time in my career, I saw all nine achieve or exceed their goals and objectives, thanks to Zempel's strength.

When interviewed in July 2004 he stated one reason behind his success.

I wasn't afraid to be unpopular. Of course this couldn't have been a working strategy unless I had good credibility with the project teams and team leaders. But I clearly was constantly inquiring about progress or lack of it and making sure intersession deliverables were being met. If I had tried to be Mr. Popularity, I don't believe we would have accomplished as much.

The Quality Leader is an essential role that has a multitude of responsibilities, none more important than ensuring team results in the first year of implementation. If the project Champion has the strategic responsibility of one team, the Quality Leader in essence has the responsibility of all teams. Sometimes the Quality Leader must override the Champion. At other times, getting the business leader to provide support during the course of DMAIC is crucial. The advantage, as we have seen with the Brian Zempels and Sean Sanders of the world, is that good business leaders keep them in these positions long enough to learn the entire business and then channel them into line positions within the company. When this is done, it sends yet another clear cultural message to the organization about the seriousness of their implementation efforts. However, a good Quality Leader must be willing to risk unpopularity at times. Without confronting those who don't see Six Sigma as a primary focus of the organization, the odds of success diminish dramatically.

Pitfall #4—Consensus Management

Consensus is the negation of leadership.
—Margaret Thatcher

We started this book with a case study featuring weak management leadership regarding a decision to embrace Six Sigma. Sadly, I see this occurrence time and again. I conduct a one-day overview of what Six Sigma is, review the three components (strategy, tactics, and culture) through a series of case studies, and then proceed to show how to launch a first-year deployment.

Usually, I'm hired by a business leader who has read one of my previous books on Six Sigma. The leader can conceptualize the value of embracing Six Sigma. Like our business leader in Chapter 1, they show a keen interest but expect me to convince their staff. Ever the competitor, I have gotten suckered into doing the work of the business leader. While my role is to sell Six Sigma, it is not my role to bring the team together. When done properly, Six Sigma can transform the organization. But, in the final analysis, consensus is rarely reached among the executive team. It takes courage and decisiveness on the part of the business leader to commit to Six Sigma if a successful launch will occur.

What I find odd is that in the last 10 years Six Sigma has been tried and tested in variety of industries. Yet, often in preliminary discussions with business leaders who show interest in Six Sigma, they do not want to make an overt commitment toward implementation of Six Sigma. Two recent examples highlight this lack of management leadership.

The CEO of a large multinational financial services company recently called me. The individual in question was highly intelligent and had carefully read two of my books. After 45 minutes of detailed, highly specific questions, I was impressed with his true interest in Six Sigma. He inquired about my availability to conduct my one-day overview and we even talked dates and cost. Then near the end of the conversation he said he had a request. "Can you provide this overview and not call it Six Sigma?" He went on to say he didn't want his staff thinking he was jumping on the new fad of the month and wanted Six Sigma not to be uttered during the overview. "Can we call this something else?" I hesitated to facetiously ask if I could call it Seven Sigma and then bluntly told the CEO that if he didn't want to call it Six Sigma then he shouldn't ask a Six Sigma consultant to provide the overview. Obviously, this organization didn't become a client of Eckes and Associates.

Another recent inquiry involved three business leaders of a large southern manufacturing firm. Our first teleconference went well while we talked conceptually about Six Sigma. Additionally, these three business leaders were candid about the need to improve both their effectiveness and efficiency, as in recent years they had become their industry's cautionary tale. Being NASCAR fans, they used the analogy that their competition was lapping them around the track. I was further impressed with their focus on improving customer satisfaction with Six Sigma and their understanding that cost reduction was a by-product of the effort, but not the primary goal. Then the roof fell in. I used the analogy from my psychology days that we have expertise in

Six Sigma and they were the experts in their commodity, so we would work together blending our individual skill sets to solve their problems. I let them know that we would not act as a traditional consulting firm, giving them the solutions to make them more effective and efficient.

At that point their enthusiasm waned considerably. "Gee, we really don't have the bandwidth to spend much time on the initiative. We thought with your experience in our industry you could come in, map our processes, determine the problems, and recommend solutions and then implement them." Clearly, this organization didn't understand how an implementation effort worked. Using the analogy of personal weight trainers, we indicated that they still needed to do the heavy lifting if Six Sigma was going to work for them. After this call we crossed them off our list of potential new clients.

Pitfall #5—Waiting until the Last Minute

Most people have an issue with procrastination. We live in a hectic world where much of our day is spent in a variety of pursuits that often lead us to fall behind. Whether it's Christmas shopping, major work projects, school activities, or an exercise program, there seems a universal tendency to keep putting off something and then rush to get things done. There are consequences to this course of action. I know I am a major procrastinator when it comes to Christmas shopping. Even though December is a slow consulting month, I put off my shopping. I pay a high price for procrastinating—not only spending more than I expected but adding to my stress level.

Six Sigma teams fall prey to the same procrastination. As detailed in Chapters 5 and 6, we assign report outs for each time project teams meet. While we indicate to the participants we want to see their progress to date, there is a built-in hidden agenda. You see, when team leaders are faced with an audience of peers, superiors, and even subordinates, there is a greater chance that work gets done. This approach has worked well, though in several instances you can see the project team rushed to complete their items, often waiting to the last week or so to complete their action items. This reflects badly upon those participants.

Of course, it is easy to spot these procrastinators. They tend to exceed the allotted 10-minute status review, excuses proliferate in their reports, and the work itself is shoddy and sometimes unprofessional. It is reminiscent of the advice I received from my mother as a child. She instructed her sons that the habits we learned in the sixth grade are often the same work habits we take into the job arena. "George," she once said, "Here is the key to success in the world: 90 percent of success is showing up on time; 95 percent of success is showing up on time with a plan; 99 percent of success is showing up on time with a plan and executing your plan."

I have passed the same lesson onto my son Temo, a near straight-A student who starts assignments right away, as opposed to most of his fellow students who procrastinate until the last moment. The word "cramming" isn't in his vocabulary. Unfortunately, many teams think they can cram Six Sigma project work into the last week before a report out, and sadly this practice results in poor performance.

At Eckes and Associates we have tried to assist teams in overcoming the procrastination urge. As part of the last day of DMAIC training, we give specific assignments as well as intermittent deadlines for deliverables so that a team can gauge if they are falling behind. Additionally, in recent years we've instituted intersession consulting and alert the Quality Leader about teams falling behind. This way, the Quality Leader can choose to lend additional assistance during the intersession and postsession periods.

Regardless of this hand holding, we continue to see teams wait to the last minute to do work. Invariably, these teams are rarely seen as successful case studies.

Pitfall #6—Neglecting Common Sense

Several years ago I was planning the kickoff Six Sigma event for a client located in Germany. They were working with a new client who had agreed to collaborate on several Six Sigma projects, so the client asked me to provide a one-day overview to the customer. The event was to take place in Madrid, Spain. However, the client asked me to fly to Dusseldorf the day before for a planning session only to fly on to Madrid that night in anticipation of the next day's session. When my son Joe saw the itinerary, he asked, "Dad, why don't they hold the planning session in Madrid, the same city you are going to do the session in?" Good question, my brilliant son. Obviously, this client was lacking in common sense. That lack of common sense proved near disastrous.

The planning day went well. The client's representative, my wife at the time (who was working with me), and I drove to the Dusseldorf airport in anticipation of our Swiss Air direct flight to Madrid. Our estimated time of arrival was 7:00 p.m., sufficient for a nice Spanish dinner and a good night's sleep. Unfortunately, a labor strike had closed the Dusseldorf airport. Our client's representative called the Quality Leader, who was not making the trip. With typical German efficiency his travel agency had rebooked us on a flight from Frankfurt to Munich, connecting to a plane bound for Madrid. But our new arrival time only allowed for two or three hours sleep before starting the Madrid sessions.

"That is unacceptable, my friend." I informed the representative. While I don't mind most of the drawbacks and compromises of consulting work, I knew traveling all over Western Europe and then getting two or three hours sleep would result in a disastrous presentation, which in turn would cause the joint supplier customer effort to lose valuable momentum. While the client was upset, we ended up taking a train to Frankfurt, staying at the Frankfurt Sheraton airport hotel, and taking the first flight to Madrid in the morning. Even though the session started late, it was better than the client's alternative. I recalled the wisdom of my son Joe. The session in Madrid would have gone better if he had been in charge of the planning meeting. Common sense is essential in any endeavor.

At the project level, too many teams make things more complicated for themselves. This greatly enhances the probability of failure. As a former psychologist I sense that sometimes this tendency to abandon common sense is a form of a fear of success. Some people either actively or passively seek to sabotage their work because they are uncomfortable achieving their goals.

This was the case for one project team in a service-related organization. The project had been chosen properly through the executives' business process management work. During the first week of DMAIC training, my team had strong feelings that this project had seven-figure ROI potential. However, our breakout visits raised some initial concerns; it wasn't until our intersession consulting that we knew something was deeply wrong. The team leader, otherwise intelligent, was making the project unduly more difficult than needed. This rubbed off on the team members, and the entire team was in a state of massive confusion over the simple Define and Measure tasks. For example, we suggest that the team use a combination of two methods to validate customer requirements. This team had decided three methods were needed. After a focus group and one-on-one interviews, they had created a cumbersome questionnaire to send customers to survey what they had learned through the interviews and focus group. During the intersession consulting, we informed the team that they had adequately validated the customer requirements and told them to move forward with validation of the process map. This request to move forward was met with resistance. They insisted on not only sending out the survey, but then weren't satisfied with the poor return rate and kept waiting for more customers to respond. They were paralyzed.

This was just the beginning of their self-inflicted complications. They continued in the Define stage to take the high-level process map and make it more detailed than necessary. We received calls after intersession coaching that they wanted to validate the map at several branches and found naturally the process was done differently at the branches. We instructed the team that they were better suited to use one branch as a pilot and see if a newly improved process could be transferred into other branches. Seeing this as a scope issue, we instructed the team leader to meet with the Champion and redefine scope issues.

With their difficulties in the Define stage, we anticipated seeing them struggle with baseline sigma calculations. Anticipating this problem, we worked with the Quality Leader to arrange a conference call to simplify the calculations of baseline sigma. Instead, confusion reigned as the team leader wanted to calculate multiple sigma measures in the multiple branches.

This continued through Analysis and even into Improve, though as you might expect this team was significantly behind each and every time we met. Project report outs were more indictments of the Six Sigma methodology instead of progress reports, and ultimately this team disbanded before even getting a chance to claim victory.

Put bluntly, Six Sigma is tough enough without making it more complicated than it needs to be. A dose of common sense as you apply the methodology will go a long way toward your success.

Pitfall #7—Stretching your Six Sigma Infrastructure after Wave I

Ironically, a successful Wave-1 rollout can make the organization too greedy as it moves forward expanding Six Sigma through the organization.

As the organization selects Wave-2 projects, I strongly suggest that they purposely choose fewer Wave-2 projects than in Wave 1. There are several reasons for this. First, as Chapter 7 suggests, Wave-2 projects should be higher profile in their contribution toward the organization. Second, there are a host of nonproject activities that will make Six Sigma a cultural phenomenon.

But most of all, the Six Sigma infrastructure (the Quality Leader and his master black belts) will be hard pressed to close out Wave-1 projects as quickly as they expect. Why? First, there will be a huge learning curve as process owners actually begin to use Response plans. It will be the job of the master black belts to ensure that new processes are used properly by the process owner and the employees who live in these new processes. Second, the Quality Leader and the master black belts will be working with Wave-1 team leaders and selected team members on what is called "next generation" solutions.

You will recall from Chapter 6 that the Improve phase of the first wave of projects demands that solutions meet certain criteria. One: they must be implemented in 90 days or less. Remember, these first-wave projects are sometimes called "show me" projects, and the quicker we generate results the quicker the initiative can gain traction and become more than a cost-reduction program. The problem with this 90-day implementation window is that many Wave-1 teams have a host of solutions that extend beyond the 90-day window, and they are forced temporarily to abandon solutions they feel strongly about.

What we recommend is to "basket" these solutions and hold the team leader responsible after the team formally disbands to work with the quality team (the Leader and master black belts) to ensure these next-generation solutions have some implementation strategy.

Unfortunately, the quality team often underestimates the amount of time it will truly take to close out these projects. Like your first true love, these master black belts and quality leaders have much invested in these projects. Typically, they will want to spend a disproportionate time working the next-generation solutions, unaware that they are starting a set of new projects as well. This was the case at HSBC Household Retail Services when I advised Brian Zempel to scale back both the number and timing of his next Wave-2 projects in year two. Ever the competitor, he patiently listened and then ignored my advice. As I've said before, feedback is a gift and some gifts can be returned. This one was returned. In retrospect, Brian later said my advice was sound and should have been followed. Don't overdo the second wave of projects despite your enthusiasm. Remember that a second-year deployment includes many nonproject activities if you are going to adopt Six Sigma as more than project work. Choose high-profile, vibrant Wave-2 projects, but don't spread yourself or your master black belts too thinly.

Pitfall #8—Keeping the Six Sigma Group in the Quality Department

While populated with talented people, the Quality department has been saddled with a bad reputation. We saw in Chapter 2 that Six Sigma at Motorola altered the reputation of quality professionals from a necessary evil to the valuable defect-reduction experts that populated Motorola. Later we saw how GE transformed Six Sigma culturally to the point that it was necessary to become a quality leader, black belt, or master black belt for advancement into nonquality positions in the organization.

We also saw how into year two, HSBC's Mike Dougherty combined the project management group with the Six Sigma function to create the Business Performance Group. This group's mission was to use the combination of project management tools with Six Sigma to create a value-added team. This team enabled the entire organization to achieve the strategic business objectives of HSBC Consumer Lending.

The same approach was taken at Wells Fargo Financial in Des Moines and WMC Mortgage in Woodland Hills California. These efforts send a message to the organization at large that Six Sigma is more than just a toolbox.

Unfortunately, we have seen too many organizations just relegate the Six Sigma team to reporting to the Vice President of Quality. In most cases the VP of Quality is schooled in Quality Control efforts.

Sometimes she is even adverse to Six Sigma. In one case several years ago, the Quality leader of a major automobile supplier had multiple years of experience in inspection duties. He knew inspection techniques backward and forward but showed active resistance to Six Sigma. He perceived it as a threat to his ability to stop the manufacturing line. When the Six Sigma program manager was placed under this Vice President rather than the business leader, I predicted the failure of Six Sigma at this organization.

Therefore, avoid this potential pitfall that could spell the doom of your effort. Make the Quality Leader someone who is already in a position of responsibility within the organization, prominently announce this "promotion," and allow the new leader to build a small team of master black belts in training for Wave 1.

Pitfall #9—Forgetting that Six Sigma is a Management Philosophy

Of course, the people responsible for the transformative effects of Six Sigma will always be the business leaders of the organization. I've said it over and over: at its core Six Sigma is a management philosophy. This philosophy embraces using facts and data to make decisions. It is a philosophy that embraces becoming more customer and process focused that then allows strategic business objectives to be met. Finally, this management philosophy empowers the workforce to utilize their common sense, technical expertise, and process knowledge to improve how work gets done in an organization.

What has made Six Sigma so popular? What differentiates it from other quality approaches? It's not the contents of the Six Sigma toolbox. Instead, it is who uses it. When a seminar participant reminds me he was taught control charts in the 1980s or received Design of Experiments training in college, I am always quick to agree. I stress that all those tools were used by the workforce but rarely understood or practiced by management. When I think of how Six Sigma is so different than my statistical process control work I did in the auto industry in the early 1980s I think of business leaders like Sandra Derickson at HSBC Retail Services, David Wessner at Park Nicollet Health Care, and Mohan Garde at HP Consumer Operations.

In the case of Sandra, she first embraced Six Sigma while being the business leader at GE Auto Financial. She then brought Eckes and Associates into the fold when she embraced Six Sigma at Household Retail Services. Sandy was the type of leader that trusted Brian Zempel to keep tabs on each and every project in Wave 1. As Brian indicates, Sandy played "Good cop" to his "Bad cop." If there was a Champion beginning to flounder, she would intervene with what only could be described as her "velvet hammer." She would clearly inquire about progress to date and provide encouragement to the Champion or team leader. With her subtle management style, she communicated her commitment to Six Sigma. To me this culminated with her full attendance during our three-day Design of Experiments training. What a beautiful message to send to direct reports that she was willing to learn and become conversant on what had to be the most difficult of all Six Sigma tools.

David Wessner has a quiet, collegial management style. Yet I learned early and often in my work with Park Nicollet that he understood his role in the deployment of Six Sigma. Health care efforts at implementing Six Sigma often neglect to include the physician. Without physician involvement, Six Sigma becomes a cost-reduction effort to eliminate inefficiencies (as anyone who has visited an HMO knows are rampant) and improve backroom processes like billing and collections. However, Wessner actively encouraged physicians to identify and select patient care projects as part of Wave-1 activities, then created incentives that resulted in not only physician involvement, but their excitement as well.

Finally, it's been my pleasure to know Mohan Garde. I have always said that you get to know someone during a long flight, and that was the case with Mohan in February 2004. During our Six Sigma overview in December 2003, he had impressed me with his gentle but forceful leadership. It was on a flight from Mumbai to Frankfurt that we bonded. He was setting up a call center in Bangalore and visiting his family in Mumbai when I heard at 3:30 a.m. my name being called out. "George, over here." I had arrived early at the Mumbai airport after a week working with the largest company in India, Reliance Ltd.

On our seven-hour flight from Mumbai to Frankfurt, we sat together in the upper deck of our Lufthansa 747. It was during this flight that I saw a visionary business leader who wanted to use Six Sigma to transform his culture. As he later said during the Analysis report outs at the Hotel Valencia, he wanted Six Sigma to be his legacy at HP Consumer Ops. While at the time of this writing it is too early to tell whether this will be the case, I am confident that HP Consumer Ops is my next client that will experience a cultural transformation due to the successful execution of Six Sigma.

Unfortunately, these types of business leaders are rare. Like so many initiatives, Six Sigma is used by too many business leaders as a quick fix. If your organization has an "instant pudding" mentality, Six Sigma will not work for you. As Brian Zempel was quoted in our July 2004 interview:

> **If an organization wants quick fixes and quick ROI, they are going to have a hard time with Six Sigma. If you want to do it right and you have some patience, then it can transform your organization. It doesn't have to take a year. We got our first ROI in six months. But sadly some management wants even quicker results. Companies that live quarter to quarter will not like Six Sigma. But if you want to influence a culture, then Six Sigma will jazz you.**

In order to be jazzed, as Brian Zempel indicates, you will need the constant nurturing of visionary business leaders to really make this work.

Pitfall #10—Whining

There is an old adage in consulting that at the end of the day if you felt you worked harder than the client, something is wrong. Sadly, I have had more than my fair share of those days. Sometimes when asked what I do for a living, I tell people I am a well-paid child care provider.

The main cause of my occasional cynicism is the excessive amount of whining about Six Sigma. While I firmly embrace the concept of overcoming resistance with the power of influencing strategies and stakeholder analysis, I sometimes take a more simplistic approach and set a ground rule to start a seminar that there will be no whining.

Too many individuals have embraced the notion that they live in ineffectual organizations and nothing can change their culture. Of course these people are wrong. Six Sigma has helped change the landscape of international business. However, too many business leaders, middle management, and individual contributors spend more time debating the merits of improving their business rather than working to change things.

It is hoped that this book on Six Sigma execution can provide the pragmatic steps to modify how work gets done in your organization. But above all else—stop the whining and get to work.

Key Learnings

There are host of pitfalls to avoid in executing Six Sigma. They include:

- Avoid the learned helplessness that paralyzes a team or manager in executing Six Sigma. This is prevalent in larger organizations but exists in smaller ones too.
- Avoid making cost reduction the major goal of a project. Cost reduction should always be a by-product of a good project. The goal of any project should be to improve customer satisfaction and ultimately impact the strategic business objectives of the organization.
- Don't strive to be a popular Quality Leader. Many times the Quality Leader will have to push and cajole the Champion, team leader, or the team itself. Obviously, the Quality Leader can only do this if he possesses credibility within the organization.
- Six Sigma can only be successful with a business leader's decisive commitment to move forward. Avoid consensus-style decision making when implementing Six Sigma.
- Budget time wisely to complete intersession and postsession project deliverables. Never wait to the last minute. Project report outs always reveal the people who try to "cram" a project.
- Always use common sense. Six Sigma is a way to tap into technical expertise and knowledge, not a way to replace it.
- Avoid trying to do too much in year two. The year-two deployment is not just a repeat of year one, where the focus was on generating ROI on projects. Year two is the year Six Sigma becomes a cultural phenomenon in the organization.

- Make the Six Sigma quality function prominent in the organization. Don't hide it.
- Never forget that Six Sigma is more than projects. At its core it's a management philosophy.
- Stop whining and get to work.

Appendix A
Generic Letter from
CEO to Direct Reports

Dear _____:

The ACME Company is ready to embark on a journey to improve our productivity through a Six Sigma Quality Initiative. Six Sigma is a management philosophy that improves the effectiveness and efficiency of our Key Processes.

The work of implementing Six Sigma begins with management, and that is why I am writing you. On January 17 and 18, we will be working with a consulting firm (Eckes & Associates, Inc.) that plans to help us align our Key Processes that impact our Business Objectives. Ultimately our work will lead to selecting 7–10 low-performing processes targeted for improvement.

As your business leader, I consider this work vitally important. I expect both your attendance and active involvement for both days. No other work will be a priority from 8:30 a.m. to 4:30 p.m. both days.

By way of preparation, please read Chapter 2 of *Six Sigma for Everyone* by George Eckes. Please pick up a copy with my assistant, Vicki L., who will also provide logistics about the event.

Best wishes, Walt L., CEO

BPM Course Logistics and Supplies

Course Materials

- Course Materials will be e-mailed to you.
- Please ensure that the appropriate video computer hardware is provided and BPM materials loaded.
- The course materials, printed in the notes view, must be copied and bound, one for each participant. (Black and white is fine).

Supply List

- Masking tape, 3 rolls
- Flip chart paper pads, 2 to 3. Post-it makes easel pads, sticks to most walls, and removes cleanly. These are preferred, not required.
- 8 packages of flip chart markers (if quantity is 4 per package). Note: Enough for each participant to have one plus markers for the flip chart stands.
- 5×7 Post-it notes—7 to 8 packages (one package usually has four pads)
- 3×5 Post-it notes—10 to 12 packages (one package usually has four pads)
- Name tags
- Two packages of ¾-inch sticky dots, any color
- 8½×11 inch Note pads, one for each participant
- Pens or pencils, one for each participant

Equipment List

- Video computer hardware
- Screen for projector
- 2 flip chart stands

Room Setup

- The room should be set up with round tables for participants, or u-shaped.
- The room needs to have a lot of wall space to tape charts and notes.
- 3-5 Breakouts rooms recommended, but not mandatory.

BPM: Day 1 and 2 Agendas

Table A.1   Day 1

Time	Topic	Speaker/Participants
8:00	Opening Comments	CEO
8:20	Introductions, Expectations, & Ground Rules	George Eckes
9:00	Business Process Management	George Eckes
10:00	Break	
10:15	Confirmation of Our Strategic Business Objectives	George Eckes/Dave Schulenberg & Group
12:00	Lunch	
1:00	Continue with Strategic Business Objectives	
2:00	Brainstorm 5-7 Core Processes	Group
4:00	Alignment check; Core Processes vs. Strategic Business Objectives	Group
5:00	End day 1	

Table A.2   Day 2

Time	Topic	Speaker/Participants
8:00	Review of Day #1	Dave Schulenberg and George Eckes
8:15	Review alignment check & modify as needed	Groups
9:15	Brainstorming of Key Subprocesses	Subgroups
11:00	Group reports & discussion on Subprocesses	Subgroups
12:30	Lunch	
1:30	Brainstorming Measures of Effectiveness and Efficiency for Subprocesses (Process Dashboards)	Subgroups
3:00	Random Report Outs on Process Dashboards	Subgroups
4:00	Next Steps and Wrap-up	George Eckes
5:00	End day 2	

Deliverables

1. Introduction and discussion about Business Process Management
2. Your core business processes identified
3. Metrics agreed for core business processes (process dashboards developed)
4. Group alignment check of strategic business objectives versus core business processes
5. Key subprocesses identified
6. Measures of effectiveness and efficiency agreed for subprocesses
7. Next steps identified and actions assigned

Appendix B
Champion Activities

**In your simulation team, create an affinity diagram
to answer the following question:**

- What were lessons learned from the Business Simulation that will be important to communicate to Project Teams in your role as Champion?
- Be prepared to report out your findings to the large group.

Champion's Role as it Relates to DMAIC Project Team's
Before/During/After

There are three flip charts in the room, one labeled "BEFORE," one labeled "DURING," one labeled "AFTER":

1. Break into three groups and proceed to a flip chart.
2. Spend five minutes brainstorming and capturing what a Champion should do based on the heading on the flip chart.
3. At the end of five minutes, rotate to the next flip chart; add ideas to the flip chart. If there is an idea written that you agree with, place a check mark by that idea.

4. At the end of five minutes, rotate to the last flip chart and complete the exercise.

Champion's Responsibilities as They Relate to DMAIC Project Team's before the Project Starts

- Selecting Your Team.
- Creating the Business Case for Your Project.
- Formulating the Preliminary Problem Statement.
- Identifying the Preliminary Scope of the Project.
- Identifying the Preliminary Goal(s) of the Project.
- Allocating Resources for the Team to Complete Its Week.
- Identify your Team Leader (Green Belt).
- Communicate the Business Case to Team Members.
- Establish the Timeline for the Project Team to Do Its Work.
- Establish Milestones for Input from you, the Champion.
- Distinguish Decisions Requiring Your Input.

Champion's Responsibilities as They Relate to DMAIC Project Team's during the Project

- Validate/Finalize the Charter.
- Monitor and Approve All Project Tollgate Work.
- Meet Regularly with Your Team Leader.
- Remove Road Blocks or Barriers.
- Maintain Momentum.
- Deal with Resistance Among the Team.
- Communicate Progress to Upper Management.
- Continuing Education.
- Recognize Efforts.
- Reevaluate Scope.

Champion's Responsibilities as They Relate to DMAIC Project Team's after the Project Completes

- Communicate New Process/Results to the Business Quality Council.
- Capture Lessons Learned.

- Monitor Performance of the New Process.
- Recognize, Reward, and Celebrate Both Success and Efforts.

Team Chartering: A charter is the collection of documents that provides purpose and motivation for an improvement team to do its work.

Team Chartering—Elements of a Good Charter

- Business Case
- Problem Statement
- Project Scope
- Goals/Objectives
- Milestones
- Roles/Responsibilities

Team Chartering—The Business Case

- How Does This Project Impact the Strategic Business Objectives of the Organization?
- Why Is This Project Worth Doing Now?
- What Are Consequences of Not Doing This Project? (Now)
- Do Other Projects Have Equal/Higher Priority?

The Business Case for My Project—Be Ready at the Appointed Time to Report Out to the Group Your Business Case:

_____

_____

_____

Problem Statement Elements

- Specific, Measurable
- Since When
- Describes Impact

- Describes Gap Between Current State and Desired State (Implied or Explicit)
- Stated in Neutral Terms
  - No Causation
  - No Solutions
  - No Blame

Problem Statement Example: "Since January 1998 Client XYZ has averaged Payment of Invoices 96.2 Days Past Due Resulting in Additional Administrative Costs."

Using the Example:

What do you like about this Problem Statement? (+)	What could be different? (delta)
_____	_____
_____	_____
_____	_____
_____	

Team Chartering—Project Scope

- What Are the Boundaries of the Process to Be Improved?
- What Are Elements Outside the Scope of the Project Team?
- What Constraints Must the Team Work Under?

Large-Team Exercise—Group the following items into the Project Scope for NASA in placing a man on the moon:

<u>IN</u>

- Space Walk
- Orbiting the Earth
- Space Station Creation
- Operate a Lunar Module

OUT

- Landing a Man on Mars
- Creating Tang
- Circling the Moon

The Preliminary Scope for My Project

IN

OUT

Team Chartering—Goals/Objectives:

- What Goals Must be Met and By When?
- For Each Goal, What is the Objective?
- What are the Milestones for Each Goal/Objective?

Team Chartering—Milestones

BY

- Define/Measure   June 14, 2004
- Analysis   August 13, 2004
- Improvement & Control   October 31, 2004

Team Chartering—Roles/Responsibilities

- Who Should the Team Members Be? Why?
- Who Is the Team Leader?
- Is There a Need for Team Facilitator?
- When Must Team Go to Sponsor for Approval? When Can Team Act Independently?
- How Often Does the Sponsor Want to be Statused?

The Team Members for My Project

- _____ *
- _____
- _____
- _____
- _____   ADHOC Members
- _____   _____
- _____   _____
- _____   _____

Team Leader (Green Belt)

Champion Responsibilities Breakout

Special Resources:

_____

_____

_____

Types of Decisions That Require Your Input:

_____

_____

_____

Types of Decisions That the Team Can Handle on Its Own:

_____

_____

_____

Appendix C
DMAIC Breakouts, Tables, and Interpost Session Deliverables

Desired Outcomes:

- Review and provide input to Champion on the Business Case.
- Review and provide input to Champion on the Problem Statement.
- Review and provide input to Champion on Project Scope.
- Review Team Membership for possible revision.

Decision-Making Method

- Consultative

Table C.1 Breakout #1—The Project Charter

Item	Method	Person	Time
Review Agenda.	Discussion	Team Leader	5 minutes
Review Business Case.	Discussion	Team Leader and Team	10 minutes
Review Problem Statement.	Discussion	Team Leader and Team	15 minutes

(Continued)

Table C.1   *(Continued)*

Item	Method	Person	Time
Review Project Scope.	In/Out? Tool	Team Leader and Team	30 minutes
Review Team Membership.	Discussion	Team Leader and Team	5 minutes
Complete Parking Lot for Unfinished Items.	Parking Lot	Team Leader and Team	5 minutes
Plus Delta of Breakout.	Plus/Delta	Team Leader and Team	5 minutes
		TOTAL	75 minutes

Team Roles

- Facilitator_____
- Scribe_____
- Timekeeper_____

Remember to post and review a set of ground rules.

Breakout #2—Customer Focus

Desired Outcomes:

- Determine Customer(s) of your project.
- Determine segmentation of customers if needed.
- Create a CTQ tree with brainstormed needs and requirements.
- Gain experience applying Kano's Model to potential customer requirements.

Decision-Making Method

- Primary—Consensus
- Secondary—two-thirds majority vote

Table C.2   Breakout #2—Customer Focus

Item	Method	Person	Time
Review Agenda.	Discussion	Team Leader	5 minutes
Determine customers of your project and determine segments if needed.	Discussion	Team Leader and Team	15 minutes
Create a CTQ tree for the primary customer.	CTQ tree	Team Leader and Team	30 minutes
Apply Kano's model for the first-level requirements.	Kano's Model	Team Leader and Team	10 minutes
Complete Parking Lot for unfinished items.	Parking Lot	Team Leader and Team	5 minutes
Plus Delta of Breakout.	Plus/Delta	Team Leader and Team	5 minutes
		TOTAL	70 minutes

Team Roles

- Facilitator_____
- Scribe_____
- Timekeeper_____

Remember to post and review a set of ground rules.

Breakout #3—Creating the High-Level Process Map

Desired Outcomes:

- Begin creation of the High-Level Map.
- Discuss plans for how the High-Level Map will be validated during the intersession.

Decision-Making Method

- Primary—Consensus
- Secondary—two-thirds majority vote

Table C.3 Breakout #3—Creating the High-Level Process Map

Item	Method	Person	Time
Review Agenda.	Discussion	Team Leader	5 minutes
Begin Creation of the High-Level Map.	SIPOC	Team Leader and Team	60 minutes
Discussion of how the High-Level Map will be validated during the intersession.	Discussion	Team Leader and Team	10 minutes
Complete Parking Lot for unfinished items.	Parking Lot	Team Leader and Team	5 minutes
Plus Delta of Breakout.	Plus/Delta	Team Leader and Team	5 minutes
		TOTAL	85 minutes

Team Roles

- Facilitator_____
- Scribe_____
- Timekeeper_____

Remember to post and review a set of ground rules.

Breakout #4—Creating the Data Collection Plan (Pt. I)

Desired Outcomes:

- Determine the potential measures for your project.
- Determine the type of measures and types of data.
- Determine operational definitions for all potential measures.

Decision-Making Method

- Primary—Consensus
- Secondary—two-thirds majority vote

Table C.4   Breakout #4—Creating the Data Collection Plan (Pt. 1)

Item	Method	Person	Time
Review Agenda.	Discussion	Team Leader	5 minutes
List the potential CTQs of the project's customers.	Discussion	Team Leader and Team	5 minutes
Determine type of measures and type of data.	Discussion	Team Leader and Team	15 minutes
Determine operational definitions for all potential measures.	Discussion	Team Leader and Team	30 minutes
Complete Parking Lot for unfinished items.	Parking Lot	Team Leader and Team	5 minutes
Plus Delta of Breakout.	Plus/Delta	Team Leader and Team	5 minutes
		TOTAL	65 minutes

Team Roles

- Facilitator_____
- Scribe_____
- Timekeeper_____

Remember to post and review a set of ground rules.

Breakout #5—Creating the Data Collection Plan (Pt. 2)

Desired Outcomes:

- Determine the targets and specifications of the potential measures for the project.
- Determine the type of data collection forms necessary to collect your team's data.
- Determine factors that will contribute to ensuring your sampling will be representative and random.
- Determine a unit, defect, and number of opportunities for your project to assist your team in calculating baseline sigma.

Decision-Making Method

- Primary—Consensus
- Secondary—two-thirds majority vote

Table C.5 Breakout #5—Creating the Data Collection Plan (Pt. 2)

Item	Method	Person	Time
Review Agenda.	Discussion	Team Leader	5 minutes
Determine the targets and specifications for your potential measures.	Discussion	Team Leader and Team	5 minutes
Determine the types of data collection forms necessary to collect data.	Discussion	Team Leader and Team	10 minutes
Determine how the sampling for the project will be both representative and random.	Discussion	Team Leader and Team	15 minutes
Determine what a unit, defect and opportunity will be for the project.	Parking Lot	Team Leader and Team	15 minutes
Complete Parking Lot for unfinished items.	Parking Lot	Team Leader and Team	5 minutes
Plus Delta of Breakout.	Plus/Delta	Team Leader and Team	5 minutes
		TOTAL	60 minutes

Team Roles

- Facilitator_____
- Scribe_____
- Timekeeper_____

Remember to post and review a set of ground rules.

Breakout #6—Data Analysis Breakout

Desired Outcomes:

- Review Discrete or Continuous Data Collected to Date.
- Create one or two Microproblem Statements.

Decision-Making Method:

- Consensus with two-thirds majority vote as fallback

Table C.6   Breakout #6—Data Analysis Breakout

Item	Method	Person	Time
Review agenda/ assign roles.	Discussion	Team Leader	5 minutes
Review Discrete or Continuous Data Collected to Date.	Discussion	Team	30 minutes
Create one or two Microproblem Statements.	Discussion	Team	45 minutes
Plus/Deltas.		Team	5 minutes
		TOTAL	1 hour 25 minutes

Breakout #7—Process Analysis

Desired Outcomes:

- Develop preliminary subprocess map for one high-level process.
- Perform value analysis on subprocess map.
- Complete summary matrix.
- Identify one or two microproblem statements.

Decision-Making Method

- Consensus with two-thirds majority vote as fallback

Table C.7 Breakout #7—Process Analysis

Item	Method	Person	Time
Review Agenda/ assign roles	Discussion	Team Leader	5 minutes
Subprocess map	Select one key high-level step from the SIPOC. brainstorm sub- process steps on Post-it notes.	Team	40 minutes
Value Analysis/ Summary Matrix	Identify each step as value add or non-value add. Record decision on the summary matrix. Calculate percentage of VA to NVA steps.	Team	40 minutes
Microproblem statement	Analyze summary matrix and brainstorm list of microproblem statements. Narrow to your top one and two.	Team	15 minutes
Plus/Deltas		Team	5 minutes
		TOTAL	1 hour 45 minutes

Breakout #8—Root Cause Analysis

Desired Outcomes:

- Develop preliminary Cause-and-Effect Diagram
- Identify preliminary suspect Xs
- Perform Five Whys

Decision-Making Method:

- Consensus with two-thirds majority vote as fallback

Table C.8 Breakout #3—Root Cause Analysis

Item	Method	Person	Time
Review agenda/ assign roles	Discussion.	Team Leader	5 minutes
Cause-and-Effect Diagram	Choose one micro-problem statement. Complete a preliminary C and E diagram.	Team	60 minutes
Suspect Xs	Use multivoting to identify the three to five preliminary suspect Xs. Put into a Pareto chart.	Team	10 minutes
Five Whys	Choose one suspect X and perform a Five Why Analysis.	Team	15 minutes
Additional C&E analysis	Time permitting, select another micro-problem statement and create another C and E diagram.	Team	30 minutes
Plus/Deltas		Team	5 minutes
		TOTAL	2 hours 5 minutes

Improve and Control—Break out Session #9

Desired Outcomes:

- Clarify and Gain Understanding of the "Must" Criteria Issued By Your Project Champion.
- Brainstorm and Gain Agreement of the "Want" Criteria For Your Project.
- Brainstorm, Clarify, and Duplicate a Set of Potential Solutions That Address Your Potential Root Causes.

Decision-Making Method

- Consultative/Consensus (Backup two-thirds Majority)

Table C.9 Improve and Control—Breakout Session #9

Item	Method	Person	Time
Review Agenda	Discussion	Team Leader and Team	5 minutes
Clarify and Gain Understanding of "Must" Criteria	Discussion	Team Leader and Team	10 minutes
Brainstorm and Gain Agreement on the "Want" Criteria	Affinity Diagram	Team Leader and Team	1 hour
Brainstorm, Clarify, and Duplicate a Set of Potential Solutions	Affinity Diagram	Team Leader and Team	1 hour
Review "Parking Lot"	Discussion	Team Leader and Team	5 minutes
Plus/Delta	Discussion	Team Leader and Team	5 minutes
		TOTAL	2 hours 25 minutes

Improve and Control—Breakout Session #10

Desired Outcomes:

- Identify and Agree on a Set of Key Stakeholders For Your Project.
- Conduct a Stakeholder Analysis Chart.

Decision-Making Method

- Consensus (Backup two-thirds Majority)

Table C.10 Improve and Control—Breakout Session #10

Item	Method	Person	Time
Review Agenda	Discussion	Team Leader and Team	5 minutes
Identify and Agree on Key Stakeholders	Brainstorming and Discussion	Team Leader and Team	45 minutes

(Continued)

Table C.10 *(Continued)*

Item	Method	Person	Time
Conduct a Stakeholder Analysis Chart.	Stakeholder Analysis Chart	Team Leader and Team	1 hour
Address "Parking Lot."	Discussion	Team Leader and Team	5 minutes
Plus/Deltas.	Discussion	Team Leader and Team	5 minutes
		TOTAL	2 hours

Improve and Control—Breakout Session #11

Desired Outcomes:

- Determine Key Stakeholders Who Could Be Potentially Resistant to Your Solutions.
- Create a Planning-for-Influence Chart for Each Potential Resistor.

Decision-Making Method

- Consensus (Backup two-thirds Majority)

Table C.11 Improve and Control—Breakout Session #11

Item	Method	Person	Time
Review Agenda.	Discussion	Team Leader and Team	5 minutes
Determine Key Stakeholders Who Could Be Resistant.	Discussion	Team Leader and Team	30 minutes
Create a Planning-for-Influence Chart for Each Potential Resistor.	Discussion	Team Leader and Team	1 Hour
Review "Parking Lot."	Discussion	Team Leader and Team	5 minutes
Plus/Deltas.	Discussion	Team Leader and Team	5 minutes
		TOTAL	1 hour 45 minutes

Improve and Control—Breakout Session #12

Desired Outcomes:

- Determine Through-Put and Standardization of Your "New" Process.
- Determine Your Method of Control for Your New Process.

Decision-Making Method

- Consensus (Backup two-thirds Majority)

Table C.12   Improve and Control—Breakout Session #12

Item	Method	Person	Time
Review Agenda.	Discussion	Team Leader and Team	5 minutes
Determine Through-Put and Standardization of New Process.	Discussion	Team Leader and Team	30 minutes
Determine Method of Control.	Discussion	Team Leader and Team*	30 minutes
Review "Parking Lot."	Discussion	Team Leader and Team	5 minutes
Plus/Deltas.	Discussion	Team Leader and Team	5 minutes
		TOTAL	1 hour 15 minutes

*With Eckes Team

Intersession & Postsession Deliverables Time Line

Intersession Deliverables (6-14)

- Confirm Project Charter.
- Validate Customer Needs/Requirements.
- Validate High-Level Process Map.
- Complete Data Collection Plan.
- Implement Data Collection Plan.
- Create 10-minute presentation for 6-14 a.m.

Eckes & Associates, Inc

Charter

- Reconfirm business case with project Champion.
- Reconfirm preliminary problem statement/goals with project Champion.
- Reconcile in/out? items with Champion.
- Add/subtract team membership as applicable.
- Completed by April 30th.

Eckes & Associates, Inc

Customer Needs and Requirements

- Confirm primary and secondary customers with Champion.
- Complete CTQ tree.
- Come to agreement on at least two ways to validate CTQs.
- Validate two to four vital CTQs.
- Completed by May 14th.

Eckes & Associates, Inc

Process Map

- Complete SIPOC the way you "think" it is.
- Create a plan to validate the high-level "as is" map.
- Implement plan for validation.
- Complete by May 31st.

Eckes & Associates, Inc

Data Collection Plan

- Identify input, process, and output measures.
- Confirm operational definitions for each measure and whether measures are continuous or discrete.
- Identify target and specifications for each validated measure.
- Implement data-collection plan and measure baseline sigma.
- Completed by June 11th.

Eckes & Associates, Inc

June 14th 10-Minute Presentation

- Using the enclosed templates (or others of your choosing) create a 10-minute presentation showing your Define and Measure work.
- Limit each tollgate to no more than two slides.
- Due date: June 14th.

Eckes & Associates, Inc

Templates

Six Sigma Project Charter
Business Case (Connection to SBOs)

Project Scope	
IN	**OUT**

Goal and Objectives	**Subject Matter Experts**

APPROVAL	
Champion:	
Date:	
Team Leader:	
Date:	
Six Sigma Director:	
Date:	

Six Sigma Project Charter (cont'd)
Problem Statement

Expected Benefits	**Target**	**Stretch**
Total Savings	$ –	$ –

Milestones Start Date	**Plan**	**Actual**
Define		
Measure		
Analyze		
Improve		
Control		
Team:		
Champion		
Team Leader		
Master Black Belt		

Team Members	**Team Members**	**Role/Percent of Time**

CTQ Tree Template

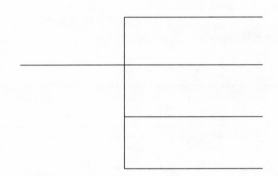

General
(Need)

Behavioral
(Requirement)

SIPOC Template

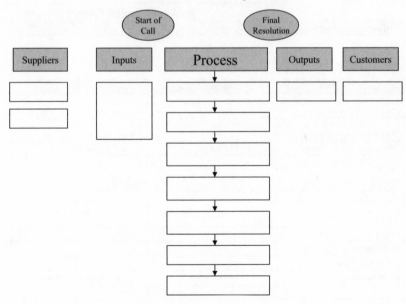

Data-Collection Plan

What to Measure	Type of Measure	Type of Data	Operational Definition	Target	Specification	Data-Collection Form(s)	Sampling	Baseline Six Sigma

INTERSESSION DELIVERABLES
Analysis

Complete D/M Work.

Create and Agree on One to Three Microproblem Statements.

Complete the Initial Work of Root Causation.

Begin Work on the Validation of Root Causation.

Determine Financial Opportunity for Your Project.

Data and Process Analysis by July 13th

- Analyze Data to Create One or Two Microproblem Statements.
- Complete and Validate Subprocess Map.
- Complete Process Summary Analysis Worksheet.
- Create One or Two Microproblem Statements from the Process Summary Analysis Worksheet.

Eckes & Associates, Inc

Root Cause Analysis

- Complete Root Cause-and-Effect Diagram(s) for all Microproblem Statements.
- Narrow List of X's to 5–15 by July 13th.
- Agree on Method(s) to Validate X's.

Validation Due Date:
   August 8—if using basic data collection or scatter analysis
   August 31—if using DOE

Eckes & Associates, Inc

Analysis Intercession 10-Minute Presentation

- Using the Enclosed Templates (or others of your choosing) Create a 10-Minute Presentation Showing Your Analysis Work to Date.
- Limit Each Tollgate to No More Than Two Slides.

Eckes & Associates, Inc

Templates

Process Analysis
Subprocess Mapping

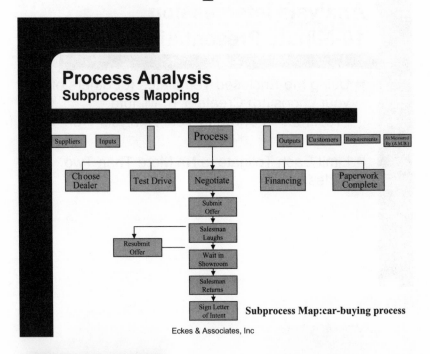

| Suppliers | Inputs | | Process | | Outputs | Customers | Requirements | As Measured By (A.M.B.) |

Choose Dealer — Test Drive — Negotiate — Financing — Paperwork Complete

Negotiate → Submit Offer → Salesman Laughs → Wait in Showroom → Salesman Returns → Sign Letter of Intent

Resubmit Offer

Subprocess Map:car-buying process

Eckes & Associates, Inc

Process Summary Analysis Sheet

Summary Analysis

Process Steps	1	2	3	4	5	6	7	8	9	10	Total
Cycle Time (min.)											
Value Added											
Non-Value Added											
Moves											
Set-up											
Internal Failure											
External Failure (Botched MOTs)											
Delays											
Controls/Insp.											
Bottlenecks											
Value-Enabling											

Eckes & Associates, Inc

Microproblem Statement(s)

1) _____

   _____

2) _____

   _____

3) _____

   _____

Eckes & Associates, Inc

The Cause-and-Effect Diagram

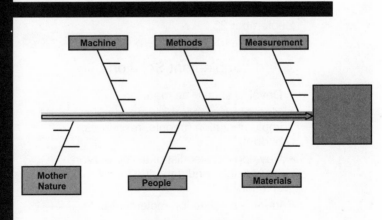

Eckes & Associates, Inc

Postsession Deliverables

Improve and Control

Technical Improve

- Generate list of brainstormed solutions.
- Finalize must and want criteria.
- Screen list of solutions against must criteria.
- Screen remaining solutions against want criteria.
- Select final solutions, completed by September 16.

Cultural Improve

- Develop list of KEY stakeholders (this should begin in Define & Measure).
- Conduct stakeholder analysis.
- Develop threat/opportunity matrix.
- Complete TPOI analysis.
- Develop influence strategy.
- Implement influence strategy, complete by September 23.

Implement Solution

- Develop should-be map.
- Identify list of resources needed for implementation (people, resources, budget).
- Develop detailed list of tasks, person responsible, and date due for roll-out of solution.
- Identify timeline for implementation.
- Execute plan, to be completed by October 15.

Control Plan

- Identify process owner if not already done.
- Develop monitoring plan (control chart, checklist, etc.).
- Develop response plan.
- Formal handoff to process owner, to be completed by November 4.

Appendix D
Conversion Tables/
Table of Constants

Abridged Process Sigma Conversion Table

Long-Term Yield	Process Sigma	Defects per 1,000,000	Defects per 100,000	Defects per 10,000	Defects per 1,000	Defects per 100
99.99966%	**6.0**	3	0.34	0.034	0.0034	0.00034
99.99946%	5.9	5	0.54	0.054	0.0054	0.00054
99.999915%	5.8	9	0.85	0.085	0.0085	0.00085
99.9987%	5.7	13	1.34	0.134	0.0134	0.00134
99.9979%	5.6	21	2.1	0.207	0.021	0.0021
99.9968%	5.5	32	3.2	0.32	0.032	0.0032
99.9950%	5.4	48	4.8	0.48	0.048	0.0048
99.9930%	5.3	72	7.2	0.72	0.072	0.0072
99.9890%	5.2	108	10.8	0.08	0.11	0.011
99.9840%	5.1	159	15.9	1.6	0.16	0.016
99.9800%	**5.0**	233	23.3	2.3	0.23	.023
99.9700%	4.9	337	33.7	3.4	0.34	.034
99.9500%	4.8	483	48.3	4.8	0.48	.048
99.9300%	4.7	687	68.7	6.9	0.69	.069
99.9000%	4.6	968	97	10	0.97	.097
99.8700%	4.5	1,350	135	13	1.3	0.13
99.8100%	4.4	1,866	187	19	1.9	0.19
99.7400%	4.3	2,555	256	26	2.6	0.26
99.6500%	4.2	3,467	347	35	3.5	0.35
99.5000%	4.1	4,661	466	47	4.7	0.47

Abridged Process Sigma Conversion Table

Long-Term Yield	Process Sigma	Defects per 1,000,000	Defects per 100,000	Defects per 10,000	Defects per 1,000	Defects per 100
99.400%	**4.0**	6,210	621	62	6.2	0.62
99.200%	3.9	8,198	820	82	8.2	0.82
98.900%	3.8	10,724	1,072	107	11	1.1
98.600%	3.7	13,903	1,390	139	14	1.4
98.200%	3.6	17,864	1,786	179	18	1.8
97.700%	3.5	22,750	2,275	228	23	2.3
97.100%	3.4	28,716	2,872	287	29	2.9
96.400%	3.3	35,930	3,593	359	36	3.6
95.500%	3.2	44,565	4,457	446	45	4.5
94.500%	3.1	54,799	5,480	548	55	5.5
93.300%	**3.0**	66,807	6,681	668	67	6.7
91.900%	2.9	80,757	8,076	808	81	8.1
90.300%	2.8	96,801	9,680	968	97	9.7
88.500%	2.7	115,070	11,507	1,151	115	12
86.400%	2.6	135,666	13,567	1,357	136	14
84.100%	2.5	158,655	15,866	1,587	159	16
81.600%	2.4	184,060	18,406	1,841	184	18
78.800%	2.3	211,855	21,186	2,119	212	21
75.800%	2.2	241,964	24,196	2,420	242	24
72.600%	2.1	274,253	27,425	2,743	274	27

Abridged Process Sigma Conversion Table

Long-Term Yield	Process Sigma	Defects per 1,000,000	Defects per 100,000	Defects per 10,000	Defects per 1,000	Defects per 100
69.100%	**2.0**	308,538	30,854	3,085	309	31
65.500%	1.9	344,578	34,458	3,446	345	34
61.800%	1.8	382,089	38,209	3,821	382	38
57.900%	1.7	420,740	42,074	4,207	421	42
54.000%	1.6	460,172	46,017	4,602	460	46
50.000%	1.5	500,000	50,000	5,000	500	50
46.000%	1.4	539,828	53,983	5,398	540	54
42.100%	1.3	579,260	57,926	5,793	579	58
38.200%	1.2	617,911	61,791	6,179	618	62
34.500%	1.1	655,422	65,542	6,554	655	66
30.900%	**1.0**	691,462	69,146	6,915	691	69
27.400%	0.9	725,747	72,575	7,257	726	73
24.200%	0.8	758,036	75,804	7,580	758	76
21.200%	0.7	788,145	78,814	7,881	788	79
18.400%	0.6	815,940	81,594	8,159	816	82
15.900%	0.5	841,345	84,134	8,413	841	84
13.600%	0.4	864,334	86,433	8,643	864	86
11.500%	0.3	884,930	88,493	8,849	885	88
9.700%	0.2	903,199	90,320	9,032	903	90
8.100%	0.1	919,243	91,924	9,192	919	92

Table of Constants
Factors for Determining from R the 3-Sigma Control Limits for X and R Charts.

NUMBER OF OBSERVATIONS INSUBGROUP	FACTOR FOR X bar CHART	FACTORS FOR LOWER CONTROL LIMIT	R CHART UPPER CONTROL LIMIT
n	A_2	D_3	D_4
2	1.88	0	3.27
3	1.02	0	2.57
4	0.73	0	2.28
5	0.58	0	2.11
6	0.48	0	2.00
7	0.42	0.08	1.92
8	0.37	0.14	1.86
9	0.34	0.18	1.82
10	0.31	0.22	1.78
11	0.29	0.26	1.74
12	0.27	0.28	1.72
13	0.25	0.31	1.69
14	0.24	0.33	1.67
15	0.22	0.35	1.65
16	0.21	0.36	1.64
17	0.20	0.38	1.62
18	0.19	0.39	1.61
19	0.19	0.40	1.60
20	0.18	0.41	1.59

References

Chapter 2

1. Zucconi, T. (2004). Interview. (Interview with George Eckes and Andrea Price, 01, July, 2004).
2. Ibid.
3. Ibid.
4. Ibid.
5. Ibid.
6. Klugman, A. (2004). Interview. (Interview with George Eckes and Andrea Price, 30, July, 2004).
7. Ibid.
8. Ibid.
9. Laux, iSixSigma, discussion forum, 2004.
10. Ibid.
11. Gabriel, M. (2004). Interview. (Interview with George Eckes and Andrea Price, 09, September, 2004).
12. Ibid.
13. Ibid.
14. L. Bossidy and R. Charan, *Execution, The Discipline of Getting Things Done,* Crown Business, New York, 2002.
15. Ibid.
16. Gabriel, M. (2004). Interview. (Interview with George Eckes and Andrea Price, 30, July, 2004).
17. J. Welch, *Straight from the Gut,* Warner Business Books, New York, 2002.

Chapter 3

1. *USA Today.* Del Jones, October 30, 2002.
2. *The 9/11 Commission Report,* Norton, 2004, page 16.
3. Ibid, page 17/18.
4. Ibid, page 18.
5. Ibid, page 28.
6. Ibid, page 31.
7. Ibid, page 29.
8. Ibid, page 36.
9. Ibid, page 74.
10. Ibid, page 77.
11. Ibid, page 76.
12. Ibid, page 77.
13. Ibid, page 79.
14. *Christian Science Monitor.* May 17, 2002.
15. The *New York Times,* "Pre- 9/11 Files Show Warnings Were More Dire and Persistent, April 18, 2004.
16. *Time* magazine, "The Bombshell Memo" May 21, 2002.
17. *Christian Science Monitor.* May 17, 2002.
18. Ibid.

Chapter 8

1. *Wall Street Journal* article July 1, 2004.

Index